SUBSMASH

SUBSMASH

The Mysterious Disappearance of HM SUBMARINE AFFRAY

ALAN GALLOP

SUTTON PUBLISHING

First published in the United Kingdom in 2007 by
Sutton Publishing, an imprint of NPI Media Group Limited
Cirencester Road · Chalford · Stroud · Gloucestershire · GL6 8PE

Alan Gallop has asserted the moral right to be identified as the author of this
work.

British Library Cataloguing in Publication Data
A catalogue record for this book is available from the British Library.

ISBN 978-0-7509-4656-8

Typeset in Photina.
Typesetting and origination by
NPI Media Group Limited.
Printed and bound in England.

This book is dedicated to the seventy-five brave officers and ratings who sailed in HMS Affray on Exercise Training Spring on Monday 16 April 1951 and never returned

CONTENTS

LIST OF ILLUSTRATIONS

FOREWORD

Few people today have heard of HMS *Affray*, the Royal Navy's 'A' class submarine which made its way out into the English Channel in April 1951 with seventy-five officers and ratings on board, dived and never again returned to the surface. And why should they have? *Affray* was the last British submarine to be lost at sea and she dived for the final time nearly sixty years ago, triggering the largest military sea-air search ever mounted in this country before, or since.

But there are sufficient numbers of people still alive *who do* remember the mysterious disappearance of the *Affray* and for some of them the memory still hurts and haunts. After all this time they still ask questions, answers to which have never been satisfactorily provided.

They ask: what really happened to *Affray*? What prevented her from resurfacing after she dived on the evening of 16 April 1951? Why were so many men summoned to join the submarine and then sent ashore again minutes before she sailed? What might have happened to her once she had disappeared beneath the waves? Was the submarine in a fit state to sail? Was she overcrowded? Was her crew experienced enough? Were there spies on board?

Perhaps there are no answers to these questions, but this book sets out to tell the true and in-depth story of *Affray* for the first time, throw new light on many issues surrounding her last 'cruise' and offer suggestions about what may – or may not – have happened to her. To do this, I have been fortunate to have enjoyed the co-operation of four people who lost a husband, father or brother on the submarine and others who either participated or observed the attempts to find and rescue her.

Experienced submariners – including a respected submarine commander – have also kindly provided me with their own professional perspectives, and a technical deep-sea diver describes what the vessel looked like sitting on the sea bed half a century or so after she went missing (and before diving was banned on underwater military graves).

There are many questions that could not be answered in 1951 because the technology needed had not been invented at that time. But it does exist today. When an underwater television camera was lowered into the sea for the first time from the deck of HMS *Reclaim* and identified a mysterious cigar-shape object on the seabed as *Affray*, it marked a great leap forward for salvage operations. Today's sophisticated, highly portable X-ray and salvage equipment could be used on the wreck to obtain those answers without any need to disturb the last resting place of seventy-five men.

If the sixteenth-century Tudor warship *Mary Rose* could be raised from the Solent in 1982, why could the mid-twentieth-century submarine *Affray* also not be salvaged, too? Admittedly, *Affray* sits in nearly 300ft of water and a metal submarine weighs considerably more than a wooden Tudor warship. But we know that the *Mary Rose* was top-heavy and sank after keeling over. We do not know what caused *Affray* to fail – and may never find the answer, even if it were possible to carry out a detailed underwater survey. Evidence of an explosion in her battery tanks or the position of a hidden snort mast valve may – or may not – provide answers. If the *Affray* failed because of human error, as is suggested later in this book, it is unlikely that any hard evidence will ever be produced.

This author is not and never has been a submariner, or even a Sea Scout. The nearest he has come to a submarine is being shown over HMS *Alliance* at the Royal Navy Submarine Museum at Gosport (which is highly recommended) and, as a child in 1958, seeing the American submarine USS *Nautilus* arrive at Portland Harbour following her groundbreaking (icebreaking?) voyage under the North Pole.

I first heard about *Affray* from a friend who, as a boy sailor in 1951, was on guard duty at the gates of the Royal Navy Dockyard at Portsmouth when news was circulated that the submarine was overdue reporting her position while on a war patrol exercise. For some reason, the record book in which names of all visiting dockyard arrivals and departures was entered was requested by a senior officer – and never returned.

Preposterous rumours began to circulate: she had been captured at gunpoint by the Russian navy and the crew taken prisoner, there had been a mutiny on board, she had been run down by a ship while cruising at periscope depth, a pair of young female 'passengers' had been smuggled onto the submarine and the Navy did not want to salvage her as it would identify serious gaps in its security. And there were others, including more realistic suggestions that *Affray* was unfit for sea, was 'a leaking sieve', had not been properly tested with a deep dive before putting to sea and had some serious problems with oil appearing in one of her battery tanks. All of this, some of this or – possibly – none of this may be true.

This book avoids 'being technical', but where a technical term must be used, I have attempted to make sense of it and appreciate that this may rankle some submariners. During my research I learned many things about submarines: that they are often called 'boats', that their commanders are often referred to as 'captains', and operating one (and maintaining its balance and 'trim') is a most difficult task requiring team work of the highest order. Which is, perhaps, why HMS *Affray* met the unfortunate end that it did in the spring of 1951.

ACKNOWLEDGEMENTS

The author extends sincere thanks to everyone who gave me their time, shared their memories, provided images and access to personal papers, opened their archives, loaned me material and took the trouble to answer my questions.

I am particularly grateful to those who lost loved ones on HMS *Affray* and were prepared to revisit that time and speak to me about their memories and feelings. Sincere thanks in particular to Mary Henry (widow of Lieutenent Derek Foster), Joy Cook (widow of Leading Seaman George Cook), Robin Andrews (brother of Marine Sergeant Jack Andrews) and Georgina 'Gina' Gander (daughter of Able Seaman George Leakey). Thanks also to Margaret Goddard, whose husband, Leading Seaman John Goddard – who retired from the Royal Navy as a lieutenant – was one of the men discharged from the submarine before she sailed and who later did much to keep the story of *Affray* alive.

I also wish to thank three special people at the Royal Navy Submarine Museum at Gosport – a visit to which is highly recommended to people of all ages, especially those who want to actually go on board a submarine – for their patience and interest shown in my research for this book: Commander Jeff Tall, OBE, MNI, RN (Director), George Malcolmson (Archivist) and Debbie Corner (Keeper of Photographs/Temporary Exhibitions Coordinator).

Many other people also took the trouble to contact me by telephone, letter and e-mail and I am grateful to: Dave Lowe, Dave March, Gordon Selby, Bernard Kervell, Brian Collis, Gordon Chatburn, Val Clements, Roma Maw, Ron Leakey, David Dyer, Alice Graham, Richard Pilgrim, Douggie Elliott, Mike Draper, Geraint Ffoulkes-Jones, Peter Stephens, Captain W.H. Kett, DSC, RD, RNR, Michael Kenyon, MBE, BEM, John Rogers, Leonard Lowe, E.V. Bugden, Peter Sampson, Jeffrey Barlow, Roy 'Tug' Wilson and 'MJS'.

Finally, I extend my appreciation to the unseen backroom ladies and gentlemen at The National Archives, Kew, and the British Library Newspaper Library, Colindale, whose swift efficiency ensures that researcher and authors always get what they have requested in the fastest possible time.

Chapter 1

1951: POSTWAR BLUES, RADIO TIMES

Although the war had been over for nearly six years, it was taking a long time for Britain to start feeling good about itself again. Times were hard and for many the country remained a gloomy place, lingering in an extended post-war depression not helped by wartime rationing, still in place in the spring of 1951 after twelve long, austere years.

Rationing of bread, canned and dried fruit, chocolate biscuits, treacle, syrup, jellies, soap and clothes had been lifted, but restrictions on the sale of petrol and most types of meat continued and it would be another fifteen months before rationing was completely lifted. Food quotas had been forced on the British public in January 1940, four months after the outbreak of the war when limits were placed on the sale of bacon, butter and sugar. Two months later all meat was rationed and clothing coupons introduced.

Slowly – very slowly – popular consumer products were creeping back into the shops. Bristow's Lanolin Shampoo had returned to shelves at all good chemists in 1949, price 1s 3d or 2s for the family size. Britons no longer needed to wash their hair using carbolic soap.

Top footballer Billy Wright told newspaper readers through advertisements that 'Quaker Oats is my food for action! (Price 9½d or 1s 7d for a bumper box)'. As there was little variety available in food, the British public took Mr Wright's word and went into action buying the expensively priced product until the shelves were bare. HP Sauce returned to 'improve all meals' while Churchman's No. 1 cigarettes had never left the tobacconist's counter during the war and in 1951 remained 'the 15 minute cigarette for extra pleasure and satisfaction'.

While the war in Europe was now a thing of the recent past, the country remained on a war footing. After six years of peace, it was still difficult for many people in large towns and cities to become re-accustomed to life again without air raids, sirens, separations from loved ones for months – sometimes years – or the possibility of a knock on the door from a telegram boy bringing bad news.

Abroad there was armed conflict in Korea. Armed communists had retaken the city of Seoul and United Nations and South Korean forces had crossed the 38th parallel. There was unrest in Malaya where rebels were attacking British-owned rubber plantations and demanding independence. China had occupied Tibet and British and American relations with Russia were heading towards a period soon to be known as 'the Cold War.' Winston Churchill had dubbed the USSR and communist countries surrounding it the 'Iron Curtain' and newspapers referred to the 'Red Menace' almost daily. Trouble was also brewing along the Suez Canal after King Farouk ordered British troops from the zone and there was talk of sending warships in to take it back.

In April 1951, the *Daily Mail* told readers there was likely to be a reshuffle in Prime Minister Clement Atlee's new Labour government following the recent death of Earnest Bevin and illness of Sir Stafford Cripps, 'compelling the PM to look for new and younger men for the cabinet.' A cabinet reshuffle, however, was the last thing on 68-year old Atlee's mind at the time. He was lying ill in St Mary's Hospital, Paddington, recovering from a major operation to remove a duodenal ulcer and instructed by physicians not to sit up and work under any circumstances.

The *Daily Mail* also said that currency restrictions for British tourists visiting the Continent would end soon. Not that many people took foreign holidays, the majority either staying at home or spending hard-earned wages at British seaside boarding houses. You needed to be posh to stay in hotels.

Other newspapers said that millions of people in India were starving and forced to eat snails and that Randolph Turpin was ready to fight Billy Brown in a middleweight championship in Birmingham (which Turpin subsequently won by a knockout in round two). Humphrey Bogart and his wife Lauren Bacall decorated the pages of the popular press after arriving in London from the United States for a few days before going on to Africa to film *The African Queen*.

Radio listeners had a choice of three BBC radio stations to tune into on their Bakelite sets powered by an accumulator. Although the BBC had been transmitting programmes into British homes since the 1920s, it was during wartime years that the corporation really came into its own. For the majority of the population, a daily BBC diet of news and current affairs, music and entertainment, education and culture were a lifeline to daily information and amusement. The country loved and trusted the BBC.

On the Light Programme listeners could tune into *Housewife's Choice* – 'popular gramophone records played for the nation's wives at home while their husbands are at work.' The programme was followed by Joseph Seal 'on the organ' and the fifteen-minute long daily radio serial *Mrs Dale's Diary* in which the star character (a doctor's wife played by Ellis Powell) told the nation frequently that she was worried about her son Bob (played by Nicholas Parsons).

The Light Programme was liberally sprinkled with news bulletins and current affairs programmes surrounding other daily favourites, including *Listen with Mother*, another fifteen-minute show featuring children's songs, nursery rhymes and a daily story introduced by a phrase asking children: 'Are you sitting comfortably? Then I'll begin . . .' By 1951 the programme was heard by more than 1 million children (and their mothers) across the nation and other countries painted bright pink on the world map.

Listen with Mother was followed by *Woman's Hour* – still a firm BBC favourite with listeners of both sexes – and later in the evening millions tuned into the latest episode of a new daily drama series, which had begun transmission four months before. It featured characters living at Brookfield Farm in a fictitious town called Ambridge and was called *The Archers*. People rushed home from work to eat their tea (most working people ate 'dinner' at lunchtime) to the sound of *The Archers*. Like *Woman's Hour*, *The Archers* still has a strong radio following in the twenty-first century.

The Home Service was more a more serious station offering plays and music. Daytime programming was directed at schools and produced to be played through large Bakelite radio sets in post-war classrooms with children sitting quietly at their desks listening to BBC academics discussing geography, history, science and literature.

Programmes lightened up during the early evening hours when the noise of rush-hour cars and buses boomed out of radio sets and an announcer shouted: 'Stop!' And the traffic noise miraculously ceased. In more modulate tones, the announcer continued: 'Once more we stop the mighty roar of London's traffic and, from the great crowds, bring you some of the interesting people who have come by land, sea and air to be *In Town Tonight!*'

Children's Hour (actually a fifty-five-minute long programme) comprised stories, talks, plays and drama serials and became a much loved national institution heard by millions of youngsters – mainly boys – eager to catch up with the latest adventures of schoolboy hero Jennings and boy detectives Norman and Henry Bones. In the evening, Home Service listeners tuned into *Twenty Questions* and *The Brains Trust* – programmes designed to fulfil the BBC's charter to 'educate, inform and entertain' the public at large.

The Third Programme was the BBC's heavyweight station dedicated to discerning or 'high-brow' listeners preferring serious classical music, concerts and plays to popular light music and 1950s' versions of today's soap operas. It was the corporation's least popular channel.

Although the BBC had started broadcasting television in 1936 and Britain was first in the world to have regular scheduling of programmes, TV was still a novelty in 1951. Less than one million people owned a television set – referred by many as 'the box in the corner' – and spent time watching eight hours of intermittent daily programmes. BBC Television opened up at 3 p.m. with a film followed by an hour-long children's programme starting at 5 p.m. This was followed by a two-hour long 'interval' before *BBC Newsreel* at 8 p.m. when most stories featured the 'newscaster' reading the news from a script like on radio with a small number of stories on film. The rest of the evening was made up of variety programmes and drama before a final news bulletin and weather forecast closed the station down at 10 p.m. sharp.

It was thanks to dramatic newspaper and radio coverage and a British cinema film that stories about submarine disasters and escapes were commonplace in the immediate post-war years. The nation was shocked in 1950 when HMS *Truculent*, a Royal Navy 'T' class submarine, was accidentally rammed by a Swedish tanker while cruising along on the surface on a cold, dark January night following sea trials in the Thames Estuary. Six men died immediately as a result of the collision and five others who had been on the bridge fell into the icy Thames water. They were rescued nearly one hour later.

Damage to *Truculent's* forward section caused the submarine to sink 60ft to the bottom of the estuary, where the sixty-seven men still on board gathered in the Engine Room to prepare for emergency escape using special breathing apparatus designed to take them to the surface. All the men were able to get out of the wreck, but only ten lived to tell the tale. The night was so cold and dark and the estuary ebb tide so strong that they quickly died of drowning or exposure. The loss of *Truculent* and her men was the Royal Navy's worst peacetime disaster and few thought that anything on a similar scale could ever happen again.

In the year before the *Truculent* disaster, British film director Roy Baker had begun shooting a feature film about a submarine disaster for the Rank Organisation entitled *Morning Departure*. It starred box office favourites John Mills and Richard Attenborough. After careful consideration, the Navy had agreed to cooperate with Baker, considering the film to be an accurate depiction of submarine life and an opportunity to show potential submariners that it was possible to escape from a trapped submarine. In return for lending a real submarine to the film-makers – HMS *Sirdar* – and allowing access to the dockyard at Portland, the Navy was allowed to suggest script changes that would more accurately reflect what was happening in the modern world of post-war submarine defence. Baker agreed and filming commenced in the summer of 1949.

In the film Mills, playing Lieutenant-Commander Armstrong, takes his submarine – named HMS *Trojan* for the story – out on a short exercise. His crew are all experienced men who get along with each other, apart from Attenborough's character – Stoker Snipe – a shy loner with marital problems at home.

At the start of the film Mills is seen telling his wife that he would be home in time for tea and later his fellow officers talk about playing cricket and meeting girlfriends when they returned to shore in the evening. Soon after diving, Mills peers through the periscope and spies an electronically operated German mine left over from the war floating on the surface. It is too late to avoid the mine and *Trojan* is rocked by an explosion sending it to the seabed. As both time and air begin to run out, Mills gathers the survivors together. The majority get out of the submarine using escape equipment, but the explosion has damaged some escape kits and a handful of men – including Mills, Attenborough and Able Seaman Higgins (James Hayter) – must remain behind in the stricken sub until help arrives.

Up on top a storm is raging, hampering rescue attempts by a depot ship. Down below air and food are running low. The captain of the depot ship says that further attempts to rescue *Trojan* would be dangerous to his men – and he orders the cables winching the sub to the surface to be cut. On hearing that rescue must be abandoned, Commander Gales of the depot ship (Bernard Lee) tells seamen on deck that the men below will die as 'a combination of two things that might happen to anyone at sea – bad luck and bad weather'.

In the stricken submarine Mills, Attenborough and Hayter sit around the wardroom table waiting for the end to come.

MILLS: I wonder what day it is?

HAYTER: Sunday, Sir.

MILLS: Six-o-clock Sunday morning. They'll be just about getting up for early service on the depot shop.

ATTENBOROUGH: What'll it be like, Sir? It's not that I'm frightened, Sir. It's just that I'd like to know. Be the end of everything, I suppose.

MILLS: Maybe the beginning. (He reaches for a prayer book from the shelf.) Don't you chaps think it might be rather a good idea if we joined those fellows in the depot ship? (Begins to read the Seaman's Prayer out aloud as lights in the submarine grow dim and the camera pulls back to show the injured *Trojan* on the seabed and a marker buoy tossing around like a cork in the stormy water above).

The End.

While the film was being edited for release, the *Truculent* disaster hit the headlines. For the Royal Navy, the true story of HMS *Truculent* and fictitious HMS *Trojan* was too similar to be true and the Admiralty asked J. Arthur Rank himself to delay its release. In the end, the Royal Navy and British movie mogul arrived at a compromise: A statement would be made at the start of the film:

> This film was completed before the tragic loss of *HMS Truculent* and earnest consideration has been given as to the desirability of presenting it so soon after this grievous disaster. The producers have decided to offer the film in the spirit which it was made, as a tribute to the officers and men of HM Submarines and the Royal Navy of which they form a part.

The Navy also insisted on a final caption at the close of the film:

> The Producer gratefully acknowledges the co-operation and facilities given by the Admiralty and the officers and men of HM Submarines and the Salvage Service in the making of this film, *which does not portray the latest developments in submarine escape and salvage.*

Morning Departure was a 1950 British box office hit and despite its occasional stiff-upper-lip approach to life in the submarine service in the face of disaster, it remains a gripping and convincing piece of cinema. The public loved the film and the press were not slow to draw parallels between what had happened in the Thames Estuary earlier that year and the story unfolding on the silver screen a few months later. Recruitment into the submarine service also doubled everywhere *Morning Departure* was shown.

Another major news story grabbed the headlines the following year. It was an event designed by the country's new post-war Labour government to cheer up British people and offer a gesture of hope for the country's future as the austerity years dragged on. It was called the Festival of Britain and took the form of a gigantic outdoor and indoor spectacle costing £11 million and celebrating the battered old country's post-war industrial, architectural and cultural achievements. The event was to be presented on two massive London sites – a bombed out area near Waterloo Station on the south bank of the Thames, which would house the exhibition, and Battersea Pleasure Gardens, which would be home to a giant fun fair. It was held in April 1951 exactly 100 years after Prince Albert's famous Great Exhibition had been staged in London's Hyde Park.

The Festival of Britain was a five-month long showcase for all things British – architecture, industry, furniture, interior decoration, cars, food and the arts. The main centrepieces were the brand new Royal Festival Hall, a 'dome of discovery' and a strange vertical sculpture looking like a space rocket with pointed ends at the top and bottom, 'The Skylon'. The official programme described this piece of art as 'symbolising the spirit of new hope . . . announcing that drab, grey, funless times are conclusively over'. At night Skylon would be illuminated from within making it appear to hang in the sky with no visible means of support.

There were pavilions celebrating 'The British land and its people, minerals of our land, power and production, sea and ships, health, sport, television, telecinema and design.'

Festival of Britain stories began appearing in newspapers months before building gangs moved onto the two sites to clear thousands of tons of *blitzkrieg* debris to make way for the wonders of modern Britain. Readers, listeners and a tiny handful of TV viewers were treated to daily updates about how work on the event was progressing. The public began planning day trips to London to experience the Festival of Britain for themselves, feeling they had earned the right to enjoy their country's achievements at first hand, determined that nothing was going to knock their favourite story out of the spotlight.

But with just nineteen days to go before King George VI was to officially open the Festival and tour the site, a Royal Navy 'A' class submarine was easing its way from its berth at Gosport and into the Solent to take part in a peacetime 'war game' exercise and signalled to shore that it was about to dive. It never surfaced again and for the next four days all excitement about the Festival of Britain was forgotten while the entire nation tuned into the radio and held its breath.

HMS *Affray*

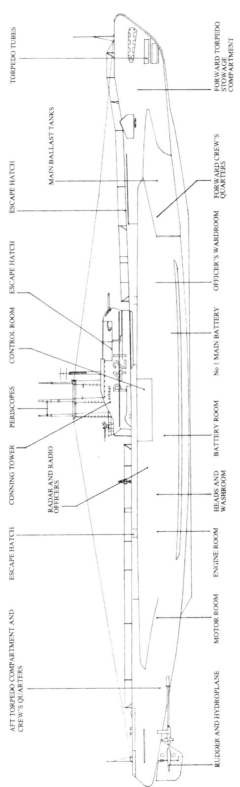

TORPEDO TUBES

MAIN BALLAST TANKS

ESCAPE HATCH

ESCAPE HATCH

CONTROL ROOM

PERISCOPES

CONNING TOWER

RADAR AND RADIO OFFICERS

ESCAPE HATCH

ENGINE ROOM

MOTOR ROOM

RUDDER AND HYDROPLANE

AFT TORPEDO COMPARTMENT AND CREW'S QUARTERS

FORWARD TORPEDO STOWAGE COMPARTMENT

FORWARD CREW'S QUARTERS

OFFICER'S WARDROOM

No 1 MAIN BATTERY

BATTERY ROOM

HEADS AND WASHROOM

British 'A' for Acheron Class Large Patrol Submarine

This illustration shows HMS *Affray* as she would have looked when finally commissioned by the Royal Navy in November 1945. *Affray* received its snort mast in January 1950 and at the same time lost its 4in and 20mm anti-aircraft weapon to create more room for the device. The mast and its hoisting gear were fixed to the port side of the aft deck and when not in use, laid flat along the deck and locked into position in a 'collar' at the side of the conning tower.

Built by: Cammell Laird & Co Ltd, Birkenhead

Laid down: January 1944

Launched: April 1945

Commissioned: November 1945

Lost at sea during Exercise Training Spring in April 1951, with 75 officers and men on board

Reason for loss: 'Unknown'

Pennant number: P421

Motto: 'Strong in Battle'

Dimension: Length 281ft 9in
            Beam 22ft 3in
            Depth 16ft 9in

Normal crew complement: 61 (75 on board at time of loss)

Propulsion: 2 sets diesel engines
            2 sets electric motors
            Twin screws

Range: 10,500 miles at 11 knots surfaced
       16 miles at 8 knots submerged
       90 miles at 3 knots submerged

Speed: 18.5 knots surfaced
       8 knots submerged

Commanding Officer at time of loss: Lieutenant Commander John Blackburn, DSC

(Illustration drawn by Gary Symes from information contained in original Admiralty documents)

Chapter 2

THE SILENT SERVICE AND HIS MAJESTY'S SUBMARINE *AFFRAY*

Submarines have been around since 1620, when a Dutchman in the service of King James I of England built a vessel, which was navigated at a depth of 12–15ft for several hours in the Thames. The first mechanically powered 'submarine boat' to successfully dive and resurface was christened *Le Plongeur* (The Diver). It was launched in Rochefort, France, in April 1863 – ten years before Jules Verne created his fictional submarine *Nautilus* in *20,000 Leagues Under the Sea* about which a character describes 'an enormous thing, a long object, spindle-shaped, occasionally phosphorescent and infinitely larger and more rapid in its movements than a whale'.

For years sailors and maritime engineers had attempted to devise ways of producing a weapon of war that could travel underwater to attack their enemies. Propelled by compressed air stored in twenty-three large tanks to power its engine, *Le Plongeur* was a super-size submarine. The engine could generate up to 80hp (60kW), enough to travel distances of up to five nautical miles on the surface. *Le Plongeur* could not travel far or fast, but she was the first of her kind.

The submarine made its first dive the following year, but the engine was unable to cope with excessive amounts of compressed air pumped into it and *Le Plongeur* ran into the quay. After modifications, it dived to 30ft a few days later. The submarine never managed to dive below 33ft, but if proof was needed that a vessel could successfully submerge and travel underwater, *Le Plongeur* confirmed it could be done.

As late as 1900 the British Admiralty declared: 'We are not prepared to take steps in regard to submarines because the vessels are only the weapons of the weaker nations.' Fortunately, a group of young English naval officers decided otherwise and their exertions compelled the Admiralty to buy early-twentieth-century submarine technology from an Irish-American designer named John Phillip Holland.

Holland's first submarine, built by Vickers, Sons & Maxim Ltd in Barrow-in-Furness in 1901, was named *Holland 1* after the designer. It was while working as a teacher in New Jersey that Holland had developed an interest in the potential of developing submarines for warfare. Sponsored by an Irish revolutionary group, the Fenian Brotherhood, he built a small one-man submarine, which the US Navy bought for $150,000.

Holland accepted a commission from the Admiralty to design an eight-man craft to assist the Royal Navy's coastal defences. It was equipped to carry and fire three 18in torpedoes and fitted with one of the first ever periscopes allowing men to watch what was happening on the surface from a safe depth below the waves. While Holland's periscope could turn through 180 degrees, the image appeared upside down.

Powered by a 70hp electric motor and fitted with 60 battery cells located beneath the deck, *Holland I* could travel up to 20 miles underwater at speeds of 7 knots and dive to a depth of 100ft. She measured 58ft in length with a beam of 11ft. She weighed 100 tons and was lifted out of the water by a crane. The bridge consisted of a handrail and on it was no protection of any kind.

When surfaced she was driven at 7 knots. Fumes were so obnoxious that, as a matter of course, officers and men either fainted or became intoxicated. The wardroom was smaller than a modern-day passenger lift and conditions on board were so dangerous that the Admiralty issued a ration of white mice to be used (like canaries in coal mines) to test the atmosphere. *Holland 1* was called 'the pigboat' and the men who sailed in her 'pigmen'. The names were used to describe submarines and submariners for several decades afterwards.

Admiralty top brass hated the submarine, branding *Holland I* 'a damned un-English' weapon of war. Although early submarines killed more of their own men than of the enemy's, it was no longer possible to regard them as freakish toys.

The first British-designed submarine, known as the '*A1*', was launched in 1902. She was lost with all hands when the steamer *Berwick Castle* rammed her off the Nab Lightship in March 1904. But despite these early disasters, the Navy became convinced that submarines had a future and this was confirmed after enemy U-Boats came close to winning the First World War for Germany.

A publication produced for the Admiralty by the Ministry of Information in 1945 to attract volunteers to the submarine service stated:

To the layman, the submarine is a novelty, strange and little understood and the Submarine Branch of the Royal Navy is cloaked in mystery. It is the most silent branch of a silent service, for many of its activities must be kept in secret and some of its finest triumphs will remain unrecorded until after the war. The men who man the submarines must not only be specially qualified and trained but peculiarly fitted for their duties. In wartime they are not all volunteers, but it is rare for a submariner to request to go back to General Service.

British and Allied submarines played a vital part in winning the war at sea in the Battle of the Atlantic. They had helped to cut Rommel's supply lines in the Mediterranean, supply Malta at the height of the siege, smuggle Allied generals to England and virtually destroy Japan's merchant shipping fleet in the Pacific. They were used to carry landing parties who demolished railways and bridges, hoping that luck would enable them to return to the submarine under cover of darkness. Submarines were used to creep into the very heart of enemy harbours and blow up warships at their moorings.

By the time HMS *Affray* – pennant number P421 – was completed by Cammell Laird & Company Ltd of Birkenhead and received by the Royal Navy 'without prejudice to outstanding liabilities' at 1600 hours on 2 May 1946, submarines had proved their worth many times over. Like all 'A' class submarines manufactured during wartime, *Affray* was intended for conflicts in distant war zones such as the Far East. Following the outbreak of war in the region, submarine designers were forced to rethink how boats should be modified since existing models were unsuitable for tropical climates or large expanses of ocean.

'A' class vessels were specifically designed for such conditions. At 281ft 9in long, a beam measuring 22ft 3in and a height of 16ft 9in, they were more streamlined than their predecessors and could travel up to 10,500 miles at surface speeds of 18.5 knots, and 10 knots instead of the usual 8 while submerged. *Affray* could dive to a depth of 500ft but could go deeper if necessary without risk of her hull collapsing.

The boats also offered better conditions for their crew of officers and ratings – up to sixty-one in peacetime and sixty-six in war conditions – and although submarines were cramped and claustrophobic, 'A' class boats were fitted with air-conditioning and refrigeration, making life inside more comfortable. Most submariners, however, felt the extra half-crown a week they were paid for working on submarines made any discomfort worthwhile and only a few regretted 'signing up to go down'.

Many perceived submarines as dark, cold, damp, oily, cramped and full of intricate machinery. Edward Young, who joined the submarine service as a sub-lieutenant in the Royal Naval Volunteer Reserve in 1940 and went on to command HMS *Storm*, remembered his first visit to HMS *Otway* at Gosport in his classic memoir, *One of Our Submarines*:

I was rather disappointed at the fragile and ratty appearance of this submarine. It was so different from the sleek, streamlined craft of my imagination. I was unaware that most of what I could see was a sort of outer shell which filled with water when the submarine dived. The whole of the long, narrow deck, and most of the bridge structure, were in fact pierced by innumerable holes, so as to allow this outer casing to flood when diving and drain away when surfacing. As we were led for'ard and told to climb down through a round hatch into the innards of this monster, I don't think any of us felt very happy about it.

Once inside, Young was astonished by the size of the boat and the fact that he was able to stand up to his full height and walk about with ease. He found the hull was wider than a London tube train and was surprised by the brightness of the lighting everywhere.

'In the messes there were wooden bunks and cupboards and curtains and pin-up girls and tables with green baize clothes. I had not expected to find so much comfort and cosiness,' he recalled.

Affray's accommodation space, divided between the fore-ends and the boat's control room, was far from spacious. While messes were crowded places and wooden bunks used by the crew were short, submarine crews were quick to adapt and there were few complaints. In addition to a kit bag, the only other item submariners brought on board was their 'ditty box' – a plain, unpainted wooden box in which they kept personal items such as photographs, a writing pad, plus a sewing and wash kit.

The bunks concealed one of the submarine's most vital systems – half of the boat's 224 large lead-acid batteries, each weighing half a ton, which powered the submarine while submerged and supplied power to numerous auxiliary circuits. One hundred and twelve batteries hidden beneath the accommodation section and held in place with asbestos string, supplied the starboard switchboard and main motor while the remainder, located underneath the heads (toilets) and washroom, also supplied the main motor and port switchboard.

Officers and chief petty officers had their own bunks near their wardroom, but junior ratings wishing to sleep after a long watch sometimes had to search for a 'hot bunk' – a nice warm bed recently vacated by the man coming on watch. Newly joined submariners quickly learned not to be too fastidious about sharing. Not that it mattered as everyone on board hummed with the same all-pervading smell of diesel fuel which clung to clothing in the open air and on shore.

The captain was the only person on board with space to himself – a small watertight cylindrical shaped 'room' positioned inside the conning tower, allowing him to gain access to the bridge or the control room equally quickly. Most captains hated this arrangement, preferring to live in the wardroom with other officers where they could be in touch with everything going on – even while asleep.

Other 'A' class innovations included an all-welded hull, radar that could be worked from periscope depth and a night periscope. The submarines were only marginally quieter than their predecessors. Engine noise has always been a dangerous thing in submarines, allowing them to be detected by the enemy or quickly located thanks to anti-submarine sonar systems. 'A' class boats, however, were hardly silent beasts. Thanks to the complexity of their engines, there was no part of the boat that officers and ratings could escape for peace and quiet. Over time, submarine crews became used to the thundering mass of metal and machinery and after a while they hardly noticed the continual engine churn night and day, above water and while submerged.

Affray could carry a larger weapon load than other conventional submarines, avoiding any need to return to base from far-flung patrol areas every time its torpedoes had been fired. Its bow section was taken up by six 21in torpedo tubes (two positioned externally) and a stern compartment fitted with four 21in diameter tubes. A further four torpedo tubes – two of them external – were positioned in the stern of the boat. Each of the twenty torpedoes on board weighed around one and a half tons and carried an 805lb explosive charge. They were moved from their storage space into the firing tubes using chains, block and tackle and a great deal of sweat and muscle from the crew.

The forward torpedo stowage compartment served as the boat's community centre. It was here that films were screened and church services held on Sundays at sea. The captain conducted services as an unpaid parson with the off-watch crew crammed into the section in between and all around torpedo tubes. The area was also one of *Affray*'s main escape compartments with an evacuation hatch positioned amidships. If crew needed to evacuate from their boat quickly in an emergency, they would hastily don specially designed Davis Submerged Escape Apparatus – invented by Sir Robert Davis in 1910 and better known as DSEA – and while the compartment was flooded to equalise pressure and allow the hatch to be opened, they would breathe pure air from an in-built system in the apparatus.

Affray's control room was positioned directly beneath the conning tower and contained practically everything necessary to dive and navigate the submarine. To a newcomer, the space was a confusion of pipes, valves, electric wiring, switches, dials, wheels, levers, pressure gauges, depth gauges, junction boxes, navigational instruments and other mystery gadgets covering every inch of the area apart from the floor.

Diving and surfacing was a simple procedure. Like all submarines, *Affray* rose on the air in its main ballast tanks, which ran along the hull on the outside of the boat. Large free-flood holes in the bottom were always open and as soon as the main vents were hydraulically released from the control room, supporting air was released and water flooded the tanks to take her underwater. The main vents were shut when fully submerged allowing the boat to return to the surface at any time by blowing water out of the main ballast tanks using high-pressure air injection.

On-board WCs – known as 'the heads' – and washrooms were positioned alongside a passageway leading to *Affray*'s engine room. The submarine was equipped with two fresh-water distillers, but they used too much electric power to run continuously and water was always in short supply while on patrol. On longer patrols it was rationed to one gallon per man per day for all purposes, including cooking and washing up. There was no spare water for bathing and crew had to rinse dirt, oil and grease from their hands in a communal bucket before undertaking a more thorough wash in one of the washroom's steel basins. Crew members on long patrols rarely washed, as the lyrics of a popular submariner's song testifies:

> *For I don't give a damn wherever you've been,*
> *Nobody washes in a Submarine.*
> *The Navy think we're a crabby clan,*
> *We haven't had a wash since the trip began.*
> *We've been at sea three weeks or more,*
> *And now we're covered in shit galore,*
> *Our feet are black where they once were pink,*
> *Three blokes already have died of the stink.*
> *We hid them in the fore-end where they couldn't be seen*
> *For to throw them in the sea meant they might have got clean.*

The heads on 'A' class boats were better designed than sewerage disposal systems found in other submarines where contents had to be blown directly into the sea by 'pulling the plug'. This occurrence occasionally failed when sea pressure overcame blowing pressure and was known as 'getting your own back'. *Affray* was fitted with a sewerage tank into which all heads drained and this was blown periodically, usually at night where there was less risk of bubbles being spotted on the surface.

A small galley catered for officers and ratings and a single chef was kept busy for the duration of a patrol cooking three daily meals plus numerous 'brews' of strong tea. Bread loaded on board at the start of a long patrol quickly went stale, so the chef was required to bake fresh bread at regular intervals, filling the submarine with a welcome aroma that made a pleasant change to diesel and oil fumes.

Despite on-shore rationing, food served on submarines was plentiful and filling and every on-board cook had his own 'signature dish' to break up the monotony of tinned pie and mash. Favourites served on *Affray* by Cook Bob Smith included 'Elephant's Footprints' (diced spam dipped in batter and deep fried until crisp), 'Kye' (a drink for anyone feeling a need to put extra hairs on their chest, made from cooking chocolate, condensed milk, boiling water and sugar all mixed together), 'Pussers Pot Mess' (a great delicacy made from tinned stewing steak, potatoes, tomatoes, baked beans and tinned spaghetti mixed in a large pot, heated 'until festering', served in a mug and eaten with a spoon), and 'S**t on a Raft' (kidneys cooked in Worcester sauce, mustard, butter, cayenne pepper, mushroom ketchup and eaten with bread which had been swimming in a fat fry).

Submarine meals were hardly haute cuisine, but hungry men working around-the-clock on watch were glad to be served anything hot and with a bit of flavour. There was little waste and rarely any leftovers. Officers ate meals in their own wardroom, sitting at a dining table covered with a cloth, and were served by a steward, while ratings consumed food anywhere available to them, often perched on a bunk or standing next to a table covered with charts or navigational equipment. Ratings queued in the passageway for meals, ate their food, returned plates and cutlery for washing and returned to work.

Following meal breaks, the highlight of any submariner's day was his daily tot of rum, one of the longest unbroken traditions in the history of the Royal Navy and dating back to the days of Lord Nelson. Each day sailors and submariners were served 1/8th pint of neat 'Pusser's Rum' – a blend specially made for the Navy – kept under lock and key in a wardroom cupboard. Officers were allowed to swap rum rations for spirits and pink gin (gin mixed with Angostura Bitters and tonic water if you could get it), a popular substitute in the 1950s.

Any free time on a submarine at sea was spent reading, writing letters home or playing cards or board games including cribbage, dominoes, draughts or chess. The most popular game was 'Uckers', played by four submariners using a traditional Ludo board and two dice instead of one. The rules were more complicated than Ludo and winning teams became submarine heroes until knocked off their pedestal by the next winning team.

Once meal times were over, it was back to work in the noisiest part of the boat for many crew members, a compartment shared by the engine room and motor room. Powering *Affray* on the surface were 8-cylinder, 4-stroke supercharged Admiralty pattern diesels, which thundered around the clock. The motor room was where speed and direction of the main motors – ahead or astern – were controlled as well as battery charging and the supply to auxiliary circuits. When submerged, *Affray* was powered by twin direct-drive English Electric motors.

As well as acting as a torpedo stowage compartment and tube space similar to the forward section, the after end also provided additional living quarters. Space in this section was much sought after, being as far away as possible from the engine room and the officers. It offered a small amount of privacy – the ultimate luxury in *Affray*.

Although life on board a submarine was far from comfortable, most submariners loved the life they had chosen to follow. As volunteers, they had signed up for the

submarine service, although many claimed that the extra weekly half-crown paid
to members of the submarine service was the main attraction.

'Underneath the Surface', a popular song among submariners in the 1950s and
sung to the tune of Flanagan & Allen's 'Underneath the Arches', captured how
most submariners felt about the service they were proud to have joined:

> *Big ships we never cared for,*
> *Destroyers they can keep.*
> *There's only one place that we know*
> *That is deep down deep.*
> *Underneath the surface*
> *We dream our dreams away,*
> *Underneath the surface,*
> *On battery-boards we lay.*
> *There you'll always find us,*
> *Tired out and worn,*
> *Waiting for the Coxswain to wake us*
> *With the sound of the Klaxon horn.*
> *Then we all get busy,*
> *The Tiffies and the 'Swains',*
> *Working vents and blows and hydroplanes*
> *And when the panic's over*
> *We'll get it down again;*
> *Underneath the surface*
> *We dream our dreams away.*

('Tiffies' is an abbreviation of the rank 'Artificer' and 'Swains' an abbreviation of
'Coxswain.')

❖   ❖   ❖

Work constructing *Affray* commenced at Cammell Laird's yard on 16 January
1944 and the submarine was launched on 12 April 1945. Under her first
commanding officer, Lieutenant-Commander E.J.D. Turner, the boat was allocated
to the 3rd Submarine Squadron on 5 November 1945, based on the submarine
depot ship HMS *Montclare* at Rosyth. It was here just sixteen days later that *Affray*
experienced the first of many mechanical problems that would disrupt her service
life over the next five and a half years.

During sea trials in the Firth of Forth, *Affray*'s number one battery flooded
without warning forcing her to return to Cammell Laird for investigation. Over

the next three months, *Affray* underwent a series of tests and alterations before being finally accepted into service on 2 May 1946 by which time the war was over and the submarine saw no armed combat, making her motto 'Strong in Battle' unproven and redundant.

The mechanical breakdowns continued. On 3 September she needed another new battery and again returned to Birkenhead where she entered the yard for a week between 6–12 October.

Later that month *Affray* was assigned to the 4th Submarine Flotilla in Sydney, Australia, as part of the British Pacific Fleet, which included other 'A' class submarines *Amphion*, *Astute*, *Auriga* and *Aurochs*. En route in the Atlantic, *Affray* reported defects in her starboard supercharger and portside air compressor that would need attention once she entered harbour at the South African port of Simonstown, near Cape Town. Despite her mechanical problems, *Affray* smashed the UK–South Africa submarine speed record travelling both underwater and on the surface.

It would take *Affray* another four months before she finally arrived in Sydney. At Simonstown she was assigned to anti-submarine exercises during which excessive wear to her stern bushes caused *Affray* to enter dock once again for another month of repair work. Her crew were delighted. South Africa in December 1946 and January 1947 was a marvellous place to be. Unlike at home, the climate was warm and sunny, there was no rationing, the beer was cheap and officers and men from the submarine soon made friends with nurses from the local naval hospital.

When *Affray* arrived in Colombo, Ceylon, on 1 March 1947, she entered dry dock for a further week of maintenance followed by another two weeks at the naval dockyard in Singapore for repairs to her stern bushes. After visits to five different Japanese seaports and Hong Kong over a five-month period, *Affray* returned to Singapore for a partial refit on 13 September and finally arrived in Sydney on 7 April 1948.

It had been a long voyage to the other side of the world and *Affray*'s crew had plenty of time to get used to the sunshine and taste of Australian beer over the next few months that the submarine was based at the naval dockyard. Several crew members were discharged while *Affray* was in Sydney and some remained behind to become new Australian citizens.

By October 1948, *Affray* had returned to British waters, travelling home via Singapore, Colombo, Aden, Malta and Gibraltar. On the voyage home she had a most unusual encounter. While cruising on the surface off the coast of Portugal, a whale suddenly rose up in front of the submarine. Unable to stop in time, *Affray* smashed into the beast at full speed, cutting the unfortunate mammal in half. The submarine, however, was undamaged.

Back in home waters, *Affray* was now part of the 5th Submarine Flotilla based at HMS *Dolphin* in Gosport. June 1950 found her in the Norwegian ports of Galesund, Bergen and Haugesund before returning to Manchester on 7 July, where the crew were allowed to invite wives, parents and girlfriends on board for a tour of the vessel, followed by tea on shore.

By now *Affray* had covered 51,000 miles criss-crossing the globe. In December 1948 she had participated in her first exercise in home waters, Exercise Sunrise, and on 22 July 1950 she took part in Exercise Seaweed, carrying a group of trainee officers out to sea in simulated wartime conditions. By now *Affray* had her fourth commanding officer, Lieutenant Leafric Temple-Richards, and the training exercise went without a hitch. Nine months later *Affray* would participate in a similar training exercise with another commanding officer in charge. It would be her last voyage and she would never again return to Gosport.

❖   ❖   ❖

After its defeat of The Netherlands in 1940, the German Navy discovered that a Dutch submarine squadron had been experimenting with an underwater 'breathing device' called a *schnorchel* or 'snort' system. This took the form of a long steel tube with a head valve at the top to prevent the entry of seawater when raised and a hull valve where the induction system entered the engine room. While on the surface, engine exhaust gases passed through muffler tanks at water level, but when snorting underwater, the gases had to be taken up through an exhaust mast whose open end was a few feet below the surface. At the same time, fresh air was drawn down into the vessel through a separate tube contained within the snort mast system. The Germans stole the idea and perfected it for their U-boats.

A 35ft long tubular snort mast was fitted to the hull by a large flange and secured to a cradle when not in use. It could be raised and lowered pneumatically from the engine room and self-locked into both positions. At the point where the air intake entered the hull was a bulbous casting housing the main induction valve and concealed from view. A float valve was designed to close automatically whenever the submarine dropped below periscope depth.

The Royal Navy claimed the snort mast as 'a first' for Britain, but failed to mention that it was invented for the Dutch navy and adopted by the Germans. It dramatically altered the amount of time submarines could remain underwater. During trials at the end of the 1940s, a British submarine fitted with a snort mast remained submerged for forty days. In 1949 all 'A' class vessels were fitted with snort masts, manufactured at the Vickers-Armstrong factory in Barrow-in-Furness.

Snort masts were regarded as a wonderful invention, but in 1951 they had some serious flaws that needed to be ironed out. Frequently, submarines cruising at periscope depth with the snort mast raised encountered swell, causing back pressure to direct water flooding down through the exhaust tube. Water could also enter the snort induction hull valve so rapidly that it could sink the submarine. The need to thoroughly train crews about correct usage of snorting equipment was paramount in the submarine service. Used and monitored correctly when raised, snorting apparatus allowed submarines to do things never thought possible beneath the sea ten years before. Used incorrectly by busy or inexperienced crew in the engine room, the snort could quickly send a submarine to the bottom of the sea.

Another drawback to the snort mast was the partial vacuum that ran throughout the entire submarine while snorting, because the engines drew air from inside the boat as well as down the snort tube. There were limitations on the level of vacuum permitted as any long-term change in conditions within the submarine placed pressure on the crew's ears and hearing.

Affray received its own snort mast in January 1950 and at the same time lost its 4in gun and 20mm anti-aircraft weapon to create more room for the new device. The mast and its hoisting gear was fixed to the port side of the aft deck and when not in use, laid flat along the deck and locked into position in a 'collar' on one side of the conning tower.

Her mechanical problems, however, continued.

Chapter 3

'DEAR DAD, I THINK THIS BOAT IS JUST ABOUT FINISHED . . .'

By the time *Affray* entered HM Dockyard, Portsmouth, for a major refit on 8 May 1950, she was an exhausted boat. Since entering service four years previously, she had travelled to the other side of the world and back, clocked up tens of thousands of miles and was badly in need of substantial repairs.

While still in the dockyard, *Affray*'s commander, Lieutenant Leafric Temple-Richards, received orders to sail and participate alongside other European navies in joint manoeuvres in Atlantic and Mediterranean waters between 1 September and 7 December 1950. Exercises in home waters were designated 'The Autumn Cruise'. Once *Affray* arrived in Gibraltar the submarine would be taking part in Exercise Crafty Corsair involved in manoeuvres spread across long days at sea and shorter ones back in Gibraltar.

It was during the Portsmouth dockyard period that experienced crew members began expressing serious concerns about *Affray*'s mechanical and structural condition. One of them was Chief Petty Officer Engine Room Artificer 2nd Class David Bennington – known to his pals as Jim – who sent regular letters to his father, Oscar, in Ilfracombe, Devon, with news about his work in *Affray*'s engine room while in the dockyard. Bennington had joined the Navy straight from school at the age of 15. In a letter written shortly before *Affray* headed into the Atlantic, he wrote:

Another full day of work today right up to 10 o'clock and will be at it all day tomorrow, too. We must be ready for sea on Monday to exercise with the French and the Portuguese navies . . . whether we will be ready in time is very doubtful as the deeper we get into this job the worse it becomes. As far as I can see these engines have had their time. It's come to the stage now when I wonder what the devil is to happen next. I'm sorry for the engineer, I think he is very, very fed up and he does work extremely hard. Well, from now on until we reach home, all

I can see is piles of work in front of us . . . I shouldn't be surprised if this boat pays off and went into reserve. By this time I'm heartily fed up with it . . .

At sea during the exercise, Bennington told his father in another letter:

I have just spent 24 hours solid working in the engine room getting one of the engines going. We are way out in the Atlantic on exercises and they made us go out with one engine only working and we just had to press on until we got the other going.

In another letter penned a few days later, Bennington described 'another crazy day, no sleep, just diving, surfacing, attacking and snorting. Water and oil pouring everywhere and everything falling over. I feel just about all in now and everyone is very, very threadbare.' 'Falling over' is a naval phrase used when pistons break down and engines grind to a stop.

The same letter relates to

another awful day at sea – we went off at 5 this morning and after continuous exercises all day we should have been in at 7 tonight. The usual thing happened though, one engine fell over and we limped in on one, and just as we arrived in the other went and we are now left with another pile of work. This is getting serious as every time we go to sea now they fall over. It really is a terrible boat and I feel very sorry for our engineer. When I get home I'll try and describe scares and pandemonium that reign at times in our engine room. Looking back on them they seem very funny but they are not as funny when they are actually happening . . . I wish they would send us home right away as I think this boat is just about finished.

According to Bennington, *Affray*'s engines continued in 'a pretty awful state' once the submarine arrived in Gibraltar in early November 1950 for the final part of Exercise Crafty Corsair, taking it onto Casablanca for two weeks. In this latest letter home, Bennington told his father:

At present the powers that be are deciding what shall be done . . . She is being used so much that we have no time to keep her in good running repair. She leaks like a sieve and when doing a deep dive the other day the water poured into the engine room faster than we could keep it out, so we had to surface with all speed . . . In my view the blasted thing rolls alarmingly.

Leading Stoker Mechanic William Day joined *Affray*'s crew in March 1950 and left the boat when she re-entered the dockyard for more repairs in January 1951. His job in the engine room was to raise, lower, open and close the snort mast's induction tube and he recalled a list of defects encountered on the submarine during Exercise Crafty Corsair:

> The starter of the ballast pump always broke down and we had to call in an electrician every so often . . . The snort induction would close much slower than it should have. The reason is because the fixed hollow ram had a leak. I know this because once when I was bending over to do a job underneath the engine room induction, there was always a drop of oil coming out . . . As regards the engine room, as soon as we surfaced from snorting there was always a lot of water in the engine. We had to blow several times to get the water out of the engine before starting off again.

Once Exercise Crafty Corsair had been completed on 16 November, *Affray* left Gibraltar and limped back to HMS *Dolphin*, diving to a depth of 300ft for part of the journey. Her crew was ready for Christmas leave, although some would return early to be present when the submarine was again booked into HM Dockyard, Portsmouth, for a full engine refit starting on 1 January 1951. She would remain there for several weeks before taking part in another manoeuvre called Exercise Training Spring with a new commander in charge, Lieutenant-Commander John Blackburn.

Blackburn, age 28 and from York, was an experienced submariner and by 1951 had been in the Royal Navy for nine years. He was the son of a famous seafaring father, Captain J.A.P. Blackburn who had commanded the armed merchant cruiser *Voltaire* when she was sunk defending a convoy in 1941 and was taken prisoner.

Blackburn was awarded the DSC in 1943 for 'great daring enterprise and skill in successful patrols in one of HM submarines'. The submarine in question was HMS *Safari*, an 'S' class boat responsible for sinking over 30,000 tons of enemy shipping in Mediterranean waters. The award was published in the *London Gazette* on 6 July 1943. Blackburn was also mentioned in dispatches for gallantry, skill and outstanding devotion to duty while serving in submarines in numerous successful patrols, often in trying climatic conditions in the Pacific, frequently carried out in shallow or difficult waters and under enemy fire.

After the war, Blackburn spent eleven months in charge of the snort-fitted submarine HMS *Token* before taking up an eighteen-month appointment on the training ship HMS *Devonshire*, including duties as a member of the submarine training staff at HMS *Dolphin*. Blackburn was no stranger to working with trainees and during command of HMS *Sea Scout* during Exercise March Flight in the spring of 1950 had regularly taken trainee classes to sea in submarines for two days each week.

While on leave in 1944, Blackburn had married a young Wren, Jean Cowan, and now the couple were living in Gosport with their two children, Anthony, 6, and Jill, 4. Their home was conveniently situated close to HMS *Dolphin* and his new command of *Affray* began on 17 March while the boat was still in the dockyard at Portsmouth undergoing repairs. An Admiralty report on Blackburn's character noted that his 'considerable wartime experience, peacetime training experience and his sterling character' made him 'perfectly suitable' for his new command of *Affray*.

Work returning the submarine to good health moved slowly during the early months of 1951. Dave Lowe from Portsmouth, who worked as a ship's civilian fitter apprentice at the dockyard in the early 1950s, recalls that the facility employed non-naval staff to work alongside service personnel – and there were often hostilities between the two factions.

'Naval staff working up on the bridge sometimes peed on civilian dockyard staff from a "pee tube" – a little device allowing submariners working up top while at sea to take a pee without having to go down below or have the wind blow it back at them.' Lowe remembers. 'The tube channelled the pee directly down – and when a sub was in the dockyard, it pointed down to civilians working below.'

Dave remembers that when no officers were present, Navy personnel often went to sleep on the job, or spent time sunbathing on deck. 'On one occasion I needed to lower the snort mast, causing a group of submarine sailors to come running down looking for the person responsible for spoiling their sunbathing session. Naturally, I didn't own up.'

There was also conflict between the many different trades working at the dockyard and a general lack of coordination between naval and civilian staff. 'When we were trying to fit hydraulics, painters would turn up at the same time to do their work in the same place,' says Dave.

Many repair jobs were conducted by civilian personnel 'on the note', requiring a written purchase order be drafted and the Navy later invoiced for the work. According to Dave, if the Navy could short cut this by doing the job themselves or manage with a half-finished job, they were happy to do so, creating more friction with civilian staff.

During this time, David Bennington was still at work down in *Affray's* engine room helping with repairs. On 5 February he wrote to his father: 'I simply had to see the doctor today and he said I had flu and was in need of a rest. I was never so glad to see the last of anything as I was to see the last of the *Affray*.' Bennington was sent to hospital and when discharged sent on home leave, returning to HMS *Dolphin* on 8 April 'to find that the *Affray* is still in the dockyard. I am wondering if she will ever get out of there.' *Affray's* logbooks confirm that repair and maintenance work was, indeed, taking far too long. Logbook entries for most

of March 1951 show that practically no repairs were completed although there
are numerous entries stating that 'cleaning' had been taking place.

Able Seaman George Cook joined *Affray*'s crew from the submarine *Amphion*
on Friday 13 April 1951. He had been loaned out to *Affray* for two weeks while
another sailor was given leave to represent submariners in a shooting contest. In
a letter to his wife Joy, George said he had been reunited with schoolfriend David
'Jim' Bennington on the *Affray*. Mrs Cook said: 'The letter said that they were
rushing about cleaning up the boat ready for sailing and while he was trying to
clean up the control room, Jim was making a mess with his oil can.'

Electrical Artificer 2nd Class Alexander Duncombe joined *Affray*'s crew at the
dockyard on Monday 2 April. Speaking about working in the engine room while
Affray was in the dockyard he later recalled:

We had one or two teething troubles at first, but the main one was the number
one battery tank. On Friday April 6 when I was duty Petty Officer, oil was
found in the number one battery tank. I put some waste down on a line and
cleaned it out. I reported to the First Lieutenant and kept the waste to show the
Engineer Officer in the morning. I was told that we would very likely go and
have the battery lifted. We looked in every four or five hours after but we did
not see any more trace of oil fuel.

When asked how much oil had been found and where it might have come
from, Duncombe said:

Mixed with water, I should say about a quarter of a bucketful . . . The First
Lieutenant told me that the oil fuel valve outside of the Chief and Petty Officer's
Mess had been refitted while in dock and the fuel might have leaked out
through one of the battery boards and so we lifted up the battery board and
inspected the tops of the cells. We found no trace of oil on the cells and the
seals were quite alright.

Leading Seaman John Goddard was on duty that same night, sitting in the mess
with four other ratings. He remembered:

Leading Electrician 'Slinger' Wood came into the mess and said, 'We won't
be leaving the dockyard for a while just yet.' So we asked why and he said that
oil had been found in the number one battery sump. The following day a mass
of engineering officers and dockyard supervisors came on board. Discussions
were held in various messes between the officers and then we took the batteries
out and the various dockyard inspectors and naval engineering officers

went into the battery tank and everything was checked out with different instruments.

A series of meetings followed on shore while the crew waited to discover what was happening. 'At 4'o clock we got the word that we were going to put the batteries back and go out as planned,' said Goddard. 'We were most surprised thinking that the problem was so severe that they wouldn't let us leave the dockyard until it was repaired.'

Following Blackburn's arrival on *Affray* in mid-March, other senior officers and ratings began reporting to the dockyard ready for service. Some were old hands who had taken part in *Affray's* previous exercise in the Mediterranean and many were surprised to discover her engine still in pieces.

On 3 April 1951 Blackburn received orders from Captain Hugh Browne, Commander-in-Chief of the 5th Submarine Flotilla, that following short sea trials on Wednesday 11 April, *Affray* would put to sea at 1700 hours on Monday 16 April for a week-long 'practice war patrol' in the English Channel. The name given to the operation was Exercise Training Spring and its objective was to provide trainee executive and executive officers with submarine experience at sea under wartime conditions. She would also carry a small number of commando cadets from the Royal Marine Amphibious School, Eastney.

For many crew already gathered, the submarine was nowhere near fit to put to sea. They worked long hours attempting to repair the faulty engine plus scores of other tasks that needed to be passed as perfect 'in accordance with regulations in the Engineering Manual RN16' before undertaking trials in eight days time, including at least one dive. Before being released from the dockyard, inspectors also needed to examine her hull, propellers and on-board equipment.

Affray's popular First Officer, Lieutenant Derek Foster – known to the crew as 'Number One' – had his own concerns about the state of *Affray* at this time. He had served on the submarine for a year and was an experienced submariner with six years' service under his belt. Aged 25 and married with a son, Foster shared his fears with his young wife, Mary, who recalls:

We were building a house in Petersfield and living in a flat at the time and regularly went up to the new house to dig the garden at weekends. I remember that Derek was so unhappy that weekend and I asked him what was the matter? And he said he didn't want to go to sea on Monday as the submarine wasn't seaworthy. They were to take cadets on board who would get in the way. He said that the men at the dockyard were 'just tatting about with her'. That's the term he used. It seemed that nobody got on and actually did anything.

This was the first time I had ever heard Derek say anything like that because he absolutely loved the Navy and submarine life. Derek and Engineer Officer Lieutenant James Alston were on board each day during the repairs, which they noticed were carried out rather half-heartedly. They were amazed when one day the 'brass hats' came down and said, 'This boat goes out on Monday.'

Many crew were new to *Affray* and had never done a 'work up' (a team-building practice exercise) which is supposed to happen before a dive. Derek was very unhappy about everything.

On the day before *Affray* was due to leave the dockyard and go out on sea trials, Bennington told his father: 'We go to sea tomorrow with half a crew for trials and then go on that big exercise on the 16th. When that is finished we come back into the dockyard for another three weeks as another defect has cropped up.' In another short note to Oscar Bennington in Devon, his son stated:

> What a day it's been getting ready for sea tomorrow. We have only half a crew and we are taking out twenty 'subbies' (inexperienced sailors) in place of seamen, so I wonder what it will be like. I can imagine everything falling over and all in one big panic. I think the boat is in a worse state than before . . .

Ready or not, on the night of Thursday 10 April a small crew brought *Affray* out of Portsmouth dockyard and across to *Dolphin* where she was secured for the night. The next morning she was cleaned and enough provisions and equipment for her day at sea stowed on board. Only half of her crew would be taking part, the rest were either still on Easter leave or working their time out on other boats.

As the submarine left Portsmouth dockyard an official report stated: 'There are no known defects or inherent weaknesses in *Affray* likely to prejudice her safety and no previous history of recurring defects, breakdown or damage likely to lead to trouble later.' The submarine's safety certificate was updated from 9 May 1950 (when she last visited the dockyard) to 10 April 1951.

As far as the submarine's Commander, Lieutenant John Blackburn, and Commander-in-Chief of the 5th Submarine Flotilla, Captain Hugh Browne, were concerned, *Affray* was as near perfect as she could be and fit for sea.

Many of her crew felt otherwise.

Chapter 4

EXERCISE TRAINING SPRING

Affray's day at sea on 11 April 1951 lasted just four hours. Blackburn was assigned a crew of twenty-two ratings from the submarine's normal crew complement, with a further ten drawn from spare crews or reserve groups. Nearly forty officers and ratings – just over half her normal complement – headed out into the Solent to conduct the first part of *Affray*'s sea trials, testing her troublesome main engines over a two-hour period. No defects were found, apart from a small leak in a cylinder head joint, which was rectified by some tightening with a spanner.

Later that morning *Affray* dived to a periscope depth of 30ft, her watertight doors, hatches and fittings subjected to sea pressure. When she surfaced fifteen minutes later it was discovered that the yellow indicator buoy at the submarine's stern – which free-floated to the surface to attract attention in the event of the vessel being stuck on the bottom – had come adrift. The 3ft-wide wooden circular hatch holding it in place had warped and Leading Seaman John Goddard hauled it in and stowed it back into position. On returning to HMS *Dolphin*, Leading Seaman Goddard secured the warped hatch with wire.

After leaving *Affray* on the quayside, Blackburn reported to his immediate boss, Captain Hugh Browne, and informed him that he was satisfied with his submarine in every way and *Affray* was ready for service. That night Bennington wrote to his father: 'We have done our trials and everything went off pretty well and consequently everyone is fairly pleased.'

Over the next four days, work preparing *Affray* for Exercise Training Spring went ahead at a frantic pace and Blackburn spent most of that time carefully studying his orders.

ORDERS FOR A PRACTICE WAR PATROL TO BE CARRIED OUT BY
HMS *AFFRAY* FROM MONDAY 16TH – MONDAY 23RD April 1951

EXERCISE TRAINING SPRING

Reference – Chart No. 1598 – English Channel and Western
Approaches

DURATION
1. From 1800 Monday April 16th to 0800 Monday April 23rd.

FORCES TAKING PART
2. HM Submarine *Affray*
    Aircraft of 19 Group

AIM
3. To give the Executive and Engineer Officers submarine
    training course experience at sea in a submarine under war
    conditions.

PRELIMINARY MOVEMENTS
4. HMS *Affray* is to sail from Portsmouth at 1600 Monday
    16 April 1951. She is to proceed to her patrol area (south
    of the Lizard and Scilly Isles) keeping clear of standing
    water areas and may proceed dived or surfaced at the
    Commanding Officer's discretion.

PATROL AREA
5. The area bounded by lines joining the following reference
    positions
              AA 50 20' N 04 degrees 50' W
              BB 50 20' N 07 00' W
              CC 49 00' N 07 00' W
              DD 49 00' N 04 50' W

CONDUCT OF THE PATROL
6. Whilst in her patrol area HMS *Affray* is to conduct herself
    as she would in war. She may be darkened at night but
    is not to hesitate to switch on navigational lights for
    safety reasons.
7. Opportunities are to be taken of carrying out dummy
    attacks on shipping encountered.

(a) Two folboats and crews will be embarked from the Royal Marine Amphibious School, Eastney. Opportunity is to be taken of landing and recovering folboats on any suitable beach in patrol area during the night, at the Commanding Officer's discretion. If this operation has been completed by 19th April, folboat crews may be returned by rail to Plymouth from Falmouth.

AIR ACTIVITY

8. HMS *Affray* may expect Anti-Submarine activity by aircraft of 19 Group RAF. The appropriate evasive action is to be taken.

9. The Air Officer Commanding 19 Group is requested to inform The Captain (S/M), Fifth Submarine Flotilla by signal of any sightings or contacts obtained of HMS *Affray*.

(a) HMS *Affray* is to signal the Air Officer Commanding 19 Air Group Royal Air Force, Fifth Submarine Flotilla, her forecast noon position accurate to within 30 miles. This signal should be cleared by 0800 daily.

COMPRESSIBILITY FACTOR TRIAL

10. A trial in accordance with SGM 276 and STM 439 is to be carried out as convenient during the patrol.

VISIT TO FALMOUTH

11. HMS *Affray* is to proceed so as to arrive at Falmouth at 1700 hours Thursday 19th April. She is to sail from Falmouth at 0800 Friday, 20th April to resume her patrol.

MOVEMENTS ON COMPLETION

12. HMS *Affray* is to leave her patrol area so as to arrive Outer Spit Buoy at 1300 hours Monday 23rd April. She may proceed clear of standing exercise areas dived or on the surface at the Commanding Officer's discretion but is to be surfaced by 0800 Monday 23rd April.

DIVING AND SURFACING SIGNALS 'ON THE SURFACE' REPORTS

13. CB 4000(2) paragraphs 203 (a) (iii) is in force.

14. Diving and surfacing signals and 'on the surface' reports are to be addressed S/M 5 in Commander-in-Chief Plymouth, Commander-in-Chief Portsmouth.

```
15. Signals are to be made as follows . . .
    A diving signal to cover the passage westward until
    surfacing to proceed to Falmouth.
    A diving signal to cover the remainder of the patrol and
    passing eastward and a surfacing signal at the end of the
    exercise.
    A report 'On the Surface' is to be signalled between
    0800 and 0900 daily. Those reports are to be prefixed
    OPERATIONAL IMMEDIATE RECORDS
16. HMS Affray is to forward a patrol report covering points
    of interest and suggestions for future exercises on
    similar lines. A track chart, in original only, to the
    scale of chart No. 1598 is also to be forwarded.

                    Signed H.C. Browne
                    Captain
```

An appendix to the order instructed Blackburn on the nature and timings of his watches and radio frequencies through which signals from the submarine should be relayed. Blackburn's orders were framed to give him considerable latitude to, more or less, proceed as he wished and make Exercise Training Spring as realistic as possible. He hoped to use the exercise as an opportunity to bond his crew into a cohesive team and provide them with experience of how a submarine operated in wartime conditions.

Dummy attacks on shipping mentioned in the orders were exactly that – a chance to simulate raids on merchant ships travelling up and down the Channel from a suitable distance. Submarine commanders had plenty of experience stalking commercial shipping to give crews experience in the event of having to make a real attack. They knew how close to get to merchant vessels while submerged and unseen and most ships spied on through the periscopes of Royal Naval submarines had no idea they were being watched by a potentially deadly vessel 35ft underwater

Dummy attacks between dummy runs and the genuine article was that no torpedoes were fired and that everything was performed in 'slow time' – meaning that if mistakes were made, everything stopped while they were rectified, explanations given and the exercise resumed. There was never any sense of urgency during dummy attacks and plenty of time was allocated to ensure that everything was being performed correctly, unlike during a real submarine attack when every second counted and a 'kill or be killed' situation prevailed.

One of the more unusual aspects of Blackburn's orders was a requirement to carry four young commandoes from the Royal Marine Amphibious School,

Eastney, as passengers – Sergeant Jack Andrews in overall charge of Corporal Edward Shergold and Marines Dennis Jarvis and Alfred Hooper. Together, Blackburn and Sergeant Andrews were to identify a suitable beach to 'hit and raid' somewhere along the Cornish coast – probably in the vicinity of Falmouth.

Wearing combat fatigues, woollen balaclavas and with faces blackened, the Marines were to slip over the side of *Affray* under cover of darkness using 'folboats' (collapsible kayaks made of lightweight material) to paddle to the beach. The precise task the commandos were to perform on the beach once they arrived was never made clear – possibly not even to Blackburn – but when completed they were to clamber back into the folboats and paddle back to *Affray*. They would later leave the submarine when it pulled into Falmouth, from where they would catch a train to Plymouth and naval transport to return to Eastney.

During wartime, Royal Marine Commandos would travel as passengers in submarines and use folboats to land as close as possible to beaches behind enemy lines on intelligence gathering missions. Sometimes they would return to the submarine or remain in enemy territory, making a rendezvous with a local agent or member of an allied resistance group who would help with their task.

On the evening of Sunday 15 April, Sergeant Andrews spent the evening at the home of his brother Robin and his wife in Portsmouth. Robin was on leave from HMS *Swiftsure* where he, too, was serving with the Royal Marines as a corporal. Robin remembers:

Jack told me that he had spent that morning on the *Affray* discussing with the Skipper the various arrangements for the accommodation of the Marines and their equipment. He was very concerned as he said that the boat – and I quote – 'was leaking like a sieve' and that he was far from happy about taking passage on her. I remember saying that that if he was that concerned I would have to go and take out insurance on him next morning. I have always bitterly regretted that remark.

Jack and I were both Marines and very close to each other. What I find strange was the fact that he refused to discuss what the commando detachment was doing on the boat. If it were a normal exercise I'm sure he would have told me what the objectives were. I certainly got the impression that it was something more than a run of the mill exercise.

❖   ❖   ❖

Two days before Exercise Training Spring began, David Bennington wrote to his father saying he had heard from an engineer on board *Affray* that the operation 'is going to be one of the most hectic ones we have yet done, so it doesn't look very hopeful. Apparently we are going to do everything it is possible for a submarine to do . . .'

The following day a note of hopeless desperation crept into his daily letter: 'I shall be very pleased when this exercise is over. I am not looking forward to it very much. I hope everything goes off OK.'

Before *Affray* sailed on the afternoon tide on Monday 16 April, Bennington sent his final letter home to his father. The letter was posted shortly before the submarine cast off from HMS *Dolphin* at 1800 hours: 'We are just about to leave so I want to get a letter off to you. I wish this was over, I am not looking forward to it a bit.' And then for the first time in years of writing home, Bennington added this simple postscript: 'GOODBYE.'

When Oscar Bennington received his son's letter in Devon the following morning, *Affray* had already been missing for twelve hours.

Chapter 5

'CLOAK AND DAGGER STUFF'

A crew of eighty-five officers and ratings, including the four Royal Marine Commandos, joined *Affray* on Monday 16 April 1951 – twenty-three more men than she normally carried on peacetime operations and twenty more than in wartime conditions. Space on board would be very cramped indeed.

Ratings wondered where they would all eat and sleep and pondered on how the submarine could function properly with so many men on board. These were the days before health and safety laws were introduced and risk assessments came into force. God forbid that a submarine might encounter problems at sea.

Officers and ratings assigned to *Affray* for Exercise Training Spring were of mixed abilities and twenty-five of them were joining the boat for the first time on that day. Second-in-command, First Lieutenant Derek Foster, and Engineer Officer Lieutenant James Alston both had extensive submarine experience and had been attached to *Affray* for twelve and twenty-one months respectively. Their previous commander, Lieutenant Leafric Temple-Richard, considered both to be 'very capable men'.

Lieutenant William Kirkwood was identified as 'an outstanding officer' by senior ranks and had spent the last year working as Principal Training Officer of 'A' Class submarines, while Lieutenant Jeffrey Greenwood had served in submarines for eighteen months and joined *Affray* from HMS *Tote* where he gained valuable experience working on a snort-fitted boat. He, too, was described as 'outstanding'.

Out of the thirteen sub-lieutenants joining *Affray* for the exercise, six had attended the same term at the Royal Naval College, Dartmouth, in 1943 – Tony Garwood, Tony Longstaff, Roderick 'Rocky' Mackenzie-Edwards, Robin Preston, Tony Rewcastle and Bill Linton. Linton's father, Commander John 'Tubby' Linton, DSO, DSC, had been awarded a posthumous VC in 1943 after being lost with the submarine HMS *Turbulent* which had sunk twenty-seven enemy ships. His son, a Dartmouth cadet at the time, accepted his father's VC from the King.

Another sub-lieutenant, Tony Frew, was a survivor from the *Truculent* accident in the Thames Estuary the previous year. A son of Engineer Rear Admiral Sir Sidney Frew, Tony had joined *Truculent* a week before she had sunk, managing to save the life of a shipmate while escaping from the conning tower.

According to the Admiralty, of the ship's company who went to sea in *Affray* on 16 April 1951, nineteen of the forty-five ratings 'had reached a high standard of efficiency' during Exercise Autumn Cruise the previous year. The remaining crew had recently been drafted from a reserve group where they had regularly been to sea in HMS *Alaric* – a submarine almost identical to *Affray*.

Although the Admiralty described the submarine's principal personnel as 'thoroughly experienced men', eleven engine room ratings and nine other ratings had never before been to sea in *Affray*. All but one of the thirteen sub-lieutenants due to embark on 16 April had spent periods working as acting sub-lieutenants on submarines in harbour – but not at sea. They had completed only half of the fourteen weeks devoted to submarine training and just one day at sea in 'A' class boats, although time had been spent in other submarines when they first joined the service. During Exercise Training Spring they would be billeted in bunks in the seaman's mess in the forward stowage compartment – already one of the most cramped areas of the boat.

Five of the engineer officer trainees due to take part in the exercise had completed twelve weeks of their fourteen-week courses, during which time they had been to sea in a submarine for just four days. During Exercise Training Spring the men would be expected to carry out executive duties under supervision, instead of their usual engineering duties, to gain further experience. All officers and ratings participating in the exercise – including the Marines – had qualified in using emergency escape apparatus and sufficient sets had been stowed on board for the operation.

Although the Admiralty insisted that the submarine's crew were 'experienced' and later claimed that trainees on board were among the best to have passed through their recent training programme, they all shared the same the dilemma as they reported for duty that day: they had no experience of working together as a crew on *Affray*. Submariners believe that to be successful, teamwork is essential with team players relying on each other. If there is a weak link in the team, something is bound to go wrong, they say.

❖　　❖　　❖

By lunchtime on 16 April all of *Affray*'s crew had registered their arrival at HMS *Dolphin* and were marched down to the submarine jetty in small groups. Lieutenant Kirkwood, in charge of the Officer's Training Course, and his assistant,

Chief Petty Officer Gordon Selby, used their time before sailing to settle their trainees down in the submarine, making sure they understood arrangements for their accommodation and the manner in which their time at sea would progress over the next few days.

At 1700 hours – just one hour before sailing – Selby was summoned to the Chief Petty Officers' Mess at HMS *Dolphin*. As mess president, he was required to sort out a problem that could not wait for his return eight days later. While at the mess, Selby suddenly fell violently ill with a gastric problem and was rushed down the road to Haslar Hospital for emergency treatment.

Selby's illness saved his life – for the fourth time. In 1942 he had narrowly missed sailing on HMS *Upholder* a month before she was sunk in the Mediterranean. He cheated death a second time when submarine *P39* was bombed in Malta shortly before he went on board and when the submarine HMS *Olympus* hit a mine he was one of eight who swam 7 miles to shore and safety.

Gordon did not sail in *Affray* in April 1951 and from his home in Australia nearly 60 years later – where he died following a fall in March 2007 – recalled: 'My only contact with *Affray* was a brief one – about two hours. I knew no one else on board apart from Lieutenant Kirkwood.'

During the middle of the afternoon, Blackburn mustered his ship's company together to brief them about Exercise Training Spring. He told them they would be heading towards the Western Approaches and simulating wartime conditions. They heard they would be snorting throughout the night at periscope depth in one of Europe's busiest shipping lanes. Referring to the commando passengers on board, Blackburn said they would be acting independently in order 'to carry out some cloak and dagger stuff'.

Blackburn told the crew that many officer trainees would be performing various tasks under supervision in the control room including 'doing silly things with valves' and that the rest of the crew should let them get on with it so they could learn from their mistakes.

The crew heard that they would be calling at Falmouth later in the week before returning to HMS *Dolphin*. The submarine would then go to the naval base at Portland to work alongside another 'A' class submarine for two weeks before returning to HM Dockyard, Portsmouth, for further maintenance work following the earlier discovery of oil in the battery sump. She would be in the dockyard for another three weeks.

They were told that aircraft from the RAF's 19 Group Coastal Command would be seen in the skies overhead on several occasions during the operation conducting submarine search exercises of their own. If they were travelling on the surface when aircraft came into view they would dive as quickly as possible. Blackburn said he would be signalling their position ahead to the Air Officer

Commanding 19 Group RAF to forecast *Affray*'s noon position accurate to within 30 miles.

Blackburn then dropped a bombshell. He informed the crew that thirteen ratings needed to recover their kit from below and return to shore because of space shortages on *Affray*. One of the crew sent ashore was Leading Seaman John Goddard. John had been trained on torpedoes and sonar, but because *Affray* was not carrying torpedoes on the exercise, he or fellow torpedo/sonar rating Leading Seaman Ronald 'Slugger' Smith – a married man from Lincoln with an 11-month old baby – would have to go ashore. Leading Seaman Smith remained on board to operate the sonar.

Goddard later recalled: 'It was a him or me situation who went. We were of identical rank, did the identical job, but he was on sonar and I was on torpedoes. We were not going to have anything to do with torpedoes on the exercise, so I wasn't needed – and he was. He often crosses my mind.'

Goddard also remembered that different electrical staff on board a submarine conducted most of the specialist work.

There was also a specialist electrician – an electrical artificer – whose job was to look after the main gyro compass and set it up before sailing. For some reason the electrical artificer was left behind with us on shore. I have no idea why. When you think what a delicate piece of instrumentation a gyro compass is and the important role it plays, it made no sense to leave the only maintainer of the compass behind. It was a very strange thing to do and often over the last half century or so I have wondered why.

Others left on the quay as *Affray* prepared to sail included Electrician's Mate Jim Johnston. He had been told that he could toss a coin with fellow electrician Eric Horwell to see who stayed on board and who went ashore. Johnston won the toss. Signalman 'Chick' Henderson was told by Lieutenant Foster: 'The boat is rather full this trip, Chick. I'll do the signalling' and with that Henderson went below, gathered up his kit and joined the rest of the group preparing to leave the boat.

Electrical Artificer 2nd Class Alexander Duncombe, who had joined *Affray* on 2 April, was working down in the engine room when he was instructed to leave the submarine that afternoon. It was Duncombe who had discovered the oil in number one battery tank on the night of 6 April.

Able Seamen Stanley Crowe and George Worden, who had both joined *Affray*'s crew exactly one year before, were among the last of the small band to leave *Affray* before she pulled away from the quay. As they made their way up the ladder and out of the submarine they were joined by Able Seamen Frank Kendrick and Peter Warriss. Kendrick remembered:

I came off leave at 1200 and reported in to HMS *Affray* at 1300 hours. The Coxswain marched me down to the boat and I heard the Captain's speech to the men. It was then decided who should go to sea and who should not. After being a member of the *Affray*'s crew for just a couple of hours, I found myself standing on the quay with the others while she prepared to sail without me. I disembarked at about 1530 hours, shortly before she left HMS *Dolphin*.

Able Seaman Edward Hickman had also joined *Affray*'s crew the previous year and remembered:

The submarine was overcrowded and of the crew that went out, 90 per cent knew nothing about the boat. The old crew came off and it was more or less a new crew that was preparing to take her out. All the seamen and stokers were the same, but it seemed rather funny taking twenty-five trainees out with a new crew. I didn't know them. They either joined the submarine on 11 April in time for the sea trials or the day before she was due to sail. Every day we saw somebody new coming on board.

Leading Seaman John Graham, 27, from Fareham, Hampshire, was also ordered off the boat because he was suffering from a heavy cold. The enclosed area of a submarine was the worst possible place for someone likely to be sneezing and coughing in a confined space for several days, so he found himself on the quay with the others less than an hour before she slipped her moorings.

In addition to the four Royal Marine commandos, nearly thirty men going out with *Affray* that day had joined her company the previous month. Twenty of those men had never previously been to sea in the submarine.

❖ ❖ ❖

At 1700 hours *Affray* slipped away from her mooring at Haslar Creek, Gosport, and nosed her way into the choppy grey waters of Portsmouth Harbour fairway and then seaward into the English Channel. John Goddard and the twelve others ordered to remain behind watched her go. It was the last time that anyone at HMS *Dolphin* would see *Affray* on the surface again.

At the end of the Channel, the submarine was sighted by the lookout at Fort Gilkicker near the entrance to Portsmouth Harbour who noted that she was passing in a south-easterly direction at an estimated speed of 4½ knots. The sighting, timed at 1725, was the final sighting of *Affray*. The submarine then swung to starboard and pointed its nose westward towards The Needles. At 2056, nearly two hours after slipping her moorings, Blackburn sent a signal to the

Commanders-in-Chief of her home waters in Portsmouth and at Plymouth, into whose waters she would be travelling in the next few days. It read: 'Diving at 2115 in position 5010N, 0145W for Exercise Training Spring.'

It was the last signal ever received from *Affray*.

With the submarine positioned 30 miles off St Catherine's Point, Blackburn would have shouted the order for 'diving stations' to be passed from compartment to compartment fore and aft along the submarine as look-outs tumbled down ladders followed by officers-of-the-watch. A klaxon hooter would have sounded indicating that the diving process had commenced. Wheels would be turned, levers pulled, valves closed off and orders passed. Blackburn would then have given orders to his first lieutenant: 'Thirty-two feet, Number One.'

Affray's main vents would have been opened, allowing air to escape through her outside ballast tanks and seawater to enter. Inside the crew would have controlled the boat by checking the internal trimming tanks and hydroplanes – movable sets of short 'wings' on the stern controlling the angle of dive, positioned so that water moves over the stern forcing it upward; therefore, the submarine is angled downward.

She would then have begun to slide away beneath the pounding waters of the grey sea.

Chapter 6

SUBSMASH

The submarine was due to send an 'on the surface' signal the following morning, Tuesday 17 April, between the hours of 0800 and 1000, prefixed by the remark: 'Operation Immediate'. By 1040 hours nothing had been received from *Affray* and at 1045 Captain Hugh Browne, commanding the 5th Submarine Flotilla, alerted his Flag Officer, Rear Admiral Sidney Raw, about his anxiety for the boat's safety.

Checks were made to see if any other wireless stations had heard from the submarine and failed to pass on the signal. When they confirmed that nothing had been received, all stations were placed on special alert for incoming messages from a submarine possibly in difficulty, but more likely experiencing some kind of problem with its radio transmitter.

When no signal had been received by 1100 Rear Admiral Raw ordered an urgent message to be transmitted to all naval radio stations containing the two-word code guaranteed to cut through the ether like a knife and still the radio chatter of every Navy wireless room: 'Subsmash One,' indicating that the safety of *Affray* was in doubt.

'Subsmash' means that somewhere a submarine is in serious trouble. Perhaps the submarine's radio had developed a fault meaning it is unable to send routine reports or perhaps the boat is lying injured somewhere on the bottom of the sea. Either way, the Navy takes no chances and a full-scale rescue operation is quickly mounted using ships and aircraft in the immediate vicinity.

The code word was rarely called into action. The Admiralty had created it in 1931 as a means of initiating a search once a submarine had either been lost or was reported to be in difficulty. If the boat had sunk and was unable to surface due to critical damage, the code signal was changed to 'Subsunk'. Modifications to the 'Subsmash' procedure were introduced in later years. 'Subsmash One' was an immediate call to action signalling ships and aircraft to begin searching for a submarine suffering from mechanical or radio failure. The code was upgraded to 'Subsmash Two' once it was confirmed that a boat was definitely in trouble and its crew in need of rescue – below or above the waves.

Emergency signals were sent to the *Affray* several times between 1112 and 1118 hours and repeated every five minutes stating: 'No – repetition no – on the surface report yet received from you. Subsmash One being initiated. Report your position course and speed forthwith on 4900 K/cs.'

Once 'Subsmash One' was initiated, orders were given for HMS *Amphion*, an 'A' Class submarine exercising off the coast of the Isle of Wight, to remain on the surface and proceed westwards in preparation for a search. Instructions were also given for the radio receiving station at Rugby to call the submarine every fifteen minutes stating: '*AFFRAY*. PLEASE REPORT POSITION, COURSE AND SPEED.'

Meanwhile, Rear Admiral Raw and his officers began calculating the submarine's possible location based on her intention to pass within 30 miles of her estimated position 77 miles south-west of her diving point the previous evening. It was generally agreed that one of two things had happened to *Affray* – she was either suffering from a wireless failure and would be making for the nearest shore signal station to report her most likely position, or Blackburn had misread his orders and she had not attempted to make an 'On the Surface' report. At the back of Raw's mind was one certainty: *Affray* was somewhere between Monday's evening's diving position and her expected surface position at noon the following day.

It was clear to Raw that if *Affray* had sunk, the area to be searched covered a rectangular district some 77 miles by 20 miles – a total area of 1,540 square miles. Not quite like trying to find a needle in a haystack, but the nearest thing in maritime terms.

In theory, the search for *Affray* should have been controlled by the Commander-in-Chief Plymouth, but a lack of suitable search ships and submarines in his division resulted in the Commander-in-Chief Portsmouth, Admiral Sir Arthur Power, taking responsibility for search operations. At 1128 hours Power ordered all ships fitted with anti-submarine devices to prepare for sea.

By 1200 *Affray*'s surfacing signal was two hours overdue and orders given to upgrade the emergency to 'Subsmash Two'. The signal was relayed to all ships along with *Affray*'s last known diving position.

At 1201 Raw handed over conduct of Subsmash operations to Commander-in-Chief Portsmouth, Sir Arthur Power – known to everyone in the Navy as the 'Block of Teak' thanks to his no-nonsense, gruff seadog manner. Power's immediate task was to ensure that as many naval ships as possible should either be pulled from their respective exercises in waters around the south coast or made ready for sea. HM ships *Tintagel Castle*, *Hedingham Castle*, *Flint Castle* and three submarines were off Portland, while HM ships *Contest*, *Boxer* and the submarine *Amphion* were off Portsmouth. The first three ships and submarines were ordered to head off in the direction of *Affray*'s reported diving position while the rest were instructed to manoeuvre towards her proposed noontime position.

The first Navy air-sea search aircraft had taken off from Lee-on-Solent – one of many Navy and RAF stations put on an operational basis – forty-five minutes after the 'Subsmash' signal had been initiated. A Sea Otter headed in the direction of *Affray*'s diving position in the hope of spotting some evidence that the submarine was stuck on the sea bottom. Submarines were fitted with bright yellow and red marker buoys which could be released to the surface to signal the spot where they lay on the seabed beneath. At 1234 hours more aircraft took off to search a 10-mile corridor either side of a line joining *Affray*'s diving and proposed noon positions.

Meanwhile a build-up of ships taking part in the search had begun. By 1255 every ship in the Home Fleet Flotilla had been summoned to join the Subsmash operation. One of them was the 1,800 ton *Reclaim*, the Navy's only deep-diving and submarine rescue vessel, equipped with underwater rescue apparatus and decompression chambers. *Reclaim*, under her captain, Lieutenant-Commander Jack Bathurst, had been refitting her engines and half her crew were still on Easter leave when she received instructions at 1130 hours to be ready to sail within twenty-four hours. Supervised by Engine Room Artificer 2nd Class, Peter Bell, her small crew struggled to put her engine back together, raise steam in defiance of all known regulations and put to sea two hours later – twenty-two hours earlier than expected. She was joined by mooring vessels, a salvage ship and tugs to help her moor over the submarine when she was found.

A message was broadcast to all commercial shipping in the area:

A submarine is missing and possibly sunk between positions 50 degrees 10 minutes north and one degree 45 minutes west and 49 degrees 40 minutes north and 4 degrees west. Vessels in the vicinity are requested to keep a sharp look out for survivors and to report wreckage or oil slicks on the surface or any other indications to the Commander-in-Chief, Portsmouth.

The first ship to arrive at *Affray*'s reported diving position was HMS *Contest*. All hands were ordered to look over the port and starboard sides for visible signs of the submarine. They saw nothing and proceeded to patrol the immediate area conducting a visual search. When HM ships *Tintagel Castle*, *Ulysses* and *Contest* arrived on the scene, they were instructed to follow *Affray*'s expected route towards the point she was originally expected to surface. The ships travelled two miles ahead of each other moving at speeds of 20 knots. They were later joined by the ships *Hedingham Castle*, *Flint Castle* and *Helmsdale* while the submarine *Amphion* was joined by HMS *Marvel* and the submarine *Scorcher*.

The first of several foreign ships to join the search was the *Victor Billet*, a frigate from the Belgian Navy, which was placed at the disposal of the Royal Navy during the late morning. At the same time the American Embassy in London asked the Admiralty if it could find a use for two of its destroyers, USS *Perry* and *Ellison*, to search for *Affray*. Both were on goodwill visits to Britain. The answer from Sir Arthur Power was swift and to the point: 'Yes please.'

The French Navy offered seven ships, which joined search operations from Cherbourg in northern France over the following twelve hours – the *Somme*, *Meuse*, *Yser*, *Lansequenet*, *Lanciere*, *Admiral Mouchez* and *Sentinelle*.

At 1300 hours the Admiralty decided it was time to contact relatives of the officers and ratings on *Affray* and called for a list of names to be brought to Rear Admiral Raw. Instead of appointing a team of people to visit homes of the next of kin to gently break the news or telephone them in person, telegrams were sent:

HMS *Affray* in which your husband/son is at sea failed to report her position by 10-o-clock this morning. Ships and aircraft are now searching for her. Will inform you at once of any developments. Admiral Submarines.

HMS *Dolphin* staff were instructed that wives, mothers, brothers, sisters and shipmates telephoning for more information after receiving telegrams, should be told not to be alarmed, that the Navy was doing everything in its power to find their loved ones and that in all probability orders had been misunderstood. They were certain to locate the submarine soon.

At the same time the following statement was issued to the press:

Submarine HMS *Affray* (Lieutenant John Blackburn, DSC) has not surfaced as expected after diving while on exercises. She sailed from Portsmouth last night unescorted and dived at 9.15 p.m. south of the Isle of Wight.

She was proceeding westwards submerged at a speed of four-and-a-half knots. She was expected to surface at 8.30 this morning, but no surfacing signal has been received and her present position is unknown.

Naval authorities have been alerted and a search is being organised by the Flag Officer Submarines, Rear Admiral S. M. Raw, acting for the Commander-in-Chief Portsmouth (Admiral Sir Arthur Power).

Aircraft, including helicopters, have begun a search and at least five destroyers have proceeded to the scene.

Every effort is being made to contact the submarine by radio and it is possible that she has misinterpreted her instructions as regards surfacing and is not, in fact, in trouble.

❖   ❖   ❖

On the morning of Tuesday 17 April, Bernard Kervell, a schoolboy from Waterlooville, Hampshire, was walking his dog in Alexander Park, Portsea – a stretch of land overlooking the HMS *Phoenix* Technical High School and providing excellent views of shipping activity in Portsmouth Harbour. Bernard remembers:

It was just after the Easter holidays and normally the harbour would have been inactive – but it certainly wasn't on this particular day. The whole place was jumping and people could be seen scurrying hither and thither. The creek and harbour area seemed to be full of small- and medium-sized motorboats going in all directions as fast as they could. I thought that some major exercise was underway.

Walking along a little further, a helicopter suddenly appeared to leap up from nearby Fort Southwick and head off in a straight line. It was either going to HMS *Dolphin* or across to the base at Lee-on-Solent. Helicopters were a very rare sight in those days and this one looked brand new, with no evident markings confirming whom it belonged to.

The whole scene gave me the impression that something major was happening and it looked as if somebody somewhere had declared 'panic stations'. Later I learned about the disappearance of HMS *Affray* and the activity I witnessed from the park would have been the early stages of the search operation getting underway. I shall never forget that day.

What Bernard witnessed was the armada of salvage ships, tugs, lifting craft, lifeboats, aircraft from the RAF and Fleet Air Arm and a Westland Dragonfly helicopter from 705 Naval Air Squadron (the Royal Navy's first helicopter squadron) all mustered together in next to no time to take part in the search. As the morning progressed further, preparations for the search gained an urgency and impetus rarely achieved in peacetime operations. At the same time service and civilian hospitals were alerted, decompression chambers made ready in case men were able to escape from a great depth and needed to be recompressed to cure them of the diver's 'bends'.

Brian Collis from Portsmouth remembers sitting in the local Gosport cinema waiting for the early afternoon matinee performance to begin. The audience were suddenly jolted into action by a message flashed onto the screen summoning all HMS *Dolphin* personnel to return to base immediately. The cinema was emptied of its audience in minutes and the afternoon screening continued playing to an empty house. A small army of men raced down the road towards their shore base and on arrival were given the news that one of their submarines was missing. Many had friends on board *Affray* and prepared themselves to go to sea to find them.

Former Able Seaman Gordon Chatburn from Waterlooville, Hampshire, a member of HMS *Agincourt*'s company berthed alongside Portsmouth's South Railway Jetty, recalls:

> We were making preparations for a 'show-the-flag' cruise around British seaside resorts as part of the Festival of Britain activities. Quite a few of the ship's company were enjoying a run on shore that lunchtime and I, along with some other lads, had decided to go to the Classic Cinema in Commercial Road.
>
> Suddenly, over the cinema Tannoy system, a message was broadcast ordering all *Agincourt* ship's company in the audience to return on board – at the double. It was quite a sight to see dozens of matelots tearing down Queen Street all heading for the dockyard main gate. The very minute that it had been established that everyone was back on board, up went the ship-to-shore gangway and we were away. I don't ever remember leaving the harbour so quickly.
>
> We soon heard over the ship's Tannoy what was afoot. The skipper informed the crew about a missing submarine called HMS *Affray* and we were to be part of a massive flotilla setting out to find her. We didn't know it then, but we were about to be part of the largest sea-air rescue ever undertaken in this country – before or since.

Other men still on leave, including essential officers, ratings and divers, received telegrams telling them that leave was cancelled and they must return to either Portsmouth or Portland immediately. No reason was given, but anyone listening to the BBC Light Programme shortly before 1400 hours that day would soon discover why.

Mary Foster (now Mrs Mary Henry), the young wife of *Affray*'s 'Number One', Lieutenant Derek Foster, was sitting at home in Petersfield with her son David, who was nearly 4. They had tuned into their favourite lunchtime radio programme, *Listen With Mother*. Suddenly the programme was interrupted by an urgent newsflash. Mary remembers:

> The newsflash said that one of our submarines was missing and that a 'Subsmash' had been brought into effect. I remember it as vividly today as I did back in 1951. There was no need to tell me which submarine it was. I knew it was *Affray*. Derek had told me he didn't want to go to sea on that exercise. He said *Affray* wasn't seaworthy. He had told me that the repairs in the dockyard

had been conducted very half-heartedly and he was amazed when the Navy had insisted the boat be taken out on the exercise.

There has hardly been a day in all those years that I have not thought of Derek and all the others on the submarine. I grew from a carefree girl to a woman during those dreadful days when they were searching for *Affray*. We were both aged 25 at the time. Hearing about it on the radio, instead of from someone who I knew, was heartless.

Joy Cook from Ilfracombe, Devon, whose husband, Leading Seaman George Cook, was on board *Affray*, had missed the lunchtime news bulletin and knew nothing about the submarine's disappearance until she switched on the radio at six o'clock. She remembers:

An announcer said that a British submarine was missing and at once I knew it was the *Affray*, and I was right. I immediately went upstairs to check that my baby son was asleep and then went to see George's mother, who lived nearby. She had no idea which boat George was on because he had been lent to *Affray* for two weeks to allow another sailor to represent submariners in a shooting contest. I had to break the news to her. No one got in contact with me. I had to get all my news from the radio.

Someone else who heard that same radio broadcast was Val Clements from Southsea, Hampshire. At the time Val and her family were living in Portsea, close to Portsmouth and Gosport. Val recalls:

I was only a young child at the time, but I knew that something was wrong. When it was announced that HMS *Affray* had gone missing, no one seemed to worry that much at the beginning because we were sure she would be found with everyone on board. But as the days wore on, the atmosphere among the people of Portsea, Portsmouth and Gosport suddenly changed.

More than anything else, I remember the terrible silence that hung like a big black cloud over the whole area. It seemed that even the birds had stopped singing. Apart from people passing the time of day with each other, no one was actually talking to one another. That terrible silence really affected all of us. It seemed to go on forever.

What made it worse was that a young lad from our street was on board the submarine. Like many of us in Portsea, he came from a large family. I know that my mother and grandmother were both praying for that lad and the rest of the men. We always said our prayers, although older members of our family would have kept this part of their prayers away from us children.

It was a terrible time for everyone in our community and something I have never been able to forget. In later years I married a submariner and used to dread him going away when he didn't know where an exercise might take him.

On the other side of the world, in Trincomalee, on Ceylon's eastern coast, a young Red Cross nurse working in the Royal Naval Hospital attached to HMS *Highflier* was told about the missing submarine on the second day of the search. Roma Maw from Swanage, Dorset, remembers:

My boyfriend was Engineer Officer Lieutenant James Hilton Alston. James was the only child of elderly parents who lived in Westmoreland. We had met in Simonstown, South Africa, in 1945 while he was serving in the warship HMS *Jamaica* and I was at the naval hospital there. Life in the Royal Navy at that time was very different to today and overseas tours of duty often went on for two years or more.

From South Africa James went on to serve in the Far East and on returning to England he transferred to submarines, serving first on HMS *Tiptoe* and eventually on the *Affray*.

He came up from the lower decks, meaning that he had to work his way up through the ranks. He must have been very conscientious to be promoted to an officer in a relatively short amount of time.

I heard about the loss of *Affray* when I was walking through the hospital in Ceylon. A member of staff asked me if I knew about the missing submarine in British waters. I said, 'It's not the *Affray*, is it?' and he said that it was. Shortly afterwards my letters to James were returned to me with a note saying they could no longer be delivered.

Ron Leakey, now living in Auckland, New Zealand, was a 16-year-old school-leaver when he learned that his older brother, Able Seaman George 'Ginger' Leakey, was on *Affray* when she went missing. Ron remembers:

At the time I was working as an apprentice boilermaker at George Wimpy Ltd in Southall, where my brother had also worked in the engine shop before he went very young into the Navy. I remember him going back from leave early on the Sunday evening (like all servicemen he normally left it until the last minute) saying he would accompany my Dad – who worked as a travelling ticket inspector at Kings Cross – part of the way back to Portsmouth. It was to be the last day any of us would ever see George again.

I'm now 76, but can vividly remember the *Evening Standard* billboards on the Monday evening when I cycled home from work – '*Affray* Sub Missing.'

I arrived home to a household in complete shock, but we still held hope. I cannot remember whether the Navy had been in touch with George's wife, Eileen, who lived with us at the time and was heavily pregnant.

That week was one of helping and waiting. I was encouraged by my very strong parents to carry on working. My workmates all knew my brother, the curly-haired boy who used to work in the engine shop, and they were very supportive. But as a 16-year-old, I hardly realised what the tragedy was to his wife and Yvonne, his 2-year old daughter. Eileen, of course, had to hold herself together for her unborn child – later to be called Georgina, after her Dad.

David Dyer from Portsmouth was a member of the Royal Navy's 705 Naval Air Squadron based at the shore base HMS *Siskin*, close to HMS *Dolphin*. He remembers:

I was a Petty Officer Artificer and being a single man, was often called upon to travel with helicopters on search-and-rescue missions and undertake between-flight servicing.

On Monday April 16, the Commanding Officer, Lieutenant-Commander S.H. Suthers, received orders to send three helicopters to the RAF radio station at Chickerell, near Dorchester, to take part in the air-sea search-and-rescue mission for HMS *Affray*.

A maintenance crew was quickly organised by the squadron to travel to Chickerell in a 15cwt truck, together with an array of spares, oils and greases required to keep the helicopters serviceable between flights. Everyone worked extremely hard to service the helicopters and get them airborne in record time.

We operated with three helicopters, two of which were Westland Dragonfly aircraft fitted with rescue winches and an American-built R6 Hoverfly without a winch.

Most helicopters were flying a sixteen-hour day, frequently returning to base for refuelling and sometimes a change of aircrew. Helicopters in those days had limited endurance compared with today's more modern ones.

❖ ❖ ❖

By early afternoon on 17 April, a team of experienced deep-sea divers from HMS *Lochinvar*, near Edinburgh, were on their way to Portsmouth in a Lancaster aircraft. Elsewhere in the air somewhere over the English Channel, the pilot of an aircraft from RAF Tangmere reported sighting an 'A' class submarine on the surface. The submarine was later discovered to be one of the vessels searching for *Affray*. To avoid confusion, all submarines taking part in the search and rescue mission were ordered to fly a large yellow flag while on the surface.

At 1646 hours a report was received from a Danish merchant ship, the *Rhodes Liang*, stating that she was positioned next to a large oil slick somewhere along the route *Affray* should have taken before surfacing. The ship agreed to remain next to the slick to mark the spot until a naval vessel arrived. Aircraft were diverted to the area along with HMS *Boxer*. On arrival at the scene, *Boxer*'s crew discovered a huge narrow slick stretching for four miles.

An oil sample was taken for examination to ascertain if it was diesel oil (the kind used on *Affray*) or furnace oil (as used by surface vessels). While the examination was underway, *Boxer* dropped grenades over the side to indicate to any crew from the stricken submarine that help was nearby and they should prepare to evacuate immediately. But there was no sign of survivors and oil from the slick was later discovered to be furnace oil.

By early evening plans had been drawn up for night-time operations. Thirty ships and submarines would work through the night in the English Channel searching for *Affray*. They were divided into three taskforce groups for the night:

Force X-ray comprised HM ships *Agincourt, Hedingham Castle, Marvel, Trespasser, St Austell Bay* and the Belgian frigate *Victor Billet*.

Force Yoke comprised HM ships *Battleaxe, Tintagel Castle, Flint Castle, Pluto, Gossamer, Ambush, Reclaim*, plus seven ships from the French fleet.

Force Zebra comprised HM ships *Boxer, Ulysses, Contest*, submarines *Sirdar* – which had been used in the film *Morning Departure – Scorcher, Sea Devil, Scythian* and *Amphion*, plus the American destroyers *Perry* and *Ellison*.

❖   ❖   ❖

As the flotilla began mounting powerful searchlights onto their decks to monitor the surface of the sea in the hope of finding traces of the missing submarine, the first editions of Britain's national newspapers were rolling off the presses. The disappearance of *Affray* was front page story nationwide and headlines screamed the bad news: 'Submarine Missing in the Channel – HMS *Affray* Fails to Surface After Night-Diving Exercises.' But the news was sketchy, containing Admiralty statements, library photographs of 'A' class submarines and little else. The first stories containing any real substance appeared in the London and Portsmouth evening papers sold at lunchtime on Wednesday 18 April.

Although newspapermen had descended on Gosport from London on afternoon trains, naval ratings – including the thirteen ratings taken from *Affray* before she sailed – were ordered to say nothing to reporters gathering outside the gates at HMS *Dolphin*. The thirteen were told to remain inside the shore base and not to leave until further notice. Worried that his mother would think he was missing on board *Affray*, Able Seaman John Goddard sent a telegram to 27 Bellevue Road, Southend-on-Sea Essex, stating: 'Safe. Did not sail with *Affray*. Love. John.'

Another person also receiving a messaged stating they had not sailed in *Affray* was Alice Graham, wife of Able Seaman John Graham from Fareham, Hampshire. She remembers:

My late husband was on stand-by to go on board the *Affray*. We lived in London at that time and I vividly remember my boss came back from lunch very perturbed and asked me what ship my husband was on. I told him he was on stand-by, but believe me, until I had a phone call – and remember, there were no mobiles in those days – I was a very worried person.

John Graham had been sent ashore less than an hour before the submarine sailed, suffering from a heavy cold. If he had not been coughing and sneezing all over the place, there is every likelihood that he would have sailed that day.

❖   ❖   ❖

The Navy agreed to give a press conference at Fort Blockhouse, headquarters of the submarine service at Dolphin, and a large room was packed with reporters from the world's press.

The reporters wanted to know:

Could the submarine have hit a mine – just like in the film Morning Departure*?*

Admiralty staff fielding the question said that if *Affray* had done so, the surface of the Channel would be covered in diesel oil and debris – but no such wreckage had yet been found.

Could the submarine have been rammed by a passing ship?

Reporters heard that if this had happened – and she had dived in the middle of one of the world's busiest shipping lanes – some collision report would have been received within the hour. But no such report had been received.

Could the submarine have been sunk by an internal explosion?

If this had happened, wreckage would have been blown to the surface and nothing has been found.

But mines have been seen floating in the English Channel after the storms last week . . .

Yes. French minesweepers have been sweeping within 30 miles of the *Affray*'s course.

Could the submarine's diving gear have become stuck?

Possible, but unlikely. If *Affray* is lying on the seabed, she is likely to be on firm sand and shingle, an ideal place from which to escape.

Why has no marker buoy been released?

If the submarine has rolled over onto her side, it is almost certain that no marker buoy or smoke signals could be shot to the surface.

What about survivors?

It is unlikely that anyone could escape from a submarine lying in that position. But we don't know what position she is in, so it's difficult to comment.

When is 'exhaustion hour' for the men, assuming that Affray's crew are still alive?

Friday morning. Even the emergency oxygen candles and compressed air bottles must give out by then.

Why have no survivors come up, if there are any still in the submarine?

Even if they hear rescue craft overhead, survivors must wait until they hear twelve depth charges exploding, signalling that *Affray* has been located.

Why is that?

In the *Truculent* disaster the survivors surfaced before they got the signal to escape. Most of them were carried away and drowned before rescue ships arrived.

How long could survivors float in their life saving suits?

For days.

Is there greater hope of bringing the survivors up from Affray *than there was from* Truculent?

Yes. Men in *Affray* are clearly waiting for the signal to surface. They have a marker buoy with a flashing light and a life-saving suit capable of bringing them to the surface – alive and afloat.

Could the Affray be raised?

It's feasible, but depends on the depth in which we find her.

How many escape hatches does she have?

Four, providing for the possibility that some compartments are flooded and others are not.

Could there have been a mutiny on board?

What a strange question; no comment.

❖   ❖   ❖

Things might have appeared bleak at the press conference, but out at sea there was a ray of hope. At 2155 hours and long after darkness had fallen, the submarine *Sirdar* reported it had picked up feint signals on its listening apparatus sounding as if someone was tapping out a Morse message from inside a submarine hull somewhere within the vicinity of *Affray*'s diving position. ASDIC – later known as sonar – was the name given to a device used for locating other vessels using sound waves (and named after the Anti-Submarine Detection Investigation Committee).

But was the tapping coming from *Affray*? And was she trapped somewhere nearby on the seabed? If the answer was yes, more than enough help was now on hand to rescue her crew, providing they could evacuate the stricken submarine.

Providing she could be accurately located, divers from *Reclaim* would take an air tube down to *Affray* and drive it into the submarine's hull through a hollow bolt fired from a powerful salvage gun. Compressed air would then be pumped down to replace the foul air inside. If necessary, a liquid food pipeline – known in the Navy as 'a bacon and eggs tube' – could also be driven into the submarine by the same means. Once this was done, the submarine could either be raised to an even keel by pumping compressed air into flooded compartments and giving the trapped men a chance to use the escape hatches, or the submarine could be raised to the surface using lifts mounted onto pontoons.

It had been calculated that there was sufficient oxygen on board for up to four days underwater, meaning there was at least two more days' supply left for the rescue flotilla to locate her and stand by while her officers and ratings floated to the surface wearing emergency escape apparatus. From there the rescue ships would help them on board, administer first-aid treatment (if required), provide hot drinks containing a little something extra to help fight the cold (definitely required), dry clothing and a square meal.

It looked like the search for the *Affray* would soon be over.

Chapter 7

'COMMUNICATION HAS BEEN ESTABLISHED WITH *AFFRAY*'

The tapping continued at irregular intervals for the next two hours. They lasted for between two and six seconds and were closely monitored by *Sirdar*'s crew using supersonic telegraphy equipment to receive and amplify the strange signals travelling through the water. But they made no sense, sounding like the letter 'S' repeated over and over. Could someone be attempting to send out the Morse signal: '... --- ... (S.O.S)' but for some reason unable to tap out the whole signal or did not know the full code?

At roughly the same time HMS *Tintagel Castle* also reported ASDIC contact in the identical area received through an electronic sound transmitter and receiver housed in a metal dome beneath the ship's hull. High-frequency beams – audible 'pings' – were sent out and bounced back when they hit a submarine. The time that passed before an echo was received showed the range of the submarine. The pitch of the echo revealed if it was approaching or moving away. *Sea Devil* and *Trespasser* monitored similar signals on their submarine frequencies. *Tintagel Castle* headed in the general direction of the signals at a slow speed while *Sirdar* attempted to send a reply confirming that the tapping had been heard and that attempts were being made to find who was sending them. It was generally agreed that the sender was an inexperienced man, most likely in some sort of trouble.

At five minutes past midnight the tapping sounds became louder and closer and Sirdar picked up the signal 'A.M.' – the accepted submarine signal for 'am stuck on bottom'. There was jubilation among the search flotilla and all ships were ordered to head in the direction of *Tintagel Castle* with HMS *Boxer* appointed headquarters ship.

Rear Admiral Raw, directing operations from HMS *Dolphin*, asked senior officers in the flotilla whether they considered the time was now right to send explosive grenades over the side alerting *Affray*'s crew to prepare for escape. Raw was worried that *Affray* might be stuck on the sea bottom some distance away and when the stranded crew heard the charge they would begin escaping into an area far away from the flotilla.

The rear admiral was also concerned about atmospheric conditions inside the stricken submarine. Calculations carried out by the Royal Naval Physiological Laboratory showed that if parts of the submarine were flooded, the number of survivors plus efficiency and life of its air purification system meant that escape should not be delayed. But it was pitch black out at sea and the weather was quickly deteriorating with a heavy surface swell, making it difficult to locate any men coming from the depths below.

The Physiological Laboratory warned that atmospheric conditions inside the submarine were probably so bad that men would almost certainly begin their escape attempt without waiting for explosive signals. Raw decided to delay the rescue attempt until first light when sufficient ships had reached the area to help find and pick up survivors from rescue rowboats. An RAF Sunderland aircraft would also begin circling the area at dawn.

Everyone was certain they were now close to finding *Affray*, but they could not be certain and as Subsmash rescue ships headed to the area at full speed, Raw issued the following signal from HMS *Dolphin*:

1. If not already done, a buoy is to be dropped accurately over the submarine.
2. When ordered, carry out following organisation for picking up survivors –
   a. HMS *Battleaxe* to illuminate buoy.
   b. All ships send all available pulling boats to vicinity of buoy.
   c. Ships to remain in a circle not less than half a mile from the buoy and illuminate water as necessary.
   d. *Reclaim* to be stationed downwind and burn NUC light.
   e. All survivors to be taken to *Reclaim*.
3. Delay is not – repeat not – acceptable. Escape should commence as soon as sufficient ships are available to ensure picking up survivors.

Raw urged *Sirdar* and *Tintagel Castle* to continue their attempts to establish contact with *Affray* and discover the extent of damage and flooding to the submarine.

At 0204 hours, Commander-in-Chief Portsmouth, Sir Arthur Power, made the bold move of sending the following signal to the Admiralty in London for circulation to the press:

Communication has been established by signal with Affray. The submarine is apparently stuck on the bottom in 33 fathoms of water. Searching vessels are concentrating on the position of the sunken submarine. The necessary signals to ships in the vicinity have been made to give the best chances of rescuing any men who leave *Affray* by escape apparatus.

The statement triggered off a bombardment of calls from newspapers and the BBC asking for facilities for reporters and photographers to go to the area and witness the rescue. They wanted to observe search operations, photograph survivors as they came to the surface and interview them. Requests were deliberately ignored.

Power was so certain that *Affray* had been found that he sent messages to RAF stations taking part in the search stating: 'The submarine has been located. Cancel all searches. Further instructions for helicopters and Sea Otters follow.' The Admiralty ordered Ministry of Transport Services to send an urgent cable to all shipping in the English Channel: 'Submarine has been located. Submarine rescue operations are taking place in 50 10N 0145 W. All shipping is warned to keep well clear of this position.'

Power and his team were now working on the assumption that all seventy-five men on board *Affray* were alive and had gathered in the forward bulkhead of the engine room where the required number of twenty CO_2 canisters were stored along with a number of oxygen candles to supplement the regular air supply.

It was only a matter of time before they found her . . .

❖   ❖   ❖

Shortly before 0330 a sports car screeched to an abrupt halt in front of security gates at HMS *Vernon*, the Royal Navy's torpedo and anti-submarine shore base at Portsmouth. The duty guard had been told to expect the car and to direct it towards the only building still with its lights burning. On arrival he was to ask for *Vernon*'s commander, Captain C.D. Howard-Johnston.

As the driver climbed out of his car, a naval officer walked towards him. The driver introduced himself as Commander Lionel Crabb. Howard-Johnston knew who he was. His reputation had come before him and he was something of a legend to almost everyone in the Navy and the public at large. As a lieutenant during the Second World War, Lionel 'Buster' Crabb had served with distinction at Gibraltar as a demolitions expert, bravely defusing limpet mines placed by enemy frogmen on the undersides of Allied ships. His work in Gibraltar had earned Crabb the George Medal and promotion to lieutenant-commander and he went on to supervise a massive operation to clear the Italian ports of Livorno and Venice of enemy mines before re-opening for shipping. For this he was awarded the OBE. After the war Crabb was sent to Palestine where he led a crack underwater explosives disposal team removing mines placed by Jewish rebels beneath British ships.

Crabb was a contemporary of Ian Fleming, who is said to have based many characteristics of his James Bond creation on Crabb, including 007's habit of throwing a hat across a room to land perfectly on the hat stand, a love of cocktails 'shaken, not stirred', fast cars – and an eye for beautiful women.

Crabb had been demobilised in 1947 and now, at the age of 42, was engaged on top-secret undercover diving operations, including work for the Atomic Weapons Research Establishment and as an underwater photographer for the Admiralty's Research Laboratory at Teddington. He had come to public attention again after volunteering to dive on the wreck of HMS *Truculent* after it had sunk the previous year. Crabb dived on the submarine in almost total darkness, hand-under-hand down an oily cable, only to find that survivors had already evacuated the submarine, most of them to perish from exposure in the icy water of the Thames Estuary. There were only ten survivors.

After hearing about the loss of *Affray* and her possible discovery, Crabb had contacted the Navy to again offer his services. He was told to report immediately to HMS *Vernon* where motor torpedo boats were preparing to depart for the search zone. Captain Howard-Johnston carefully briefed Crabb on the submarine's possible whereabouts and difficulties he might encounter. Crabb claimed that if *Affray* was found in less than 120ft of water, he could reach her faster wearing his frogman gear than a standard diver wearing cumbersome underwater apparatus. Crabb was offered a meal before sailing, which he refused. He wanted to get on with the job in the small amount of time *Affray*'s men had left to be rescued.

By 0440 hours Crabb was travelling out into the Channel on a motor torpedo boat. Only after leaving *Vernon* did he learn that Captain Howard-Johnston's eldest son, Lieutenant Richard Howard-Johnston, was a member of the missing submarine's crew. Nothing had been said by his father at the shore base.

❖   ❖   ❖

By 0355 the Admiralty had agreed to consider allowing some of the reporters and photographers now filling Portsmouth and Gosport's boarding houses to visit the search area. They would board the tug *Capable* at 1040 to be taken out to HMS *Starling*, where they would remain on the frigate for just one hour before returning to shore.

Another upbeat press statement was circulated at 0513:

Affray has been definitely located and positioned by HM ships assisted by US, French and Belgian vessels with support from British and French aircraft. Ships sent to the vicinity are all ready for rescue. Rescue operations will have the best chance in daylight.

At 0527 someone at the Admiralty thought it wise to slightly rephrase the statement, striking out the word 'definitely'.

At 0555 in a clear dawn and greatly improved sea conditions, the twelve-charge signal was dropped over the side of HM ships *Agincourt*, *St Austell Bay* and *Hedingham Castle*. At 0614 more hull tappings were heard, but they made no more sense than those monitored during the night. Scores of men from twenty-nine ships and seven surfaced submarines leaned over the railings of their respective vessels straining their eyes to see one head, and then another followed by dozens more break the surface into daylight. But they saw nothing more than an empty sea.

Knowing that the BBC and every newspaper in the country was pressing for more information, another statement was drafted:

Acting on the best information at daylight, sound signals were made at 0645 over the position where *Affray* is believed to be lying. These signals told crew that surface craft were ready in position to pick up any men who surfaced by means of escape apparatus. No survivors have been seen up to 0630.

Ships and submarines in the flotilla remained in their watching circle for several more hours while circling aircraft and Dragonfly helicopters were diverted in case survivors had come to the surface further west.

By now the country was reading positive banner headlines in their morning newspapers which must have cheered families and friends of those on board *Affray*: 'Submarine is Located – Contact Made After Day and Night Search' (*Daily Telegraph*), '*Affray* is Found: Crew Send Message' (*Daily Mirror*). The nation rejoiced.

It is not recorded if Sir Arthur Power regretted authorising press statements claiming that *Affray* had been found and communication established. The hearts of families with husbands and sons on the submarine sank when they read early editions of the same day's evening newspapers and Power's latest communiqué, now casting doubt about the 'discovery'. Power told the press:

Although *Affray* has been heard making signals intermittently, her precise position has not been fixed. Surface ships have formed a ring covering a wide area of probability and are waiting to rescue survivors who may be able to escape. Aircraft fitted with airborne lifeboats and helicopters are also searching the area.

By 1215 hours Power began to introduce a further shadow of doubt into his statements:

Search is continuing but it is regretted that no survivors have yet been sighted. There is increasing evidence that the search is being carried out in the correct place. The fact that the submarine has been submerged for such a long time reduces the prospects of success.

Power now demanded a report from every ship and submarine claiming to have heard hull tappings or received mystery signals. In a message to the submarines *Sirdar*, *Sea Devil* and *Trespasser*, he demanded to know: 'In light of events and as a basis for further planning, are you completely convinced that you did have SST communication with *Affray?*'

The replies came back quickly: *Sirdar*, 'Yes!'; *Sea Devil*, 'Yes!! and *Trespasser*, 'Signals heard but too feint to read.'

As the morning progressed, Power was quickly coming to the conclusion that communication had never been made with *Affray* in the first place or any reliance given to the noises and signals – 'but they cannot be discounted,' said an official Admiralty document. 'Hammering in machinery spaces can well be mistaken for hull taps and it is probable that echo sounders and/or short transmissions from ASDIC sets or surface craft were also being used at the times stated.'

It was time for another telegram to be sent to disappointed and grief stricken wives and mothers waiting for news of their men on *Affray*:

Much regret I cannot at present give you any information beyond that already broadcast but you may rest assured that everything possible is being done and you will be informed as soon as any definite news of your husband/son is established. Ends.

❖   ❖   ❖

On the afternoon of Wednesday 18 April, James Thomas, MP, stood up in the House of Commons and asked Parliamentary Secretary to the Admiralty, James Callaghan, whether he had any statement to make about *Affray*. Callaghan – later to become Leader of the Labour Party and Prime Minister – was expecting the question and had spent most of the previous night and that morning being briefed over the telephone by the Admiralty and Sir Arthur Power. He told the House:

HM Submarine *Affray* left Portsmouth on Monday for a practice wartime patrol designed to give officers of the Submarine Training Course experience at sea in a submarine under war conditions. She has on board her Captain and four ship's officers and a crew of 46 naval ratings, together with 20 officers from the training course and 4 Royal Marines other ranks of a Marine Training Course. At 8.56 p.m. on Monday evening she signalled that she planned to dive at 9.15 p.m. She was then south of the Isle of Wight and her intention after diving was to proceed westwards through the Channel.

She was expected to surface and report between eight and nine-o-clock yesterday morning, but no report was received. A search was at once organised by the Flag Officer, Submarines, acting on behalf of the Commander-in-Chief Portsmouth. All available ships of the Royal Navy, aircraft of Coastal Command and naval aircraft, including helicopters, took part in the search. I also gratefully acknowledge the assistance given by ships of the United States, French and Belgian navies.

The *Affray* is fully equipped with the latest type of escape apparatus, including sufficient escape chutes for all on board. She is also fitted with a marker buoy at each end, which can be released from inside.

Just before 1.00 a.m. today, HM Submarine *Sea Devil* reported that she had heard signals *which were definitely from Affray.* Further signals were heard at 2.35 a.m. by another submarine. She is apparently lying on the seabed at a depth of about 200ft, near the place where she dived, but her precise position has not yet been fixed.

Explosive sound signals were made at 5.45 a.m. this morning over the position where the vessel is believed to be lying. These signals told her crew that surface craft were ready in position to pick up any men who surfaced by means of escape apparatus. Forty-four surface ships and seven submarines taking part in the search formed a ring covering a wide area and are ready to proceed to the rescue should any survivors escape and appear on the surface. So far none has been sighted. Aircraft from 19 Group RAF and five naval air stations are also taking part in the search, while RAF and Royal Naval helicopters are standing by. Some of the helicopters are fitted with airborne lifeboats.

The Board of Admiralty would like to extend its sincere sympathy to the relatives of the officers and men on board in their ordeal. I should also like to record the untiring and self-forgetful efforts of all those who have organised and are engaged in the search.

The relatives can be assured that everything humanly possible will be done by those who are carrying out the search as long as there is any hope that lives can be saved.

On that same day, Richard Pilgrim, from Cosham, Hampshire, was serving as a 21-year old signalman on board HMS *Nightingale*, a coal-burning minesweeper attached to the shore base at HMS *Vernon*. He remembers:

I remember seeing HMS *Affray* in drydock on a number of occasions, including the day before she sailed for the last time. A few days later HMS *Nightingale* sailed to the Scilly Isles covering much of the same route that *Affray* should have followed. We saw much of the search and rescue operation taking place in the English Channel and when we arrived in the Scillies we learned that the submarine had still not been found.

When we returned to HMS *Vernon*, we were told that the shore-based commander, Captain Howard Johnston, would be coming on board to inspect us. We had learned that his son, a sub-lieutenant, was on board *Affray*. Even though he had broken his wrist in an accident and could have stayed on shore if he wished, Captain Howard-Johnston still came on board. Our hearts all went out to him, but obviously we could not let him know about our feelings. He acted as if nothing so terribly tragic had happened to him and his family. But duty had to be done.

❖   ❖   ❖

Captain Bill Shelford, a specialist in deep diving and submarine escape methods, was rushed back to Britain by air from his base in Malta to help oversee the *Affray* search operation. He later remembered:

At the time the great mystery of the *Affray*'s disappearance bid fair to equal that of the *Marie Celeste* . . . Eight hours after taking off in a Lancaster bomber, I walked into the operations room at Portsmouth. Still in my white cap cover and tanned after two years in the Mediterranean, I must have made strong contrast to the strained white faces of staff officers who had not left their post for the last twenty-four hours.

Admiral Power told me straight away to take over the organisation of the search for *Affray* and any rescue operations that might be necessary. I quickly learned that the greatest search operation ever laid on for a missing submarine was in progress in the Channel, involving nearly forty ships and dozens of aircraft. But that so far it had proved completely fruitless.

There was one emergency with which we might yet have to contend – *Affray* might have dived into one of the many wrecks which strew the bottom of the Channel and be jammed, unable to surface, but otherwise undamaged. Admiral Power wanted plans made in this event to pass a wire around her stern with which to try and drag her clear. The Director of Salvage from the Admiralty forecast that such an operation would take four months and was practically kicked out of the Admiral's office for his pains. I said that it might well take four months but, on the other hand, if everything went in our favour it might be done in twelve hours.

I gathered together a team of salvage experts and although they were at first sceptical, we worked out a plan to make the attempt if the situation arose. It would have been a very desperate attempt, but hourly the situation of the men in *Affray* was growing grimmer and more desperate. I had faith in the divers and equipment on board *Reclaim*. . . . I knew they could get down to the wreck and get a wire on her if only we could transfer the wire to one of the heavy lifting ships to make the haul.

Orders were issued for a full sweep of the sea bottom to be undertaken by five naval minesweepers. But there was a problem. The English Channel was, and remains, littered with the wrecks of scores of ships – some dating back centuries – and submarines including German U-boats from both world wars. Larger wrecks would easily register with minesweepers as a possible location for the wreck of *Affray* and demand further investigation. This would take time, and time was something the Navy had little of on the morning of 18 April, twenty-four hours after 'Subsmash' had first been called.

The search now covered the English Channel from the Isle of Wight to the French coast, down to Land's End and the Channel Islands. By 1000 the search flotilla had split up and gone off in different directions and at the same time back in Gosport, a *Daily Mirror* reporter was knocking on the door of Blackburn's wife, Jean, 'sitting – alone – in her cream painted home in Foster Road'. Mrs Blackburn told the reporter: 'It's this awful waiting. If only we knew something.'

Her children, Anthony, 6, and Jill, 4, were playing with a ball in their grandmother's garden just 200yd around the corner and knew nothing of their father's peril. 'My daddy's a naval officer,' Anthony told the reporter, 'but now he's at sea.'

Mrs D.L. Cowan, Blackburn's mother-in-law, said: 'Jean hasn't even got a photograph of John. He took them all to sea to paste into the family album.'

The same newspaper also reported that Stoker-Mechanic Robert Cardno, 21, and his bride Jean Bratton, from Leeds, Kent, had been married only ten days before *Affray* went missing. The *Mirror* said that the new bride 'sat weeping' while waiting for news about her husband. It continued:

> For the third time a mother sat by the phone last night waiting for news from a missing submarine. She was Lady Frew, mother of Sub-Lieutenant Anthony Frew, an officer in the *Affray*. Sub-Lieutenant Frew was one of those saved when the submarine *Truculent* was wrecked in the Thames Estuary in January last year. Her husband, Engineer Rear Admiral Sir Sidney Frew was serving in the submarine *K.12* in the 1920s when it was reported sunk off the East coast. It was later found to be safe.

Lady Frew told the newspaper: 'We have had such a lot of this in our lives. We can only hope that there will be good news.'

The *Daily Express* took a more sensitive line in an editorial leader column:

> Somewhere in the Channel a submarine is lying on the seabed. A submarine which carries the loved ones of seventy-five wives and mothers throughout the country. To those who are waiting, the nation's heart goes out. Their prayers are ours.

Hope rose again when a search aircraft reported 'many yellow and white objects in position 135 degrees Portland Bill 29 miles'. There was every likelihood that the objects could either be men bobbing about on the surface of the water wearing their brightly coloured escape apparatus or marker buoys sent up by the stricken submarine. All ships in the vicinity were immediately diverted to the spot and ploughed their way through the water at top speed. On arrival they found nothing more than a large school of cuttlefish and empty boxes probably thrown over the side by a passing ship. Spirits plummeted again.

As the second day of the search drew to a close, the Admiralty issued its final statement of the day:

> As a result of operations during daylight today, there has been no rescue of any survivor from *Affray*, although continuous search and watch has been carried out by surface craft, submarines and aircraft. This search and watch will be continued throughout the coming dark hours but chances of success are now very small. There will be no further report issued by the Admiralty until tomorrow morning unless something of importance occurs.

The statement was broadcast on the BBC's 10 o'clock radio news bulletin and heard by King George VI at Buckingham Palace. As Commander-in-

Chief of the country's armed forces, the King had been following progress of the 'Subsmash' search operation on radio news broadcasts and pondering the question of how she might be stuck on the sea bottom. Before retiring to bed for the night, he instructed an aide to send the following telegram to the Admiralty: 'From Windsor to Admiralty – Re: Submarine *Affray*. Humbly suggest get biggest explosives possible disturb seabed area possibly release to surface. Try it.'

❖   ❖   ❖

That night, Admiral Sir Arthur Power sent a message to Rear Admiral Raw reflecting on the day's events: 'A large amount of today has been wasted by a false alarm which initially appeared to give grounds for the greatest hope since the operation started.'

Captain M.J. Evans, commander of the search flotilla and based on HMS *Agincourt*, wrote in his report on that day's activities at sea:

I was not myself convinced that there was positive evidence of the presence of HMS *Affray* . . . Silence was impossible and the indistinguishable or poorly made Morse . . . smacked to me of transmissions from other searching ships heard through the back and sides of the oscillator. Echo soundings and ordinary ship noises can well be mistaken for hull tapping when operators are anxiously hoping to hear just such noises. I also felt that if the supposed operator in HMS *Affray* was sufficiently in command of his senses to look up groups out of the *Submarine Signal Pamphlet*, he would have sent a more useful message than 'AM'.

Things might have been very different if an order had been issued to maintain total underwater silence among all rescue vessels – but no such order was issued or even requested.

By Thursday 19 April Captain Evans had 'formed the opinion that the chances of survivors coming to the surface by their own efforts had, to all intents and purposes, ceased and that the problem was now one of finding and identifying the wreck on the bottom with the outside chance that, if found, one or two men might still be alive.'

❖   ❖   ❖

During the night of Wednesday 18 April, a sailor on board the destroyer HMS *Myngs* – sent out the previous day to replace another that had returned to shore – jotted his thoughts about HMS *Affray* on paper in the form of a poem. Penned while on watch in the English Channel, the poem is now in the archives of the Royal Naval Submarine Museum at Gosport. The author is identified only as 'MJS', but his words probably summed up the feelings of scores of others also on watch that night searching for a submarine which by now was almost certainly not going to be found with its crew still alive.

Lest We Forget

Perhaps somewhere 'neath us who search,
Seventy-five souls are now at prayer,
With words not heard in any church,
Of alternative hope and then despair.
Thoughts of sweethearts and of wives
Who cry and know not restful sleep
For thinking of those feared lost lives
Who lie in waters enclosed and deep.
Give to them, my God, I pray
Swift rescue and the light of day.
Not my will, but thine be done,
Help us cry 'The Battle's won.'
Perhaps such is not your will at all,
But on their sins, please do not frown
And when your Bo'sun sounds the call
Give your blessing to their last pipe-down.
R.I.P.

Chapter 8

THE FLAME BURNS LOW

There was egg on the faces of Admiralty officials on the morning of Thursday 19 April when they read the front page of the *Daily Mirror*. The paper's headline 'Six Mysteries of the *Affray*' sought answers to questions that many readers across the country were also asking that morning – why was the Navy, with all its ships, technology, experience and know-how, unable to resolve a series of mysteries surrounding the submarine's disappearance? The paper challenged the Admiralty to address each mystery in turn:

1. The *Affray* was equipped with marker buoys, which could be released to the surface within seconds if she was unable to rise. Why hasn't she released any?
2. Why, if she suffered an underwater explosion or hit a wreck or a mine, has neither oil nor wreckage been found?
3. Why has nothing more been heard from members of her crew who were thought to be alive in her control room when signals were picked up by underwater supersonic telephone in the search submarine *Sea Devil*?
4. Why was there no response to the 12 explosive grenade signals made a few hours later by surface vessels over the spot from which the *Affray* was thought to have sent out the signals? The explosions were to tell her rescuers were above her.
5. She was equipped with Davis escape apparatus sufficient for every man on board. Why has none of her men escaped by this method?
6. Why have nearly 50 surface and undersea vessels and planes, between them carrying every known submarine detection device and scientific aid, failed to place her position?

The paper added: 'The fate of the *Affray* has, in fact, become one of the biggest riddles in submarine history. The only explanation that can be advanced is that she may have lost her trim in diving, nosed over and crashed upside down on the sea bottom.'

The Admiralty had no answers. They had no idea what had happened to *Affray* and bitterly regretted issuing misleading statements declaring that communication had been established with *Affray* – claims repeated in Parliament by James Callaghan. Twenty-four hours earlier, the nation rejoiced in the knowledge that it was only a matter of time before the missing submarine would be found and its seventy-five officers and men brought to the surface. Now, the whole prospect of saving the men and their submarine had been cast into doubt.

Matters were made worse by rumours in circulation for the past thirty-six hours that *Affray*'s crew had been captured and forced to sail at gunpoint to a Russian port. It had become common gossip in Portsmouth Dockyard that some merchant seamen had actually seen the *Affray* in Vladivostok, close to Russia's frontier with China and North Korea and home of the USSR's Pacific Fleet. It was also a fact that a Russian warship had been travelling outside territorial waters through the English Channel on the night of 16 April.

Another version of the rumour was that the submarine had been sent on a secret mission to the White Sea – an inlet of the Barents Sea on the north-west coast of Russia – where the Soviet Navy had captured it and the story about a submarine accident in the English Channel was a smoke screen put out for diplomatic reasons. Rumours proliferated to such an extent that the Admiralty was forced to release a statement:

> It can be stated categorically that these rumours are without the slightest foundation. All relatives are assured that, if there were the slightest hope of the men being alive, they would have been told by the Admiralty.
>
> We are well aware of these malicious rumours and are most concerned with the effects they may have on relatives. It is shocking to add to their grief.
>
> The stories are, of course, preposterous. It is inconceivable that seventy-five officers and men of the Royal Navy would allow themselves to be forced at the point of a pistol to sail their submarine to Russia. Anybody knowing the interior of a submarine would know the whole idea is ludicrous.

Fifty-six years after the tragedy, Ron Leakey, whose older brother George, was on board *Affray*, remembers the Russian rumours. 'Sometimes we wished they had been true because there was always hope that he would come back one day. Alas, it was not to be,' he said.

Joy Cook, wife of Able Seaman George Cook, said: 'Rumours about being captured at gunpoint by the Russians kept our hopes up. It kept us going for a while longer. Prisoners they may have been, but at least our men might still be alive and the government in a position to negotiate their safe release.'

Other families and friends of the *Affray*'s crew also preferred to believe the rumours. The thought of their husbands, sons and boyfriends as prisoners in a Russia gulag were preferable to thoughts of them lying dead at the bottom of the sea.

It seems to have passed everyone's notice that it would not have been possible for *Affray* to have reached the White Sea, let alone far-flung Vladivostok, within hours of sailing from Gosport. But the western world's growing fear of communism and the 'red menace' threat was a passable excuse for any unsolved mystery and the *Affray*'s disappearance provided rumour-mongers with perfect material for their fantastic stories.

❖　　❖　　❖

Knowing that the Admiralty was dangerously close to cancelling the Subsmash search-and-rescue operation, a *Daily Express* leader article, under the headline 'The Flame Burns Low', told its 4 million readers:

> For HMS *Affray*, the flame of hope has dwindled in these last hours to near exhaustion.
>
> With the grief that all will feel if the fatal pronouncement is made and Operation Subsmash is ended comes a sense of frustration and bewilderment.
>
> For it is on these occasions that the layman realises the vast organisation, the array of safety devices employed to avert such tragedies.
>
> How can they all have failed? The ships, the aircraft have combed and recombed the area in which *Affray* must lie, with all the instruments of power and delicacy that have been evolved in war for the detection of submarines.
>
> The *Affray* itself is fitted with a multitude of safety devices, both for showing her position on the seabed and for saving the lives of the crew if the submarine is abandoned.
>
> You would think that in the time that has passed since Tuesday morning the contact would have been made and developed into some hopeful effort at rescue.
>
> Yet the news of sound signals is followed by long silence – a silence which may never be broken.

It is at times like these that the proud ingenuity of man stands chastened, amid the sorrow and despair of the fathers, mothers, wives and children of the brave men the sea has claimed.

> *Roll on, thou deep and dark blue ocean – roll!*
> *Ten thousand fleets sweep over thee in vain;*
> *Man marks the earth with ruin – his control*
> *Stops with the shore* (Lord Byron)

Is it true? If it is, Man will never believe it. He will go on striving for mastery, even in the ocean depths.

Today let us honour all men who choose the Submarine Service. And all the women who wait for them at home.

❖   ❖   ❖

At first light, HM ships *Welfare*, *Pluto*, *Marvel*, *Squirrel* and minesweeper *1788* were ordered to form the 5th Minesweeping Flotilla and carry out a 'bottomed search' of the 'best probability area, 6 miles either side of her last known diving position' – a system whereby sound waves were sent through an underwater transmitter on the bottom of the ship down to the seabed. The highly pitched sound – beyond human hearing – strikes the seabed and bounces back as an echo to a receiver. The time taken for the sound to reach the seabed and return dictates depth of the water.

Bursts of sound are fired as ships move forward so that objects on the seabed can be monitored and recorded on a chart. A submarine lying on the bottom would show up clearly as a cigar-shaped shadow. The system was far from perfect, but it made sense to give it a try even though the seabed was littered with everything from large rock formations and shoals of fish to a sixteenth-century Spanish galleon or a stricken submarine a few days late in reporting her position.

By the end of the day the minesweeping flotilla had covered a strip of just 11 miles long by half-a-mile wide and recorded just one possible contact, found to have been too small for a submarine.

At 0840 hours the 3,300-ton merchant ship SS *Andalusian* found itself ploughing through a massive oil slick in the English Channel. It radioed that the slick was located 10 miles away from The Casquets, a group of small rocky islands about seven miles west of Alderney – for centuries the graveyard of many unwary mariners. A searching aircraft from Coastal Command flew to the area, dropped a marker buoy and the American destroyers USS *Perry* and *Ellison* were sent to investigate.

Before the American vessels arrived, a second aircraft flew over the site, unaware that the slick had already been reported, spotted the marker buoy and reported that he had found the spot where *Affray* had gone missing. Hopes soared once again, to be quashed moments later when the confusion was discovered.

USS *Perry* and *Ellison* found the slick to be 15 miles long but narrow in breadth. Sailors on board the *Perry* scooped up a sample of oil and took it below to be tested. It was discovered to be bunker oil and not the hoped-for diesel oil used on *Affray*.

During the previous night, the Admiralty had begun the task of drafting a statement containing the news that nobody wanted to hear, particularly the mothers, wives, girlfriends, friends and neighbours of the crew of *Affray*. If there was no further positive news to report by 1000 hours and once they were absolutely sure nothing more could be done to find survivors from the *Affray*, it would be released to the BBC, Press Association and Exchange Telegraph news agencies. Once it was confirmed that the statement would be made public, it was agreed that next-of-kin, HM the King and the Prime Minister would be informed one hour before the rest of the world. The draft statement read as follows:

Full-scale operations have been conducted throughout the night and are continuing. In addition to other means of search, sweeping the seabed is now being carried out.

It is with the deepest regret that Their Lordships must state that there is now no reasonable hope of their being any survivors.

The statement was sent to Rear Admiral Raw for comment and he immediately insisted that only the first paragraph be issued to the press with no mention of there being 'no reasonable hope' of finding survivors delayed until the last possible moment. The Navy had had their fingers burned badly the previous day. Raw was determined not to let it happen again.

By lunchtime the search flotilla was no nearer locating the lost submarine and at 1300 hours Admiral Power telephoned Rear Admiral Raw and asked if he agreed that 'a very sad signal' should now be made.

Where possible, next-of-kin were informed personally by HMS *Dolphin* staff not necessarily known to grief stricken families. Mary Henry remembers:

The Navy sent a complete stranger to see me at my home in Petersfield and tell me to give up hope as my husband Derek and the rest of the crew could not possibly be alive after all this time. I had many friends at HMS *Dolphin* who could have been sent to break the news in a much kinder way. But they sent a total stranger.

That, plus hearing the news that the submarine had gone missing over the radio instead from a naval person, was heartless. I thought so then and still feel the same after all these years.

An official messenger informed the Prime Minister, still in his hospital bed at St Mary's Hospital, Paddington, recovering from a duodenal ulcer operation. As soon as the message had been delivered a nursing sister ordered the messenger out of the Prime Minister's private room, but Atlee ordered him to stay while he dictated a telegram to the Admiralty that could also be issued as a press statement:

Please accept my most sincere condolence on the heavy loss of life which the Royal Navy has suffered in the sinking of HM Submarine *Affray*. I shall be glad if you will send a message of sympathy on my behalf to the relatives of the officers and men involved in this tragedy.

King George asked the Admiralty to

please convey the heartfelt sympathy of the Queen and myself to the relatives of all those who have lost their lives in the tragic disaster that has befallen the submarine *Affray* – signed George R.

In a telegram to Admiral Power, First Lord of the Admiralty, Lord Hall, said:

I am most deeply distressed by the tragic news that all hope has now been abandoned for the survival of the personnel in HM Submarine *Affray*. Please convey to the relatives of all those gallant officers and men who have lost their lives in the execution of their duty the sincerest sympathy of myself and my colleagues on the Board of the Admiralty.

Joseph Francis, the Navy Minister, said that he

trusted that the families of those lost would find some consolation in the fact that they had died in the service of their country while learning to defend it and, as so many other men in the Navy had done through succeeding generations, had sacrificed their lives in the cause of duty. They are deserving of the highest tribute, for they have given all they had, just as men who had died in the war.

As soon as the BBC reported the tragic news, telegrams began flooding into the Admiralty from the great, the good, the powerful and ordinary men and women. They came from heads of state, foreign governments and navies, commercial companies, associations, clubs and individuals across Great Britain and the rest of the world. And after the telegrams came letters – thousands of them – many wanting to know how they could contribute to a fund which would help the widows and children of those lost at sea in *Affray*.

At 1945 on Thursday 19 April, sixty-nine hours after *Affray* had dived for the last time, Subsmash was cancelled. The searching ships and aircraft, salvage vessels and tugs, divers and doctors returned to shore after which a systematic search would begin for the wreck of a submarine containing seventy-five dead men, whose pay was officially stopped that day. *Affray*'s officers and men were officially 'discharged dead' on the same date.

The search had cost over £1 million and ships taking part had steamed 24,000 miles and covered an area the size of Kent. They had made 120 underwater contacts, 24 of them wrecks, each one offering the glimmer of a chance that *Affray* had been found and each one ending in disappointment.

Aircraft and helicopters had flown a total 475 hours on 258 different sorties over the search area. On the way back to the airfield at Hamble an Avro Anson search aircraft developed a mechanical fault over Torbay and ditched into the Channel. The Brixham Lifeboat rescued its crew of four who had managed to abandon the Anson and climb into an inflatable dinghy before the aircraft sank.

In a message to the Admiralty, Rear Admiral Raw said:

The disappearance of HMS *Affray* is a complete mystery. In spite of widespread sea and air searches in good weather conditions, not a trace of her was sighted. Neither wreckage of a submarine character, nor tell-tale slick of diesel oil, nor indicator buoys, nor smoke candles, nor bodies were seen. It is the considered opinion of officers in surface vessels and aircraft taking part in the search that any of the indications mentioned above must have been sighted in the weather conditions prevailing. It is idle speculation even to guess at the cause of the disaster and the mystery must remain unsolved until HMS *Affray* has been located and examined. It can, however, be stated with full confidence that submarines of the 'A' class, which have operated successfully and without loss for five years in most parts of the world and in all extreme weather and climate, are in every way satisfactory operational ships on the surface, submerged or resting on the bottom. The cause of the disaster must have been an accident; it could not have resulted from any inherent defect in material or design.

Lieutenant-Commander Douggie Elliott, a member of 705 Naval Air Squadron, which had flown multiple helicopter sorties over the Channel hoping to spot members of *Affray*'s crew in the sea, describes the end of the search as 'the most disappointing time of our lives'.

David Dyer, a member of the same squadron, recalls the frustration he and his colleagues experienced when the mission was cancelled:

> We were crushed, deflated. Of course, we were all looking and searching in what turned out to be the wrong place. So the helicopter maintenance crew packed up their equipment and returned to base in their truck, the helicopter went back to its base at HMS *Siskin* – and the rest is history.

Gordon Chatburn, part of HMS *Agincourt*'s search crew, recalls the ship returning to port 'with everyone's spirits at rock bottom'. He remembers:

> Our skipper, Captain Martin Evans, spoke to the ship's company over the Tannoy and informed us that the Admiralty had reluctantly decided to call off the search. The atmosphere on board was absolutely dreadful and on entering Portsmouth Harbour our spirits were as low as they could possibly go. Our crew, to a man, realised that seventy-five brave companions would never enter that same harbour again. It was such a dreadful loss of life and the realisation that families and friends of the *Affray* crew would soon be told that the search had all been in vain really hurt us.
>
> I'm now 76 years old and I have never forgotten the search for *Affray* and I'm sure there are many others who still feel the same. We thought we could find her, rescue her men and bring them home. Instead, they tragically lost their lives. This is the memory that I'm left with fifty-six years later.

Although search and rescue crews were exhausted and discouraged, they were still determined to find *Affray* because they knew she was out there. Somewhere.

❖   ❖   ❖

As the luxury liner RMS *Queen Mary* made its stately passage from Southampton towards the Atlantic and New York, a passenger named Eric Thompson leaned over the railings and observed all the activity in the English Channel. He knew what was going on and later in his cabin he wrote the following lines:

Salute to the Men of the Affray

Hail Submariners! Gone to rest below,
*   Not in the throes of battle bravely borne*
Thro' green-tinged depths our signal halliards fly
*   'Blow Negative!' – and rise to greet the morn.*
Another silent victim of your calling's fate,
*   Where liest now the 'Boat' which bore you down?*
And we who pass o'erhead and stand and wait
*   All help to share the burden of your crown.*

Farewell, our comrades of the heaving deep,
*   Bless'd with the key of Neptune's high estates;*
Farewell you 'Pigboat' men and may you sleep
*   In peace below until you stand before the Golden Gate.*

So let each one stand stalwart there and proud,
*   Commander, Coxswain, ratings – British men,*
Drop not your heads, but lift them high and say
*   'We did our solemn duty, as we saw it then.'*

Come to salute! My shipmates standing in to land,
*   Our island gateway lights have raised their loom,*
Whilst, neath our keel the yellow moving sand
*   Drifts quietly round your mystic silent tomb.*

Chapter 9

HEARTFELT SYMPATHY, PERSONAL EFFECTS, INVENTIONS AND VISIONARY SUGGESTIONS

O n the morning of Saturday 21 April postmen brought special delivery letters to seventy-five different homes across the country. The letters – carrying an embossed Admiralty crest and typed on green paper – were from Flag Officer Submarines, Rear Admiral Sydney Raw. They all conveyed the same sad news that had been communicated to the rest of the world via newspapers and the BBC days before. Only the names of recipients and loved ones lost on *Affray* were changed. But the letters made it 'official' – their husbands and sons would not be coming home again.

The following letter was sent to Winifred Ashley, widow of Leading Stoker Mechanic George Ashley, and her children aged 5, 4 and 9 months, at their home in Blyth, Northumberland:

Dear Mrs Ashley,

It is with the deepest regret that I have to confirm that it must now be presumed that your husband lost his life in HMS *Affray*.

As you will have heard, HMS *Affray* sailed from Portsmouth at 4.30 p.m. on Monday evening, 16th April, to carry out a practice training patrol between Portsmouth and Falmouth. She dived at 9.15 p.m. south of the Isle of Wight with the intention of proceeding westward at a speed of four and a half knots. She was expected to surface between 9 o'clock and 10 o'clock next morning to make a daily routine report. As no signal had been received from her by 11 o'clock that morning, the organisation for the search and rescue of a missing submarine was put into force at once and search and rescue operations were commenced without delay by all suitable surface ships, submarines and aircraft from Naval Aviation and Royal Air Force, including helicopters.

A full-scale search has been going on continuously over the whole of the area in which the submarine may have gone down. British ships were joined at once by ships of the United States, French and Belgian navies and ships, aircraft and submarines have been working unceasingly with the object of finding HMS *Affray*. But despite everything that has been done with every modern device, their efforts have not been rewarded with success.

At the present time therefore I am unable to say how HMS *Affray* was lost: she was one of our newest submarines and diving tests and exercises carried out a few days before she sailed confirmed that she was in perfect condition in every respect for the operation for which she proceeded.

But whatever happened, I have no doubt that all on board lived up to the highest traditions of the Royal Navy, traditions which have been handed down to us over fifty years and which we who have the honour of belonging to the Submarine Branch treasure very highly.

Many messages of sympathy have come from all over the country and special telegrams have been received from Their Majesties, the Prime Minister and the First Lord and Members of the Board of Admiralty. I am sending you a little later, copies of these special telegrams and the replies I have made on your behalf.

May I ask you to accept the heartfelt sympathy of myself and all the officers and men of the Submarine Branch of the Royal Navy in your great bereavement.

Yours sincerely,

S.M. Raw
Rear Admiral

❖   ❖   ❖

At HMS *Dolphin* a row of lockers containing personal effects of men lost on *Affray* were waiting to be opened and the contents returned to families of the missing men. This could only be done once the men were officially pronounced dead. Outside, several cars belonging to officers lost on the submarine had been parked and relatives of the dead men wanted to know when they could come and drive them away. Nobody in the Navy seemed to know the answer due to the number of 'what ifs' that existed in the aftermath of the accident.

What if the submarine was eventually salvaged and a number of Wills, scratched out at the last minute, found on board bequeathing items, however small, to particular people?

What if more than one relative had claim to an item once owned by a member of the crew – such as a car?

What if no one claimed the contents of a locker? Should the goods be sold by auction, and, if so, who should receive the money?

What if goods were sold and then a relative of the dead man claimed ownership of the goods?

The Department of Navy Accounts was charged with the task of dealing with the problem, having had plenty of experience handling similar issues during the war. True to form, a memo was written laying out options that might be pursued and seeking advice from naval lawyers. The memo stated:

In the absence of any knowledge of the circumstances in which *Affray* was lost, the possibility (however remote it may be) of her being ultimately salved and wills made on board after she sailed coming to light, cannot be entirely overlooked and until either the ship is salved or the search for her finally abandoned, the issue of a certificate authorising the payment of the Naval Assets of an individual officer or rating would have to be made with the knowledge that the disposition of those assets might be at variance with his wishes as expressed in a will that may later be found. On the other hand, the issue of a Certificate cannot be held up for an unduly long period because of this possibility.

Because of the natural desire of the relatives of a deceased officer or rating to receive 'personal possessions' as soon as possible, it is the usual practice to authorise their early release to whoever appears, on the evidence available, to be the person entitled to them.

Details of the effects of the officers and ratings in *Affray* have not yet been reported to this department, but it is understood that they range from motor cars to articles of small intrinsic (though doubtless of great sentimental) value and that many enquiries concerning them, and requests for their release, have already been received from the relatives.

In view of the protests that will inevitably be received if the effects of those lost in *Affray* are retained by the Admiralty for any appreciable time, it may be considered advisable (whatever may be the decision regarding the 'assets') to proceed with their distribution in the usual way – i.e. on the information now available, notwithstanding the possibility of further wills being found.

Naval lawyers

could foresee a shoal of protests, both Parliamentary and otherwise if we propose to stand on this and the possibility of wills being recovered from the wreck if and when it is found. It is noted that many enquiries concerning the 'effects' are being received by the Director of Navy Accounts and, as it is understood that the cars referred to are being kept in the open at HMS *Dolphin* and will inevitably deteriorate if held for long, it is considered that these should be disposed of as soon as possible.

Concerning the possibility of wills being found when the wreck is recovered, Naval Law considers that this is remote. Had the vessel been located and it had been known that some remained alive in her but could not be rescued, the possibility of wills being made by those who survived the initial impact could not be ignored. All the circumstances of the loss of HMS *Affray*, however, point to the probability of the disaster being sudden and unexpected.

Where possible, spare sets of car keys were found and the small number of cars parked near the quayside were claimed and driven away by relatives or appointed representatives. Lockers were opened and a list made of personal items found inside. Relatives were told that the Navy could either arrange to have the items returned to next of kin or sell them to their colleagues and the money forwarded with the balance of their wages for the period 1–19 April.

It is not recorded how much was raised from the sale of clothing, pen knives, cigarettes and a hundred and one other things discovered in the personal lockers of dozens of missing seamen. Wages owed and money raised from the sale of personal effects were sent to dependants with official Certificates of Death, dated 2 May 1951.

So it was that the wife of Leading Stoker Mechanic George Ashley, from Blyth, Northumberland, received a Certificate of Death because her husband 'is presumed by the Admiralty, for official purposes, to have died on April 19, 1951 following the loss of HMS *Affray*'. With it was attached a cheque for £34 18s 0d – £11 15s 0d in wages owed and £23 3s 0d from the sale of his personal effects to the mates he left behind at HMS *Dolphin*.

❖   ❖   ❖

Scores of well-meaning people who felt they had special skills that might help to locate the wreck offered their services to the Admiralty. They included experienced divers and salvage experts and others claiming to have the ways and means of detecting a large object recently deposited on the seabed. Others claimed to be in a position to categorically state the exact position of the lost submarine and locations offered ranged from the Dover Straits to the Bristol Channel. Correspondents introduced themselves as inventors, scientists, dowsers, spiritualists, clairvoyants, mystics and others claiming to have had dreams in which *Affray*'s position was clearly given to them by 'a messenger' in their sleep.

Letters arrived from all parts of the country, as well as from Germany, Spain, Holland, France and Canada. They were all sincere, even if some were hoping to use the *Affray* tragedy as a means of earning money. Most were crude attempts by amateurs who were trying to tell the Navy how to do its job. Many were ridiculous and unusable ideas. But each letter was read, politely acknowledged and then carefully placed in a file marked 'HMS *Affray* – Inventions and Innovative Suggestions'.

Realistic and authoritative proposals originating from people who appeared to know what they were writing about were taken more seriously. Captain Shelford, the deep-diving expert who had overseen part of the search-and-rescue operations, painstakingly entered these suggestions onto a map and discovered that they all met in one small area outside the scope of the main search. He suggested that time be set aside to investigate and Captain Roy Foster-Brown, Commander of the 6th Frigate Flotilla, later reported that his ship had picked up such loud echoes on the ASDIC that 'they nearly knocked me off the bridge'. A fuller investigation revealed absolutely nothing in the area.

Among the letters sent to the Admiralty was one from First Petty Officer Theodir Galleski, Hamburg, Germany – who claimed to have worked under Grand Admiral Donitz, head of Hitler's Navy – introducing himself as 'a minesweeping official'. Herr Galleski said he considered 'remuneration to me of five thousand English pounds would not be too high' in return for his 'logical and simple' scheme using fifty lifting tugs and buoys to bring the submarine to the surface once it was discovered.

He received a reply from the Admiralty stating: 'I have to say that a number of similar proposals have been considered in the past and it has been found that the inherent objections to schemes of this nature are such that further action with a view to their development for use in the HM Naval Service would not be warranted.'

E. Tuffield, from Birmingham, sent in a large drawing of a supersize salvage ship complete with ten cranes, ten lifeboats, a landing deck for helicopters, a fully equipped hospital deck and lifting gear designed to haul up the submarine from the floor of the seabed. He wrote:

> This idea may appear to be fantastic but on the other hand may give experts food for consideration. I trust you do not think that I am a crank or impertinent. If you think that a personal interview would be necessary, please make it for a weekend as I cannot afford to lose time from work. I sincerely hope that this will be treated in a way that I have put my hope in my endeavour to be of some use to my fellow man.

The Admiralty thanked Tuffield for his proposals 'which are similar in principal to a number of others received from various sources and found to present no novel feature of which the Admiralty can make use'.

A letter from Martinus P. Scott, Inventor, Edmonton, Canada, and addressed to 'The Prime Minister of England, the Hon. Clement Atlee, London, England,' told the PM that 'I have the honour to submit herewith a certain matter which is self-explanatory and which I think might be of interest to you. I have invented a submarine lifeboat designed to be contained in a cell which forms an integral part of the submarine.' He enclosed a series of drawings produced in a child's colouring book showing a single-seat mini-submarine contained within a larger vessel.

The Admiralty replied that 'the invention is not of interest to the Naval Service and it is therefore not desired to take any further action in regard to it'.

One of the more unusual letters came from Wing Commander D.A.K. Yiend, RAF Yatesbury, Wiltshire, who wrote 'to forward some information which it is hoped will assist in tracing HMS *Affray*.' The wing commander explained that he had 'recently become interested in a branch of science related to radiation. . . . Which has led me to pin-pointing the location where I am of the opinion the missing submarine now is.'

Wing Commander Yiend claimed his system to be 'more rapid and reliable and direct than radar, ASDIC or supersonic transmission . . . and when proved by you and your scientific departments, may alter the whole course of the future in regard to the submarine service.'

He disclosed the geographic coordinates where the missing submarine would be found, adding:

My difficulty has been that my map is a very small one and, accordingly you will appreciate that my plotting cannot be too precise at this stage. However, if you will be so good as to arrange to send me two charts with a big scale I would be pleased to make a more precise effort in obtaining a very close approximation of her position as found by myself.

He added:

By my system I have also apparently found the following information:

   a. The bow would appear to be damaged.
   b. The centre section – i.e. the control and conning tower – appears to reflect much confusion and I am unable to explain the difficulty there.
   c. The stern would appear to be undamaged.

Wing Commander Yiend's 'system' was a complicated one 'based on radiation emitted by almost every element of matter'. He said that no instrument had been made which could detect micro frequencies emitted.

However, there is an instrument which can do this – the human network of nerves based on the sympathetic and central nervous system acting as the equivalent of a radio reception antennae with the brain controlling the probing frequency of thought and which resonates with the continuous frequencies emitted by objects we wish to contact.

He likened his system to a dowser or water diviner, 'who has for centuries been able to find water in a manner usually inexplicable to the uninitiated'.

The wing commander suggested that his letter 'be treated as secret, because it is considered that after development, this system may be able to follow known submarines all the time they are submerged and their routes and positions can be checked at any time. The enormous importance of this fact will be apparent at once.'

The Admiralty was uncertain how to deal with the wing commander's letter. After all, the correspondent was a person of rank within the RAF and quite unlike some of the 'crackpots' claiming to know how to locate the *Affray*. As a result the letter was passed to the Navy's Director of Operations, Head of the Military Branch and the Director of Research Programme & Planning. The latter scribbled a note on the back stating: 'Wing Command Yiend's letter from a physicist's point of view is sheer bunk.'

A draft reply, composed by N.D. Imrie on behalf of the Director of Research & Planning, thanked the wing commander for getting in touch, stating that after 'careful examination, your letter reveals nothing of practical value to the Naval Service and it is not considered necessary to furnish you with the charts for which you asked.' Imrie continued:

Since any scientifically-based system by which the position of a submarine can be fixed is likely to be of interest to the Royal Navy, you are invited to send this department full particulars of the system known to you, showing clearly how and upon what data you are able to determine the vessel's position. You will realise that to be of any value, your disclosure of the system must be complete and in detail and it is agreed that you should at this stage treat it as 'secret'. Your suggestion of an interview will be reconsidered when we have had an opportunity of examining a written exposé of your system.

As there is now no hope of saving life, a systematic search of the most likely area is proceeding until *Affray* is found. Your location of the submarine has been noted and should *Affray* be anywhere near this position, you will be informed.

A handwritten note on the draft suggested: 'It might not be advisory to include the last sentence since it might prompt Wing Commander Yiend to claim for some award!'

Chapter 10

'ONE OF THE GREAT UNFATHOMABLE MYSTERIES OF THE PRESENT TIME'

Everyone was mystified about what had happened to *Affray* – and why it had happened. Parliamentary Secretary to the Admiralty, James Callaghan, on a visit to East Woolwich, told reporters:

> I can say that every device known to modern science for finding something on the bed of the sea has been used this week. No more could have been done. This is one of the great unfathomable mysteries of the present time. I have spoken to senior naval officers of very great experience and not one has formed a coherent theory about it. We can only speculate.

The Admiralty asked Captain Shelford to speculate on the possibilities in a confidential paper circulated to naval top brass. Assuming that the submarine had dived – as she had indicated in her final message to the shore – Shelford said that she could have lost her trim almost immediately and sunk to the bottom. 'In view of the nature of the bottom, sand and shingle, gravel and stones, it is most unlikely that the submarine would have stuck on the bottom. Nor is it likely that the contact with the bottom would have been so hard as to penetrate the hull,' he wrote.

Another of Shelford's theories speculated that if the submarine was already underwater – perhaps snorting at periscope depth – she might have been rammed by another vessel passing overhead. 'In the absence of any report from a ship of ramming, the accident must have been caused by some sort of mishap. It is unlikely to have been caused by hitting a wreck when submerged,' wrote Captain Shelford. He added:

> Had she been sunk early in the night, it is possible that some personnel may have escaped and have been taken some distance away by tides before the search was started.

The fact that no marker buoy or smoke candles have been released from the submarine, nor any trace of diesel oil found would indicate that the submarine was completely flooded. A further indication that the submarine is flooded is that no personnel attempted to escape after the 12-charge signal had been dropped. Against this, however, are the signals and the tapping on the hull which are said to have been heard.

Shelford referred to the oil slick reported by the SS *Andalusian* and investigated by USS *Perry*. 'Although this was found to be furnace oil, it may, however, have escaped from a merchant ship after a collision of which she is not aware. The oil tank being holed below the water line and oil escaping until it had been compensated by sea water.'

The possibility 'that some mishap occurred when the submarine was practising embarking her folboat through the fore-hatch and that the submarine dived suddenly causing the submarine to flood through the conning tower and the fore hatches' was also considered.

Shelford assumed that *Affray* sank 'within 10 miles of a line joining her diving position and her estimated 10.11 position. It will be necessary to search this area and examine all bottom contacts . . . The submarine may have to be salvaged to discover the cause of the accident. Such a search may take several weeks.'

Parliamentary Secretary to the Admiralty, James Callaghan, told Parliament that 'hopes that any lives will now be saved are dwindling. The search is continuing.' In his hands he held answers to questions he anticipated fellow MPs might ask him. There were none. If he had been asked questions, however, his notes tell us exactly what he would have said in reply. On the subject of how many men were on board *Affray*, he would have told the House:

The normal peacetime complement on 'A' class submarines is five officers and fifty-eight ratings. This would be increased slightly in war and there are minor variations in peacetime in different vessels according to the equipment carried. It would be true to say, therefore, that *Affray* has at present ten more men on board than she would normally carry and there may be supplementaries to this. This additional number should make no difference to the possibilities of escape. There is sufficient escape apparatus for everyone on board.

If asked about marker buoys on board the submarine, Callaghan's notes would have prompted him to declare:

Marker buoys are fitted at each end of the submarine and can be released from inside. No marker buoy has, so far, been found and no smoke candles, which can also be released, have been seen, neither are there any oil slicks in the position in which the submarine is believed to be.

On hull tappings:

Hull tappings were reported . . . but it cannot be certain that these came from the submarine.

On the question of sabotage, one of Callaghan's aides had written:

Should this be raised the answer is presumably that there is no evidence at present – rather than any answer which would rule out this possibility. A submarine containing twenty officers of the Submarine course would be a worthwhile target.

That morning, the *Daily Express* reported:

The planes were recalled last night and the little ships came back – there was no reasonable hope of rescuing survivors from the submarine *Affray*. A wind rose over the dull Channel and the sea had won again. Sixty-six hours after the *Affray* had dived with seventy-five souls on board an ASDIC contact was reported. A diver was going down. But the diver did not go. The reported contact was not confirmed. The sea was too rough. A gale blew in the Channel. When it drops, the search goes on – for the submarine and her secrets, but with no hope for the lives.

And so the search continued using fewer ships and with the deep diving and submarine rescue ship *Reclaim* at the centre of operations.

Gale force winds and high seas interrupted operations on 21 and 22 April. Small craft working in the search area were ordered to take shelter while other ships remained at anchor, unable to perform any useful task in such conditions. Diving resumed at early evening on 23 April when a diver attempted to investigate a contact made by HMS *Helmsdale*. The strength of the tide and depth of the water did not allow the diver to spend much time on the bottom to confirm without any doubt the exact nature of the wreck. While mooring above the wreck, *Reclaim* lost an anchor and damaged her mooring wires. The spring tides were considered too strong for further diving and the salvage group was ordered to return to harbour on 24 April to re-equip and await more favourable tides.

❖ ❖ ❖

From *The Times*, 21 April, 1951:

> The opening of a fund on behalf of the relatives of the men who lost their lives in the submarine *Affray*, by which it is hoped to raise at least £100,000, is announced by Albert Johnson, Lord Mayor of Portsmouth and Mr Charles Osborn, Mayor of Gosport. In a joint appeal issued yesterday, they state:
>
> 'The nation as a whole will join with us in offering their profound sympathy to the relatives of those who lost their lives on the tragic disaster to HM Submarine *Affray*. It will be generally known that *Affray* was based at HMS *Dolphin*, the submarine depot at Gosport and manned with a crew from three naval ports – Portsmouth, Plymouth and Chatham.
>
> 'We feel sure that the whole country will wish to assist us in the efforts we are now making to alleviate the distress and sorrow which this terrible accident has inflicted on so many of the young wives and children of the gallant crew. No words can describe the anguished thoughts during these last few days of those whose dear ones are now lost to them, nor can we measure in terms of money or any other help we can give the magnitude of their loss.
>
> 'We are inaugurating a fund in an endeavour to ease the financial stress which must inevitably follow as a consequence of their bereavement. We have set as our target the sum of £100,000 which would, in a small measure, help to bridge the gap in the income of those widows and orphans who are left to sorrow.'

April 21, 1951 – From Commander-in-Chief, Portsmouth to the Admiralty:

> The Lord Mayor of Portsmouth and Mayor of Gosport have decided to launch a joint appeal in aid of the dependants of officers and men lost in HMS *Affray*.
>
> It is felt that the Navy will wish to subscribe generously to this appeal and it is suggested that all commanding officers be invited to collect subscriptions from their commands and to remit them to the Supply Officer, HMS *Dolphin*, or direct to the Lord Mayor of Portsmouth or Mayor of Gosport.

Trustees of the Portsmouth Naval Disasters Fund contributed £6,000 towards the fund and despite rationing, food restrictions and the post-war shortage of just about everything, the British public also dug deep into their pockets, wallets, handbags and piggy banks to donate. The day after the fund was announced, the postman delivered bundles of letters to the Lord Mayor of Portsmouth's parlour containing contributions from sympathisers all over Britain. The Mayor was inundated with telephone calls from societies and individuals wanting to contribute to the fund.

Early donations were received from the Prime Minister's office, the Cammell Laird yard where *Affray* had been built five years earlier and the Trades Union Congress.

Popular entertainers Bud Flanagan and the Crazy Gang, Chesney Allan, Arthur Askey, Tommy Trinder, Jack Warner and Elsie and Doris Waters teamed up with the stars of *Morning Departure* John Mills and Richard Attenborough to stage a Sunday night benefit performance at London's Victoria Palace Theatre. Stars of stage and screen, including Margaret Lockwood, Kay Kendall, Phyllis Calvert, and Susan Shaw volunteered their services as programme sellers. The sell-out evening raised hundreds of pounds for the fund.

Divers on board *Reclaim* donated the danger money they were paid while searching for *Affray* to the fund. A total of £40 from the ship's company was handed over to the Lord Mayor of Portsmouth.

Across the country dances – everything from ballroom to bebop – whist drives, charity football matches, sponsored silences, choral singing, drama productions, coffee mornings and poetry recitals were held with proceeds sent directly to the fund. Mums, dads and children living in the Portsmouth and Gosport districts got to work on a range of fund-raising activities. Children from Kilmiston School, Fratten, danced and sang for two hours watched by 100 people and raised £2 5s. The Sunday League second division club Red Lion played a charity football match with HMS *Implacable* and a £25 cheque from *Implacable* was sent along with the £16 17s 6d match proceeds. A performance of *The Middle Watch* by the West Amateur Dramatic Society raised £56 12s 9d, while Portsmouth Spiritualist Medium Fellowship donated £7 to the cause.

Other donations were received from Mother Shipton Men's Darts Club (£5), a Junior Spotlight concert (£15), a Pompey Revellers Concert organised by the West Portsmouth Conservative Association Club (£13 18s) and the Order of Woodcraft Chivalry, Porchester (£12 0s 1d). The Football Association donated the ball used during the Blackpool *v* Newcastle championship match, complete with autographs of the players. It was later auctioned with the proceeds donated to the fund.

Before long, Fund Chairman, Albert Johnson was telling the press: 'So generous has been the nationwide response to our appeal that we are now in the happy position of being able to announce that our original target of £100,000 has been exceeded.'

The *Portsmouth Evening News* paid a visit to the Lord Mayor's Parlour to see how the fund was being handled. It reported:

Among the thousands of letters which have poured into the council's offices is a poignant little note from a woman who thirty-four years ago waited for news of her sailor sweetheart. Eventually it came. She has written to the Lord Mayor, 'May I offer this enclosed mite in memory of my fiancé whose submarine was lost in January 1917.'

Here was another from a little Somerset village which simply said, 'As one who is receiving a pension from a similar disaster fund, I know well what a difference such financial help makes to the widows and children.' Wolf Cubs, Scouts, schoolchildren, ambulance brigades, ex-Wrens, office girls are among those who have made collective efforts. The fund also brought residents of various streets in Portsmouth and Gosport together and their collections have raised good sums of money which have been donated.

The BBC declined to broadcast an appeal over the airwaves, stating that 'where charitable institutions already exist, we do not normally arrange for appeals'. It was explained that various naval and seaman's charities existed for such disasters and the disaster fund ought to be talking to them. BBC radio's main rival for teenage listeners, Radio Luxembourg, however, came to the rescue and an appeal by the popular actor, Wilfred Pickles, generated hundreds more pounds for the fund.

By July more than £150,000 had been raised and cash, cheques, postal orders and foreign currency dominations were still coming in daily. Sixty-two dependants registered to receive payments from the fund – thirty-three widows and children and twenty-nine parents of lost *Affray* seamen. The families of ten officers and three ratings declined payment of any kind.

The first payments were made to dependants on July 24 'to help meet their immediate needs'. Widows each received an initial grant of £200 plus £50 for each child (there were thirty-six in April 1951) or unborn child (three widows were pregnant at the time of the disaster). Other dependants – mostly parents – also received £50. Later each dependant received a monthly sum, the amount determined by the rank of their late husband or son in the submarine service and number of children under the age of 21 living at home. The widow of an able seaman with two children, for example, would receive a monthly sum of £27 19s 2d. The widow of an officer would receive 10 per cent more. Naval pensions would be paid on top of these sums.

The fund was officially closed in November 1951 with £176,673 3s 11d in the bank. It allowed appointed trustees to administer the fund to buy homes already lived in by widows or allow them to move to other accommodation. Money was available to pay for new furnishings, cover removal costs, legal fees, home insurance and rates. Fees were also available for children of *Affray*'s crew to attend private schools if their mothers decided this was best for their sons or daughters. The fund provided money for school uniforms, educational materials and trips. Fees for children later going on to higher education at university were also covered.

Bonus payments were made to dependants at Christmas: £20–£25 for adult dependants and £10 for children. In later years Christmas payments were increased to £50 in 1960, £70 in 1970 and by December 1999 widows still eligible for payments received £100.

A booklet issued to each dependant stated: 'The allowance to a female dependant (whether widow, mother, sister, child or other dependant of one of those lost) shall cease on her remarriage or cohabitation.' Payment to children stopped when they reached the age of 18.

After initial payment had been made to dependant families, the trustees elected to invest some of the money in institutional stocks and shares guaranteed to provide healthy and regular returns. Shares were purchased in Unilever, Imperial Tobacco, ICI, the Manchester Ship Canal, Distillers and the brewing company Courage-Barclay-Simonds. Equity was also purchased in British Electricity, British Gas, British Transport and corporation and county stocks. Ten years after the *Affray* disaster, the fund's investments totalled £121,963 9s 2d which generated an annual income of £5,045 12s 7d.

Affray's widows, children and parents had to pay a price for their financial aid and account for every penny spent from their income from the fund. Each year they received an official visit from a fund representative who questioned them closely about their financial circumstances. Some – but not all – of the dependants dreaded the annual visits fearing giving wrong answers to pages of questions about their annual expenditure; everything from shopping and utility bills to the cost of wallpaper and paint, petrol and public transport. Every item had to be accounted for and if it appeared that additional income might be coming into a household from another source, money received from the fund was reduced accordingly. Children had to be present at the meetings, wearing school uniform and clutching a copy of their latest school report. If visits took place in term time while children in boarding schools were not present at home, fund officials travelled to the schools to interview children and their teachers. There was no doubt, however, that all dependants were grateful to the fund and the people from across the country – and the world – contributing to it.

Following these visits, fund officials wrote detailed reports about their findings for circulation to the trustees. Their comments were often cruel. After visiting one widow, the visitor recorded that 'the house was very untidy, smelly with washing strewn all over the furniture'. At another home she observed that a child's 'school report clearly shows that he is a real plodder who will probably go nowhere in life'. Another widow was challenged as to how she could afford a seaside holiday with her children 'and was unable to tell me how she could afford the trip'.

Not every *Affray* widow found the official visits a trial. Lieutenant Foster's widow, Mary, always found her representative, Miss Gilmore, 'a charming and sympathetic lady and when she retired, a Miss Rhodes equally so'.

Members of the disaster fund committee met annually, under the chairmanship of the Lord Mayor of Portsmouth, and produced a press statement for circulation to local papers. In November 1963, twelve years after the disaster, the media was told:

The Annual General Meeting of the HM Submarine *Affray* Disaster Relief Fund was held at Guildhall, Portsmouth, on Tuesday 26 November 1963, under the Chairmanship of the Lord Mayor of Portsmouth (Councillor H. Sotnick, JP).

Payment of regular allowances to widows, children and other dependants were approved and in a number of cases additional grants were awarded. The cost of supplementing the education of the child dependants continues to be a major call on the fund. As usual, each dependant child will receive a Christmas gift.

Fourteen widows and thirty-five dependant children will benefit by the receipt of these allowances. The children of mothers who have remarried continue to receive allowances from the fund.

The Committee learned with pleasure that a number of the dependant children, with whose education the Fund has assisted, have achieved considerable success and, in particular, a Naval Scholarship at Dartmouth has been awarded to one of the boys.

Reports were received from the Almoner on other beneficiaries of the Fund who, whilst not falling within the above categories, were at the time of the loss of HM Submarine *Affray* in receipt of financial assistance from a member of her crew. Again, the reports showed that in a number of these cases, hardship had arisen as a result of diminished income, ill health or infirmity – and in each such case the Committee authorised the payment from the fund of a monetary grant sufficient to relieve individual hardship.

By 1978, remaining funds were invested in new annuities to ensure there would be sufficient money available to pay remaining dependants their allowances. But dependants were put through a means test and told they were 'no longer entitled to the money, which was paid at the discretion of the trustees'. Widows learned that annuities had been purchased to give them 'peace of mind' for the rest of their lives.

In 1982, the late Kathie Johnson, MBE, Alderman of the City of Southampton and widow of the former Lord Mayor of Portsmouth, contacted John Marshall, Leader of Portsmouth City Council, expressing concerns about how the fund was being managed. She reminded Mr Marshall:

When my late husband, Albert Johnson, was Lord Mayor of Portsmouth there occurred a great disaster when the submarine HMS *Affray* went down and my husband set up an appeal for the widows and dependants . . . The money poured in from the good people of Britain, many, many thousands of pounds – and then along came a law about only being able to distribute sufficient funds for ordinary needs of widows and dependants . . .

I drove my husband to a meeting of the *Affray* fund committee in Portsmouth in 1969, just before he died, and on the way home I recall how unhappy he was, saying there was still this terrific amount in the fund. He said that seventeen years after the disaster, all the offspring had completed their education and there was only one widow left. There was some discussion about giving her £10 for Christmas. My husband said, 'Why not give her £1,000? What are we saving it for? It was raised for the likes of this widow.'

I told the present Lord Mayor, Councillor Frank Sorrell, that I thought any funds still in hand should be handed over to something like the British Sailors Society or King George's Fund for Sailors for the benefit of all sea-faring widows and asked if it were permissible to tell me how much was still in the fund.

I received a reply from the Lord Mayor saying: 'I do recall the establishment of the *Affray* Disaster Fund and that your husband was Chairman of that committee for some years. I have only recently attended the 1981 meeting and whilst the beneficiaries have now diminished considerably, there is some money left, which is, of course, administered by the Public Trustee Office. However, in order that you may have the up-to-date situation, I am sending a copy of your letter to the Secretary of the Fund who will give you a current resumé of progress.' Since then, I have received nothing at all.

And so it goes on. In 2007 the HM Submarine *Affray* Disaster Relief Fund Trust remains active – although Portsmouth City Council is coy about revealing how much money is still in the bank. All enquiries to the council are referred to the Office of the Official Solicitor at the Public Trustee Office, whose department works at the speed of a snail and then chooses to be economical with information it divulges, even when approached under rules governing the Freedom of Information Act.

When formally approached by this author with a raft of questions, Mrs J. Kearney for the Public Trustees gave little away, stating that just because the *Affray* fund was established by subscription,

does not in itself mean that it is subject to public scrutiny in all respects. . . . The accounts of the fund are not open to public scrutiny although the investment of the fund is in accordance with the powers/limitations of the trust instrument and the general law relating to trustee investment and in force from time to time. . . . Prima facie the fund comes to an end on the death of the last dependant. If there are any monies remaining in the settlement on the death of the last dependant, the trustees will consider which legal principal must apply to the disposal of these monies in the light of the law and general circumstances obtaining at the time. It is possible that any such monies will be applied for charitable purposes, but this will be determined by the trustees at the appropriate time, possibly in conjunction with the Charity Commission.

This author has learned that nearly sixty years after the fund was established, only three *Affray* dependants are still alive in 2007 and entitled to a monthly allowance. One of them is Joy Cook, from Ilfracombe, Devon and widow of Leading Seaman George Cook. Mrs Cook, who never remarried and is today an invalid, now receives around £2,000 a year – £166 per month – from the fund. Inflation has clearly failed to keep up with the needs of a disabled widow whose husband was so cruelly snatched away from her after just thee years of marriage more than half a lifetime ago. Her allowance is classed a 'war pension' as *Affray* had been on a war exercise. Her Christmas bonuses stopped a long time ago.

Mrs Cook no longer receives annual visits from trustee representatives. They also stopped long ago. She said:

The last time I had a personal visit from a fund representative, the lady asked me what HMS *Affray* was. She had no idea what it was all about. She had done no research. It's obvious that the present fund managers haven't a clue about its history, where the money had come from or the price paid by our husbands and their families all that time ago.

When the day finally comes when people are no longer drawing money from the fund, I would like to see it put to some good use. It ought not to just sit there; it needs to be used – preferably for submariners and their families.

Lieutenant Foster's widow, Mary, agrees.

Any money left should, without a doubt, be looked into and distributed to those for whom it was originally intended. Failing that, it should be given to Naval charities for deserving cases. I feel that we treat our service personnel abominably, a national disgrace for which our government, whatever their colour, should be shamed.

Chapter 11

'NO ESCAPE WAS POSSIBLE BY ANY MEANS'

Just when it looked as if news about the disaster might slip from newspaper front pages, a new Admiralty statement ensured that the story would remain there for the time being. On 22 April, it was announced that all fifteen of the Royal Navy's remaining 'A' class submarines would be prevented from going to sea until further notice, 'pending investigations into the reasons for the loss of *Affray*'. Construction of up to thirty more submarines at Cammell Laird's Birkenhead shipyard was also put on hold.

Like the *Affray*, all 'A' class vessels in the fleet were given names beginning with the letter 'A' – *Anchorite, Artemis, Astute, Aeneas, Alaric, Artful, Alcide, Alderney, Alliance, Ambush, Amphion, Andrew, Auriga, Aurochs* and *Acheron*.

The statement gave little away and the Admiralty refused to elaborate when questioned by the press. However, a top-secret communication from the First Sea Lord, Sir Bruce Fraser, to Parliamentary Secretary to the Admiralty, James Callaghan, is more revealing:

Submarines from the 'A' class were stopped from going to sea because further detailed calculations of their stability when flooded and on the bottom showed that if two-thirds or more of the submarine were flooded, she might lie over at such a large angle that escape in the ordinary way would become extremely difficult – and in some cases impossible.

It has always been known (and accepted in the Navy) that if a submarine sinks in over 150ft of water or if she is badly flooded, escape by any means is rendered most difficult and hazardous. *At depths greater than 300ft it is impossible to escape and survive. This fact is not generally known outside of naval circles and the public believe that escape by Davis Submerged Escape Apparatus is possible at much greater depths.* While the cause of the loss of HMS *Affray* is as yet not known, the fact that no survivors, wreckage or indicator buoys have been sighted suggests that the submarine was so rapidly and extensively flooded that no escape was possible by any means.

After full examination of all possibilities, it is confirmed that 'A' class submarines are operationally safe under all undamaged conditions (surface, diving or on the bottom).

From the escape aspect, it is confirmed that 'A' class submarines suffer as compared with other British ships because with their fine underwater lines they have a tendency, if heavily flooded, to take up a large list on the bottom.'

While the 'A' class submarines stayed in port, the search out in the English Channel went on using fourteen ships attempting to cover an area of about 1,000 square miles of water. They included four frigates, minesweepers and two groups of survey and salvage ships.

A helicopter and eight naval aircraft from Lee-on-Solent and the naval station at Ford, Sussex, maintained dawn-to-dusk searches. A civilian Handley Page Hermes aircraft equipped with a new magnetic detection device was brought in to fly over the search area and attempt to make 'contacts' with any large metal objects lying on the seabed. On its first day out, the four-engine research plane recorded five contacts. By the end of the week this had increased to thirteen with three of the positions designated as priority diving areas.

On closer investigation divers discovered the barnacle-covered wreck of a First World War submarine, remains of a coasting steamer thought to have sunk a century before, a merchant vessel lost in the 1920s, the fuselage of a wartime bomber and a pair of D-Day landing barges all lying in their weed entangled underwater graves. Every positive contact was investigated and divers went over the side in some of the roughest April sea conditions recorded for many years. Every contact was a possibility and every possibility offered the chance of locating the lost submarine. Captain Shelford, on *Reclaim*, remembered this time as

a tough one for the divers who took incredible risks, often going down in conditions never before thought possible. I saw them diving one night in such rough weather that the seas were sweeping waist-deep over the sill of the big door in her side through which the diving ladders were rigged.

In the huge diving compartment under her fore well-deck, we stood knee deep in water and watched the angry white horses (waves) rearing suddenly from the darkness in the glare of the deck lights and come cascading through the door. The whines of the electric pumps picking up the water and chucking in back in the sea, the clatter of sea boots on the steel deck, shouted orders and curses and the hiss of the compressed air in the diving machinery almost drowned the metallic voice of the diver coming from the loudspeaker telephone. Two hundred feet down in the black water under this fury, a lone and grotesque figure groped his way over a rusted and barnacled wreck and told us the depressing news that once again we had not found the *Affray*.

One diver nearly lost his life in a watery grave while searching a wreck thought to be the *Affray*. During one of his dives, Petty Officer Robert 'Nobby' Hall, Chief Bosun's Mate on *Reclaim* had the unbelievable experience of being blown to the surface from a depth of nearly 200ft after a cable linked to his voice-piece had been wrenched from his diving helmet. The incident occurred when Nobby was about to leave the wreck. His voice-piece cable – allowing him to speak to *Reclaim*'s crew on the surface – became entangled with a jagged piece of wreck and he became trapped with his feet higher than his head. His voice grew fainter through the voice-piece as he began to lose consciousness in his efforts to free himself.

Nobby just managed to tell *Reclaim*'s commanding officer, Captain Jack Bathurst, that he might just clear the wreck if everyone pulled hard together on the cable. This was done with such vigour that the cable suddenly went slack and instead of finding Nobby on the end, they discovered the mouthpiece wrenched from the diver's helmet, leaving a hole 1in wide through which seawater began to enter. Fortunately, Captain Bathurst knew what to do, even though communication with Nobby had now been severed. He ordered his crew to increase the amount of air being pumped down to the diver and within moments there was a huge cloud of bubbles alongside *Reclaim*, in the middle of which Nobby appeared – feet first.

The diver was rapidly hauled on board, unconscious but alive. The fact that he had come up feet first had caused air in his diving suit to blow water out of the hole in his helmet. Had he come up the correct way, he would undoubtedly have drowned.

'It's all in the day's work,' Nobby later told the *Portsmouth Evening News* with a huge grin on his face. 'I thought for a while that I might be a gonner. I suddenly found myself upside down looking up through the hold of the ship. Then I realised that I couldn't move my head. My chums on the ship saved my life. They sent down so much air that it kept the water out of my suit.' The brave diver was later affectionately re-named by his shipmates Nobby 'All In A Day's Work' Hall.

❖   ❖   ❖

On Sunday 22 April special prayers were offered and silent tributes paid to *Affray*'s officers and ratings in churches and chapels in Portsmouth and Gosport. All ceremony was cancelled during a visit to HMS *Sheffield* by the Duchess of Kent at

Portsmouth. Royal salutes were to have been fired from naval batteries around the port while warships should have been dressed overall in special colours. But pomp and ceremony was put to one side while the shadow of mourning for *Affray* continued to hang over the country.

The following morning, Kirkcaldy Police in Scotland was alerted that two notes written on the back of empty cigarette packets stuffed inside a bottle had been found on Pathhead Sands. The first note read:

We have been submerged for eight days. Air supply exhausted. Two of the crew ill, six of the crew dead. Fumes in escape hatch. Signed P.O. Nigel. Captain is dead, has been for three days. Please send help. HMS *Affray*.

The second note read:

62 degrees 6 mins W of Bass Rock. Escape hatch out of order.

The police alerted the Flag Officer Scotland at the HM Naval base on the Clyde, who forwarded the information to the Admiralty with the following note: 'This is considered to be a disgraceful hoax and the information is communicated in view of possible press enquiries.'

❖   ❖   ❖

The ban on 'A' class submarines leaving port was announced in Parliament a few days later by Callaghan, who spoke about the escape options available to *Affray*'s crew members. He conveniently avoided mentioning that it would be impossible to escape from a submarine stranded in over 300ft of water. This was too much information for the *Affray* widows and children left behind and hundreds of submariners about to return to 'A' class submarines and dive deep beneath the waves.

Out at sea a diver gazed from the deck of *Reclaim* and told the *Daily Mail*: 'Somewhere down there is the *Affray*. And we mean to find her.'

Chapter 12

THE UGLY DUCKLING

 One week after the disaster had seized the headlines, the Festival of Britain was back on the front pages again. The fact that a large flotilla of ships and aircraft were still engaged in attempting to find the missing submarine was no longer news and only a few smaller stories about the *Affray* search found their way onto the inside pages of the country's newspapers. News that HM The King would be opening the Festival of Britain in London on 3 May was deemed a better – and much happier – story.

Out at sea three destroyers, four minesweepers, a radar ship, salvage vessel and *Reclaim* had begun sweeping an area shaped like an oblong box 90 miles long and 14 miles wide. This latest 'area of probability' was split into twenty-eight different 'boxes' – measuring seven square miles - and each thoroughly searched. It was similar to searching for something underwater measuring 290ft long and 25ft wide and sitting who-knows-where on the sea bottom somewhere along a 14-mile long corridor between Southampton and Exeter.

❖   ❖   ❖

It was announced that a memorial service for the crew of *Affray* would be held at Portsmouth Cathedral on 2 May 1951. Admiralty top brass would be there with Commander-in-Chief, Portsmouth, Admiral Sir Arthur Power – aide-de-camp to HM The King – who would be representing His Majesty, now too busy preparing his Festival of Britain inauguration speech to attend in person. The Army and Air Force would also be represented along with MPs and twenty-six attachés from Dominion and foreign navies – including two from the USSR.

The Revd Douglas Wanstall, a senior naval chaplain, told a packed cathedral that the tragedy 'is deeply embedded in our hearts because it has occurred so near home. Perhaps it is wise to view the disaster in the context of what is happening in Korea and elsewhere where so many young men are giving their lives in the cause of freedom, which is the very essence of Christianity.'

As a remembrance wreath was placed on the altar by two ratings as a token of remembrance, the words of the Navy Prayer was spoken:

O Eternal Lord God, who alone spreadest out the heavens, and rulest the raging of the sea; who has compassed the waters with bounds until day and night come to an end; be pleased to receive into thy Almighty and most gracious protection the persons of us thy servants, and the fleet in which we serve.

They then sang the hymn synonymous with tragedy at sea:

Eternal Father, strong to save,
Whose arm hath bound the restless wave,
Who bidd'st the mighty ocean deep
Its own appointed limits keep:
O hear us when we cry to thee
For those in peril on the sea.

No relatives of those who had died in *Affray* were present in the cathedral. A private service for immediate family and crew members dismissed from the submarine before she sailed was held at the same time in a wardroom at HMS *Dolphin*, close to the jetty from where *Affray* had set out on her final voyage. Drawn together in a common grief and with no graves over which to mourn their loved ones, the wives, parents, fatherless children and mates of *Affray*'s crew heard the Last Post sounded, interwoven by a ship's band playing Rock of Ages, followed by reveille.

John Goddard, one of the seamen left on the quay when *Affray* sailed, remembered the occasion as 'a heart-rendering experience, especially when the Last Post was played, which will never be forgotten by anyone who was there'.

Many attending the services wondered what might happen if – and when – the submarine was discovered. Would she be brought up to the surface? Would the remains of husbands and sons be buried in a mass grave somewhere or allowed to finally rest in family graves closer to home? It was a question the Navy would only address once the missing submarine was located – and the depth of water in which she was found.

❖   ❖   ❖

Commander Lionel 'Buster' Crabb was still on *Reclaim* during the early days of May – and most of her crew wished he was elsewhere. Crabb was disparaging of his fellow divers and their reliance on heavy diving suits that slowed them down. He considered himself superior as a 'frogman,' someone who dived using a lightweight rubber wetsuit, face mask, flippers, air tubes giving him the ability to swim underwater with ease and speed.

Seventeen other divers on *Reclaim* were suspicious of Crabb's methods because they had yet to see him in action. Until then, they had to go over the side in their heavy gear, taking three to five minutes to sink to the bottom, holding onto their 4½in thick guide rope and staying on the bottom for half an hour or less if tides were strong. It took five minutes for a diver to return to the surface, but he then had to stay in *Reclaim*'s decompression chamber for a further half hour.

Underwater conditions were difficult and hazardous. On the seabed, silt and mud was often so thick that even strong lights were unable to pierce the gloom. Startled fish would often peer through the diver's glass visor and have to be repeatedly waved away – an exhausting job in itself. A diver's only equipment was a knife to help him out of trouble. Wrecks had to be investigated by divers feeling their way around, often leading them into danger, making the extra 4*d* a day they earned a small price for situations they often encountered.

Crabb was on board *Reclaim* in the event of *Affray* being found in shallow waters. That was his speciality and he was probably the best and fastest diver in the country when it came to swimming down to depths of no more than 20 fathoms – or 120ft. But the search for *Affray*, so far, had been in waters much deeper than those that Crabb was used to. So the civilian diver spent his days on *Reclaim* sleeping late, staying dry, enjoying leisurely breakfasts and lunches while deep-sea divers worked around the clock investigating every possible wreck which demanded examination.

Crabb later admitted: 'I'm afraid there was a certain amount of backchat between myself and the other divers.' But he also accepted that the world's diving record – to a depth of 535ft – had been made from the decks of *Reclaim* 'and here was I coming aboard with a pair of swimfins (flippers) and a few bottles of air'.

Reclaim's crew were glad when Crabb left the ship and hoped to have seen the last of him. It was not to be. Instead of going home, Crabb made his way to the Thameside town of Teddington and headquarters of the Admiralty's top secret Research Laboratory, home of the Royal Naval Scientific Services, where he had arranged to meet a staff scientist, Rosse Stamp.

For some time Stamp had been experimenting with underwater cine photography at Teddington using specially adapted 16mm movie cameras. Crabb had dived to the muddy bottom of the Thames to shoot film using different equipment and underwater lighting developed at the laboratory. But since May and while Crabb was away on *Reclaim*, Stamp and three colleagues had made attempts to take underwater photography a stage further – using a television camera to beam 'live' pictures back from the bottom of the sea. The camera was the first of its kind to be developed in Britain.

Stamp wanted to know from Crabb if the Navy might be interested in his idea. It would mean that each time underwater contact was made with a large object, a television camera would be lowered over the side instead of a diver and everyone on board would see the images transmitted back. The camera could be operated for several hours, whereas divers were limited to just three-quarters of an hour or less on the sea bottom at any one time. It also meant that as soon as an image of an old barnacled wreck was transmitted back to a television screen, no further time was wasted. Once images confirmed that *Affray* had been found, deep-sea divers could then be sent for further investigation.

Crabb encouraged Stamp to use the shore-to-ship telephone link to talk to Captain Bathurst on *Reclaim* – but not to divulge his own involvement at this stage. He was worried that if word got around to *Reclaim*'s divers that Crabb was returning to the ship, there might be withdrawal of goodwill – or even a mutiny.

First, Stamp needed to 'borrow' a portable television camera for a long period of time – and in 1951 there was only one company in Britain producing equipment for television, the Marconi Wireless Telegraph Company of Chelmsford, Essex, owned by English Electric. Each camera, made from steel, Bakelite and other assorted metals, cost £5,000 – so expensive in fact that BBC Television had to lease the equipment from the Marconi company in 1951 for its outside broadcasts.

The Marconi people were intrigued by Stamp's idea of using one of their cameras for such an unusual purpose. They agreed to loan the camera to the Royal Navy on the grounds that it might help locate the *Affray*'s final resting place. If the exercise was successful, however, they made it clear they would attempt to interest the Navy in purchasing a camera outright for use on *Reclaim*. Television technicians at Chelmsford viewed the loan as an experiment, a sprat to catch a mackerel and, if successful, provide Marconi with an excellent shop window from which to sell their products to non-broadcasting organisations.

Stamp designed a specially welded watertight 17ft diameter metal cylinder for the camera, which would send pictures from the bottom of the sea illuminated by a 1.5kW tungsten diver's lamp lashed to the side. The entire rig would be operated by remote controls and Stamp persuaded a local garage to weld it all together for him. Although it looked like a giant dustbin measuring 24ft long, it would allow the camera to work in depths of up to 200ft. If lowered any deeper, there was every chance that water pressure would crush the camera and its case – meaning that the Navy would have to compensate Marconi for thousands of pounds.

Unlike other outside broadcast television cameras in 1951 with four lenses, the one to be used searching for *Affray* had a single lens, 1in thick and encased in ⁵/₈in thick plate glass which peeked out from the bottom of the 'dustbin' casing.

As well as providing a camera, Marconi also offered a television monitor on which to view pictures transmitted back through a cable along with a remote 'joystick' to control the lens in any direction – forwards, backwards, sideways, up and down. They also offered a technician to work alongside Stamp, installing it and keeping it all in running order. The camera would be lowered into the sea from a derrick mounted to *Reclaim*'s well-deck to pay out 500ft of multicore cable supplied by the British Insulated Cable Company and covered in an extra heavy protective sheathing of PVC.

It was time for Stamp to contact Bathurst and Shelford on *Reclaim* and offer them the underwater television kit. Shelford remembered:

I was extremely sceptical and told them so, but by then I was ready to try anything and arranged for the camera to be installed aboard *Reclaim*. It was accompanied by a small team of experts headed by Commander Crabb and a young scientist called Rosse Stamp, who in the next few weeks hardly left the side of his beloved camera.

Reclaim returned to Portsmouth so that the camera and special frame allowing it to be turned in any direction could be loaded on board. By now the entire kit weighed in at around one ton, described by Stamp as 'a marvellous piece of knitting'. He, in fact, had no idea if it would work – but he believed that it would and he was going to give it his best shot.

Three weeks after the equipment had been delivered to Teddington, the completed underwater television apparatus had been installed on *Reclaim*. Stamp did not claim to know much about television, but he was a born optimist. He recalled:

Since speed was an essential factor in the construction, no attempt was made to refine the design beyond the bare essentials. Indeed the design of the casing was influenced more by expediency than elegance, but the resultant contraption – nicknamed the 'ugly duckling' – justified the methods used.

No information was available, of course, on the design or performance of underwater television . . . but our extensive experience of underwater cine photography enabled the work to proceed with some hope of success.

Before departing for Portsmouth, Stamp put his 'ugly duckling' and rigging through its paces – and found that the watertight casing was far from leak-proof. In a desperate bid to have everything ready for the following day when the equipment was to be delivered to Portsmouth, Stamp and his colleagues worked through the night lining the inside of the 'dustbin' casing with specially cut screws and rubber mountings bound together with pints of household Bostic glue.

One of the team quickly devised a 'dampometer' to ensure that if the case leaked again they could hoist it out of the sea before the camera was ruined. At one end of the case he placed a piece of ordinary blotting paper. If it became wet it would create a short-circuit which would show up on a voltmeter rigged to the control box on *Reclaim*.

When *Reclaim* returned to Portsmouth to collect Crabb, Stamp and the television equipment on 27 May, Shelford was informed that two young girls had asked to see him and were sitting in the waiting room. They claimed to be the young wife and sister of a man lost on *Affray* and begged Shelford to take them to sea where they were certain to know when they were directly above the lost submarine.

Shelford gently led them across the room to a window and told them to look out to sea. 'Look in any direction,' he told them. 'Do you really think you could find the *Affray* if it was anywhere out there?' The girls shook their heads. 'All of that is about 20 square miles. We're looking for *Affray* in over 1,500 square miles of water.' The girls thanked him for listening and quietly left the building.

❖   ❖   ❖

Reclaim's divers were not best pleased to hear that Crabb would be rejoining the ship, bringing equipment that would make their jobs almost redundant. What were they supposed to do while the television camera was sent to the bottom of the sea to do their job for them? Learn how to knit? Write poetry? Read cookery books?

At sea, *Reclaim*'s crew soon found that the camera allowed them to speed up their search. It worked like a dream, sending back images of the sea bottom, wrecks and marine life at least 15ft away from the lens when a diver's normal visibility was usually around 5ft. By the end of the month *Reclaim* had had completely covered the original 'probability area' and opened up another one further south – without once ever having to send a diver overboard to check contacts.

Crabb insisted on being placed in charge of coordinating underwater television surveillance and personally supervised lowering and raising the derrick on which the camera rig was attached. As soon as the camera began to beam images back to the television monitor in Captain Bathurst's cabin, he would join Stamp and together they carefully scanned the screen in the hope of spotting something that looked like part of a submarine stranded on the seabed.

Stamp was violently seasick almost from the moment *Reclaim* pulled out of port and the only time he felt well was when seated in front of the monitor – sometimes for up to twelve hours at a time.

By 12 June, *Reclaim* and other ships were searching an area on the edge of the latest 'probability area', to the south of *Affray*'s expected route and 30 miles from the Channel Island of Alderney. At 1911 hours the frigate HMS *Loch Insh* made contact with a large object on the seabed – a contact which, for some reason, had previously been missed when the American ship USS *Ulysses* and HMS *Contest* passed over the spot at 1705 while conducting a visual search on 17 April and within twelve hours of the accident. Ships from the 4th Destroyer Flotilla and the two American destroyers had also been within one mile of the site at 1900 hours on 18 April and carried out ASDIC searches for over an hour at 2040.

A printout of HMS *Loch Insh*'s ASDIC reading revealed a long cigar-shaped object, estimated to be approximately 260ft long (*Affray* was 281ft) and 20ft at its highest point (*Affray* was 19ft) and sitting in approximately 300ft of water.

There had been so many disappointments and false alarms during the past weeks that everyone on the search flotilla that day expected this latest contact to be yet another rusting wreck. They knew they were directly over the northern edge of Hurd Deep – a 70-mile long underwater valley, the bottom of which plunges to a depth of 564ft below the surface of the sea. It stretched from the western coast of Guernsey to an area three miles north of Alderney before continuing along the English Channel to a point north-west of the Cherbourg peninsula. It was known as 'Wreck Valley' and the 'graveyard of the English Channel' thanks to the number of hulks littering the sea bottom.

Hurd Deep had also been used after both world wars for dumping redundant weapons and drums full of chemical and radioactive waste. Thousands of tons of unwanted ammunition, guns and tanks from two German divisions garrisoned on the Channel Islands during the Second World War ended up at the bottom of the undersea valley after the War Office decided it would be quicker and cheaper to dispose of it this way instead of taking it to incinerators on the mainland.

This was the first time since the *Affray* search had begun that ASDIC equipment had generated an image that matched the shape and – more or less – dimensions of a submarine so closely. Underwater visibility was poor and it was decided that before sending the television camera down to take a closer look, an observation chamber containing three divers would be lowered over the side at first light on 13 June. The site was named 'Contact J for Jig' for future reference.

As the chamber slowly travelled to the bottom, powerful searchlights attached to the side were switched on to illuminate the gloom. At first the divers saw nothing more than fish, but as the chamber came closer to the seabed, Lieutenant

Bill Filer, *Reclaim*'s Chief Diving Officer, suddenly saw a gleaming white rail emerge from the gloom – the first time anyone searching for *Affray* had seen something on the seabed not smothered in barnacles, rust or weeds.

For the next seventy-five minutes, the divers relayed comprehensive reports back to *Reclaim* through their telephone link, describing in detail what they were seeing and the state of the stricken submarine.

When it was time for the observation chamber to be hauled up, Crabb ordered the 'ugly duckling' to be hoisted into position and gave the signal for the cable to be lowered. There was every risk that the container holding the camera might buckle under the weight of water at 300ft, but he was prepared to take that chance as he gave the signal for it to be lowered away. The rest of *Reclaim*'s crew then shouldered their way into the Captain's cabin to catch a glimpse of pictures about to come back to the small monitor.

Crabb watched the cable pay out at the rate of 10ft at a time . . . 100ft . . . 150ft . . . 200ft . . . 210ft . . .

'Stop lowering, stop, stop, stop,' yelled Stamp from his chair in front of the monitor. The cable yanked to a halt and the safety brake applied. 'By one of those rare strokes of good fortune, the camera had arrived above a conning tower and then we got a glimpse of a periscope and radar aerials,' remembers Stamp.

Crabb burst into the cabin where he found the crew totally silent as they bent over to make sense of what they were seeing on the black and white screen: a set of white painted railings of the kind running around the top of the hull on 'A' class submarines. Then, without any assistance from the surface, a current caused the camera to swing forward revealing large letters on the starboard side: Y – A – R – F – F – A.

Someone produced a camera and began taking still photographs of what was appearing on the monitor. Once processed, they were found to be poor quality images, yet clear enough to reveal a section of a once proud 'A' class submarine – and the last resting place for seventy-five brave men. The pictures were never shown to the public and found their way into a 'top secret' file.

The search was over. The missing submarine had been found fifty-nine days after her final dive. The 'ugly duckling' had withstood pressure in what was later confirmed to be 278ft of water – 78ft deeper than the camera was designed to withstand.

A signal was hastily sent back to the Admiralty: 'Contact J for Jig is the *Affray*.' Wisely, the Admiralty sat on the information for the time being until further underwater investigations were carried – just in case.

Chapter 13

THE BROKEN SNORT

Much to his annoyance, the water was too deep for Crabb to dive down in his frogman's suit, so next morning he shook hands with the deep-sea diver chosen to be the first person to physically come into contact with *Affray* since she was last sighted on 16 April.

The diver went down at the same time as the television camera and together they found *Affray* laying on a shingle and hard muddy sand sea bottom, slightly listing to port at an angle of 35 degrees. Her surface detection radar aerial and after periscope – the one usually used to keep an all-round lookout when cruising at periscope depth – were both raised. All four escape hatches were shut indicating that no successful attempt at escape had been attempted. There was no obvious damage to her hull.

Captain Shelford recalled that the underwater camera transmitted pictures back to *Reclaim* showing that a release mechanism on the emergency buoys had not been moved into the 'Free' position. Both pairs of hydroplanes were at 'Hard-arise – forward edge up' indicating that someone had made a final frantic effort to hold the submarine up in an attempt to prevent her from smashing into the sea bottom. The forward planes were at 30 degrees to rise and after planes at 25 degrees.

Affray's main motor telegraphs on the bridge were photographed at 'Stop' showing that someone in the engine room had anticipated a violent impact with the seabed. A trench in the gravel seabed was discovered a short distance away on the submarine's starboard side, as though part of the submarine had hit the floor and then bounced to port. It appeared that the vessel's after part had hit the seabed with some force.

The diver reported that the undamaged starboard propeller and after plane were 8–10ft clear of the seabed and that underwater guns used to fire smoke candles had not been fired.

It was obvious that whatever had happened to *Affray*, had occurred quickly, taking her crew by surprise, leaving them no time to save their submarine – or themselves. Another diver was sent down the following day with the television camera to continue where his colleague had left off. One of the first things he discovered was the great 35ft long snort mast lying on the seabed. Shelford recalls:

> It was seen to have snapped off like a carrot a few feet above deck level and was leaning over the side into the dark shadows beneath her hull. A truly remarkable photograph by underwater television showed a break so clean that only material failure could explain it.

On closer examination the diver found the snort mast had fractured immediately above the crutch and was laying over the port ballast tanks at right angles. The mast was at an angle of approximately 30 degrees from the vertical with the head on the seabed. Only a small sliver of metal about 3in long connected the fallen tube to the rest of the boat, leaving a 14in diameter hole above the engine room exposed to the sea, allowing thousands of gallons of water to flood into the submarine.

Reclaim was instructed to make every effort to recover the snort mast before the tides turned and bring it to the surface for close examination by expert metallurgists. This was going to be a tricky business requiring the help of a salvage ship to work alongside *Reclaim*.

Recovering the mast involved divers attempting to grapple with a 5in thick heavy-duty tarred shot-rope – known as a strop – shackled around the top of the snort. This would be attached to a hook on the end of a recovery wire, winched to the surface and laid on *Reclaim*'s deck. The difficulty was that once the rope had been placed in the water and taken to the bottom, its weight was about as much as a diver could carry at such depths.

The recovery attempt was a hazardous diving operation and six attempts were made. The current was so strong during the first dive that the diver became distressed and wanted to return to the surface after only sixteen minutes. A second diver managed to stay down for a few minutes longer, but the strong pull of the current made it almost impossible to remain upright. The final attempt took place on a brilliant sunny afternoon, with a heavy sea running in from the west. Shelford recalled:

> *Reclaim* was an impressive sight with clouds of spray breaking over her decks while the signal flags at her yardarm, warning shipping to keep clear, added colour to the scene as they streamed in the wind. Her two mooring craft rolled sickeningly as they carried the mooring wires from the buoys to the diving ship.

I was anxious lest the weather should prevent us diving, but towards evening the sea fell away and *Reclaim* completed her operation.

Suddenly away to the north, I saw the great bulk of the liner *Queen Elizabeth* working up speed for her run to New York. Her colossal wash might well have swept *Reclaim* off her hard-won moorings. We signalled her, 'Please go slow,' and such is the camaraderie of the sea that we immediately saw the huge plume of her bow wave dying away as she eased right down and gracefully slid past dipping her ensign to our little fleet.

To reach the broken mast, a pair of divers first had to get down past the overhanging periscope, radar aerial and a tangle of wires. The underwater camera was used to make sure the diver's shot rope went down to the seabed clear of obstructions. It took two days for divers to loop the strop around the head of the snort and onto the recovery wire. One diver landed in the middle of the submarine's periscopes and had to be hauled back again. But on Sunday 1 July in flat calm weather, *Reclaim* began slowly to hoist the snort to the surface. Shelford said:

It was an exciting and awesome moment as the head of the great tube broke the surface alongside *Reclaim*. Here was the only part of *Affray* ever to see daylight again. Her name had been in our sleeping and waking thoughts ever since April and although we had found her, we still had no more idea as to the cause of her fate that we had on the night of her disappearance. Would this snort tube provide the answer?

Gently, the great tube was laid along *Reclaim*'s narrow deck. A quick end-to-end examination by *Reclaim*'s senior officers showed there was no sign that it could have been hit by a ship or entangled in floating wreckage as many had suggested. The fracture at the other end of the case seemed to indicate that the material had simply failed due to metal fatigue.

Before returning to Portsmouth, marker buoys were positioned over the wreck. Divers would return to the spot and make many more visits to the watery tomb in an attempt to seek and gather more evidence to tell the Admiralty about what had caused *Affray* to fail.

Admiral Power and a gathering of experienced metallurgists were waiting on the quay ready to examine the mast. In next to no time, it was lifted from the ship and removed to the Admiralty's Central Material Laboratory at Emsworth for tests. It was also carefully photographed and some of these images now see the light of day for the first time in this book.

❖   ❖   ❖

Affray was back in the news and the press began speculating about what had happened on the night *Affray* dived for the last time.

Marshall Pugh, a close friend of Commander Crabb and author *The Silent Enemy*, an account of the frogman's wartime exploits, wrote in the *Daily Mail*:

Senior submarine officers formed a theory on what had happened to *Affray*. In public they said nothing. In private their beliefs were never shaken.

In the early hours of the morning, the *Affray* had been cruising at periscope depth. Before the arduous patrols of the day to follow, the great part of the submarine's company had been asleep.

Looking after the engine room there would probably be an artificer and a stoker. The chances were that the artificer was forward when the snort cracked open . . . cracked open, just like that.

Almost immediately water flooded in the submarine through the intake valve at the base of the snort, roaring into the submarine at 100 gallons a second, increasing to 200 gallons a second and more as the submarine dropped. Before the stoker could close the valve, he was stunned and drowned.

While the *Affray* went down fast by the stern, the water flooded through the submarine, drowning men before they could even begin the drills of submarine escape. As she struck the bottom, the snort snapped off.

It was one thing for the submariners to form such a theory, another to prove it and another still for the Admiralty to accept that seventy-five men and a submarine could be lost through a fault in a piece of piping. For one thing, it might infer that this was partly the Admiralty's fault, that the snort was not only faulty, but badly designed.

The *Portsmouth Evening News* reported:

A former submariner with many years of experience, suggested last night that as the course and speed of the submarine were within circumscribed limits in order to comply with her training programme, it is most unlikely that she would have arrived at her last resting place near the Hurd Deep before the accident occurred.

On the other hand, had the vessel met trouble while she was actually diving, she would have holed and immediately sunk to the bottom and stayed there.

The fact that she has been found nearly 40 miles away from the spot from where she was reported to have dived on that fateful night of April 17, indicates that any buoyancy remaining in the submarine was sufficient for tides and currents to carry her well away from the track she would normally have followed.

It seems fairly certain that the vessel must have been flooded from end to end in a matter of seconds because had any one compartment been shut off with anyone in it at all, there would have been some means of indicating their presence to the men on the surface.

As soon as the men inside her were immobilised, the submarine may well have been carried either along the bottom or through the water to the position in which she has now been located.

Having found the *Affray*, the Navy must now at all costs discover the cause of the disaster to guard against possibilities of future tragedies, but if that can be done by divers, then there seems little point in embarking on what would become one of the biggest salvage jobs tackled in the English Channel.

What of the recovery of those inside her? It is certain that the majority of the relatives of those 75 gallant sailors would prefer their men to rest in peace, although it is equally certain that if salvage becomes necessary in order to discover the cause of disaster, they will be the first to wish that this should be so.

Chapter 14

ENGINEERS EXAMINE THE SNORT MAST

T he mast was carefully examined by naval engineers and scientists working at the Navy's metallurgical laboratory, who put it through a series of rigorous tests in a bid to discover why it had broken away from the hull. The cause soon became apparent and a report circulated on 17 July states that it was

> principally due to a brittle fracture taking place in the circular tube of the snort, with its origin at or near the longitudinal weld between the tube and the port fairing plate [a section which secures the snort to the hull]. . . . The fracture would be followed by a shearing of a weld in the starboard fairing plate and, finally, by the failure of the elliptical tube and a weld in the port fairing plate in a ductile manner.

The report stated that the whole sequence of events leading to the snort becoming detached would have taken place 'with great rapidity, in fact almost simultaneously. The position of the failure corresponded with the point of greatest weakness of the mast.'

Metallurgists confirmed that materials used in the mast were mild steel 'of satisfactory chemical composition'. However, they discovered that the circular tube

> possessed an exceptional coarse microstructure indicative of gross overheating and had not been heat treated after being welded at a very high temperature. As would be expected from such a microstructure, mechanical tests on specimens from the tube showed the material to possess little resistance to shock at normal operating temperatures.

In addition to the principal cause of failure, transverse welds which had sheared in the fairing plates were found 'to be of poor quality and in view of their location at the point of greatest bending moment of the structure, must have constituted a secondary source of weakness'. In other words, metal fatigue was the cause of the problem.

The experts were unable to state if the fracture had been caused by 'normal stresses in service or by the snort mast receiving a blow' and added that this was considered 'a matter of little significance'. The report added: 'The real point at issue is that the complete failure of the mast was due to the combination of two factors, namely the metallurgical condition and secondly the presence of indifferent welds at the point of greatest weakness.'

It was judged that 'the complete and sudden failure of the mast could not have occurred if the circular tube of the structure had been in the correctly heat treated condition; in all probability total failure would not have taken place if poor transverse welds had been absent at the critical area.'

❖　　❖　　❖

While tests on the snort mast were undertaken at Emsworth, the divers and crew of *Reclaim* were allowed a long period of leave to recover from their round-the-clock work. When they returned to sea, it would be their job to try and ascertain if anyone in the submarine had attempted to shut off the big induction valve fitted at the point where the snort trunking entered the pressure hull. If divers discovered this to be shut, then there must have been some other cause for her sinking. If it were open, then a real possibility existed that the snort was the main culprit. It was vital, therefore, that the true position of the valve be confirmed. But the valve was located in an almost inaccessible position and difficult for divers – or a television camera – to get anywhere near it without resorting to using explosive charges that might destroy the evidence needed.

When *Reclaim* put to sea again – this time without Crabb on board – she encountered bad luck almost every day, none of it of her own making. The weather for the remainder of the summer was the worst for years with gale force winds making any further diving attempts impossible. When the gales subsided, a period of strong tides meant that the divers could only go over the side for short periods.

It was during one of these short dives that a diver noticed that *Affray* had increased its list to port on the seabed and there were fears that she might topple over completely, making further work on the wreck a potential death trap.

Chapter 15

THE FIRST SEA LORD AND COMMANDER-IN-CHIEF COLLUDE

I t was agreed that a Board of Inquiry would be convened to investigate the loss of *Affray* and while it was in session the First Sea Lord, Sir Bruce Fraser, met Admiral Sir Arthur Power to discuss the possible outcome. Together they agreed that if further investigations by divers confirmed that *Affray*'s snort induction valve was definitely in the 'open' position, it would be possible for the Board to conclude that the submarine had been lost as a result of the snort mast breaking off due to metallurgical faults. But they knew that if this were the case, the Admiralty would either be criticised for accepting a badly designed snort tube or failing to identify those responsible for welding the device to the hull.

Before the Board had an opportunity to deliver its findings, Sir Bruce and Admiral Power together agreed that water rushing into the submarine through a hole in the stump of the mast was ultimately responsible for the accident – and further investigation by divers no longer necessary. They claimed that the latest television pictures seen on *Reclaim* showed *Affray* listing at a greater angle, making it dangerous for divers to continue working on the wreck. *Reclaim* was scheduled to return to *Affray* on 25 July for eight days and future work on *Affray* was now in question.

The outcome of the conversation between the First Sea Lord and Commander-in-Chief, Portsmouth, was relayed to the three senior officers chosen to head the Board of Inquiry. They were also ordered to place proceedings on hold for the time being while an interim report was produced confirming their findings so far. This was delivered on 19 July.

Senior officers within the Navy's engineering branch were quietly asking if the broken snort mast provided sufficient compelling evidence to confirm the real reason for the *Affray*'s loss. Many suggested that the accident might have been caused by a battery explosion triggering off shock waves throughout the submarine, which, in turn, resulted in the snort mast breaking away, sending the submarine to its doom.

Admiralty bosses knew that a battery explosion carried a different set of implications about British submarine design and workmanship failures – and potential embarrassment for the Royal Navy. A broken snort mast, however, would be more acceptable for relatives of those lost on *Affray* – and the British public – to swallow as the reason for the submarine's loss.

The Admiralty had, therefore, made up its mind why *Affray* was lost long before the Board of Inquiry had presented its completed report, while witnesses were still providing evidence and naval engineers continued examining the fractured snort mast.

In a memo to the Secretary of the Admiralty dated 7 August, in which a copy of the Board's full and final report was enclosed, Admiral Power stated:

As regards alternative causes of the accident, it can only be said that no evidence has been brought forward. Other theories about collision, explosion and so forth can be suggested, but as regards fact there seems no definite evidence on which to start a different line of investigation based on such possibilities as some weakness in the condition of the ship herself, failure to obey orders, indications of collision, folboat exercise or similar lines.

The recommendations put forward hold good whether or not the Board's theory is accepted since they arise from the effects consequent on the positive fact that the snort mast snapped off and the recommendations are confirmed to those in connection with the breaking of the snort mast and to other lessons which have been learnt in the course of the Inquiry.

Chapter 16

THE BOARD OF INQUIRY INVESTIGATES

June 26, 1951 – Memo from the Office of the Commander-in-Chief, Portsmouth, Arthur J. Power (Admiral):

The following officers are to assemble at a Board of Inquiry at Fort Blockhouse at 1000 on Wednesday the 27th day of June 1951:

    Rear Admiral R. M. Dick – President

    Captain G. P. Claridge, Royal Navy

    Captain F. Lister, Royal Navy

The Board is to hold a full and careful investigation into the circumstances attending the loss of HMS *Affray*, including in their investigation

    1.   The condition of the *Affray* and her crew on sailing

    2.   The instructions and orders covering her movements

    3.   The search operations

    4.   The results of the survey of the wreck

and calling before it such witnesses as it may appear necessary to enable a correct conclusion to be formed. Before the hearing of evidence begins, consideration is to be given to the question whether any person concerned in the result of the Inquiry should be present throughout the proceedings.

The report is to be accompanied by the minutes of evidence taken and is to contain an expression of the Board's opinion on the merits of the case, as disclosed by the evidence, including a statement of the causes of the occurrence.

Two shorthand writers are to be detailed by the Commodore, RN Barracks, Portsmouth. A shorthand writer from the office of the Flag Officer (Submarines) will also be available to assist the Board.

The Board of Inquiry would meet over the next month. Nearly forty witnesses would be called and asked 759 questions. They ranged from senior naval officers to junior ratings, metallurgists, engineers and scientists. Some would be asked a few simple questions before being dismissed. Others would be interrogated more closely and challenged with long and complex questions. Several would be summoned back before the Board two or three times.

The Board visited the submarine HMS *Ambush* on 29 June 'to acquaint ourselves with the layout of an "A" class submarine' and on 2 July they viewed the broken snort mast at the Emsworth laboratory. To assist Board members, a scale model of *Affray* was built from metal to allow witnesses referring to various parts of the boat to explain points they considered useful to the investigation.

Once the Inquiry was completed, the Board had to write a lengthy report, including conclusions and recommendations, which would be bound together with transcripts of question-and-answer sessions with witnesses. The final version, running to hundreds of pages, was rubber stamped 'Top Secret' and circulated to just a handful of senior officers and Royal Naval specialists. It was locked in an Admiralty vault and not seen again for another thirty years when it resurfaced as a de-classified document at the Public Record Office (now The National Archives) in Kew.

The Board met in private and behind closed doors. Family members of those lost on the *Affray* were not invited to attend, or even informed that the Inquiry was taking place. In a note in the preface to the completed report, it was stated: 'We considered whether any relatives should be invited to give evidence . . . but decided that as no evidence of fact could be so produced, no useful purpose would be served.' The press was also kept away but, if challenged, the Admiralty would say that it intended to make a public statement about the Board's ultimate findings at a later date – assuming there would be something to say. They never did.

The Board had three aims: first, to state for once and for all what caused *Affray* to be lost at sea; second, to lift any blame for the loss from the Admiralty's shoulders; and, third, to lay the blame at someone's feet.

The Admiralty in Whitehall did not think Board of Inquiry worked fast enough. On 12 July – roughly half way through the Inquiry – the Board of the Admiralty demanded an 'interim report' be produced 'giving your opinion on the cause of the accident'. Proceedings halted while notes and transcripts were pulled together into something resembling a report.

It has been necessary to edit the contents of the report down to a manageable length for this book, because of the document's length. What follows is a selection of excerpts, quoted verbatim from the report, and interview transcripts.

The final report opened with remarks about the state and condition of *Affray* and the ship's company on sailing, reflecting on the level of experience its commanding officer, first lieutenant, engineer officer, training first lieutenant, training engineer officer and third officer had in 'A' class submarines. It noted that of the ship's company who went to sea in *Affray* on 16 April, nineteen out of the forty-five ratings 'had reached a high standard of efficiency' during the September – December 1950 exercise in the Atlantic and Mediterranean.

> The rest of the remainder had recently been drafted from a Reserve Camp where they had regularly been taken to sea in HMS *Alaric*, a submarine almost identical to *Affray*. The key personnel were all thoroughly experienced men. The ship went to sea with the whole of the engine room complement of 24 embarked, no engine room rating having been landed to make room for passengers.
>
> It is noted, however, that of the ship's complement of 45 ratings, 22 only were at sea on 11 April during trials (the number to take her to sea for that trip having been made up from spare crew from the Reserve Group, the remainder having been on seasonal leave at the time of the trials). Furthermore, of those who finally sailed in the ship, 11 engine room ratings and 9 other ratings had never been to sea in *Affray* before. It is normal submarine practice frequently to appoint officers or draft ratings to submarines at short notice in case of sickness and so on and a trained spare crew is allowed in each flotilla for this purpose.

The report noted that *Affray* was at sea for one day on 11 April between leaving the dockyard and proceeding for the exercise on 16 April.

> The ship was at sea for four hours during which time she dived for 30 minutes to periscope depth. We have found no suggestion that anything was other than completely normal on this occasion or that the way the duties were carried out by the officers and the ship's company was other than satisfactory.

It was acknowledged that *Affray*'s records for the month of April 1951 had been lost with the submarine, but

> as far as could be ascertained, her general condition on sailing on 16 April, was entirely satisfactory; there were no important defects outstanding, no inherent weaknesses and there is no particular reason to suppose that there had been any laxity in carrying out periscope tests and examinations.

A footnote states:

Reference was made by four witnesses to a small quantity of oil mixed with water in the sump of number one battery tank. Oil had dripped from a test cock. The Board are satisfied that the defect is neither important nor relevant to the Inquiry, apart from it having initially led to an assumption that the submarine may have been returning to the dockyard after the patrol, which probably would not, in fact, have been necessary.

The subject then arose about private letters written by Chief Petty Officer Engine Room Artificer 2nd Class David Russell Bennington to his father in Devon.

There has been some suggestion in private correspondence that the submarine was not in a sound condition. We received late in the Inquiry correspondence from Mr O. Bennington consisting of a number of extracts from letters written by his son during the autumn cruise, 1950 and prior to sailing in *Affray* on 16 April.

We have read these letters with care and in view of their statements that the ship was in an unsatisfactory condition as regards the engine room and that she was constantly breaking down and also that she was leaking badly, we called the Captain of the submarine (Lieutenant Leafric Temple-Richards) to 11 December, and Engine Room Artificer 3rd Class Summers who was also on the ship until January 1951. These two witnesses appeared to us to be the most responsible persons available to speak on the condition of the ship.

If the letters are read as a whole, the impression that will be given to the reader is of a thoroughly conscientious man who had been progressively overcome by his job until he became in an unsettled condition of mind which caused him to magnify troubles which do not appear to have been serious. Other evidence we have indicates that there was, in fact, no major trouble in the condition of the submarine. It is pertinent to observe that both officers and men in a submarine are as likely to be concerned with the safety of their ship – and, incidentally, themselves – as the writer of these letters, and, that being so, that some other indication of dissatisfaction with the condition of the submarine must have emerged if the conditions described by Engine Room Artificer Bennington were even anywhere near those pictured in his letters.

These letters show him to be a hard working, most conscientious and progressively worried man. It is perhaps worthy of note that he was, during the Autumn Cruise, preparing also for an examination, that his wife was expecting a child and that he obtained 15 days compassionate leave from RN Hospital, Haslar (while sick with influenza in February 1951) due to his anxiety about his wife's condition.

We are, therefore, of the opinion that these letters do not represent the condition of the ship and that the trouble to which this rating refers were not the cause of her loss. Indeed, the specific troubles of the engines constantly stopping and similar matters were not ones which would directly affect the safety of the ship and in any event the engine defects in question were made good during the period *Affray* was in the dockyard (January – April 1951).

We also feel that Mr Bennington was right to bring his son's evidence forward which, in the prevailing uncertainty of the cause of the loss of the submarine, certainly needed full investigation.

We suggest that Mr Bennington's father and wife have handled this matter in the most helpful way as regards the Navy and submarine service. The whole affair must have been excessively painful for Bennington's widow in particular, and we feel that she is owed a debt of gratitude for this action and the manner in which it was taken.

While it is not directly a matter for the Board of Inquiry, we suggest that a letter might be sent to Bennington's father and wife somewhat on the lines above. This should not be difficult to draft, observing that the Board is satisfied that the cause of the accident was nothing to do with the matters described by Bennington in his private letters.

This was by no means the last word on David Bennington's private letters home and they would reappear in a more visible way later in 1951, as a later chapter explains.

The report examined the orders given to Lieutenant Blackburn on 3 April for Exercise Training Spring, noting that 'the orders were deliberately framed to give the Commanding Officer considerable latitude so as to carry out the patrol to the best advantage for the benefit of the ship's company and trainees'. It continues:

Consequent on the latitude referred to above, it is evidently difficult from the orders to piece together what actually might have been expected to be done during the first period on the way to the patrol area. Certain conclusions can, however, be drawn. The first is that it seems unlikely that the folboat exercise would have been carried out on the first night since this period might have been expected to be used for settling down and to have carried out the folboat exercise would have meant a considerable diversion of course.

Furthermore, it would appear more convenient to do this exercise when the submarine would have been approaching land on her way into Falmouth. We now know that the Captain had expressed his intention to snort through the night and this would, because of the time factor, rule out the folboat exercise.

As regards the question of whether the submarine was snorting or not, our impression is that she would have been snorting through the night, steer a course to the southward of the line from his diving position to the position given to 19 Group for the exercise and to defer carrying out the folboat exercise until later in the patrol.

In conclusion to this part of the report, the Board stated:

We are of the opinion that the orders were clear and adequate for the work to be carried out, that there was good reason to suppose they were properly understood and are unlikely to have led to any action which might be a direct cause to the loss of the ship. We recollect that press reports have given the impression that the submarine when found was miles off course. In view of the latitude specifically allowed by the orders, this statement is not, of course, correct.

A section of the report referred to how close the search operation had come to passing over the spot where the submarine was eventually discovered during the first few days of the operation:

A 'probability area' was laid down and the centre line of this area was a line drawn from the expected diving position to the point within 30 miles of which *Affray* was intended to be at noon on 17 April – an area 77 miles long and 20 miles wide, 10 miles each side of the centre line. This area did cover the actual position of *Affray*, some three miles inside the southern limits of the area. But the tendency was naturally to start the ASDIC search along the centre line of the area given. In consequence, an ASDIC search never reached the actual position of the wreck until the forenoon of 19 April. Had the entire line of the search been 245 degrees instead of 250 degrees, the ASDIC search would have passed over *Affray*. It should, however, be remembered that it is exceedingly unlikely that the wreck would have been located observing the great difficulty which was experienced in the actual location weeks later when a thorough 'slow time' search was being carried out on this spot.

The 'false scents' that had led members of the search operation – as well as the newspaper-reading public – to believe that *Affray* had been discovered on 17/18 April had been provided by 'a multiplicity of reports of smoke candles, oil slicks, floating boxes and so on. All these had to be investigated which broke up continuity of the search.'

Later hull tapping and signals 'changed the whole picture'. The report stated that the signals had been heard by 'responsible people and had been affirmed and re-affirmed'.

The report said that as a consequence

> the whole weight of the search was shifted to the eastward under the impression that the wreck had been found, the air search to the westward was stopped and all efforts concentrated on what was believed to be the position of the wreck. We now know that this assumption was incorrect, but the result was that the search operation really ceased for the moment. We are of the opinion that it was correct to concentrate ships in the vicinity of the area where SST signals were reported. The time factor was ever present. There were probably only eight hours at most before escape be made and this was the only clue.

The first part of the reported concluded:

> We are of the opinion that the search was carried out with the utmost rapidity, persistence and devotion to duty by all concerned. Had there been any survivors, they would have been seen by visual search and the wreck would probably have been found.

The next section addressed possible causes of the accident and the Board stressed that

> this portion of the Inquiry is the most difficult as our views must be based to a considerable degree on conjecture building up from such relatively few established facts that are available to us. We are thus presenting what seems to us the best theories among the numerous possibilities that might be put forward.

Possible causes of the accident were divided into five different headings: battery explosion, material failure, drill failure, mines, collision.

On the question of a possible battery explosion, the report reminded Admiralty officials that after an accident in the submarine HMS *Trenchant* in June 1950,

> when she suffered a severe battery explosion followed by a bad fire, the Board examined evidence as to the electrical condition of *Affray*. In the case of *Trenchant* there was definite evidence of a faulty battery evolving an excessive amount of hydrogen and the evidence regarding the battery ventilation system was inconclusive. Batteries in *Affray* were likely to have been in very good condition and that if the ventilation system was in good order and correctly operated, a battery explosion is very unlikely to have occurred, even with batteries in

poor condition. As the evidence suggests that both the batteries and ventilating system were in good order, the likelihood of a battery explosion is discounted.

The material condition of *Affray* was discussed. The Board had made close inspection of the submarine's 'defects list' produced when it went into HM Dockyard, Portsmouth with the submarine in January and work undertaken during the period January – April 1951.

We found here no indication of anything unusual or unsatisfactory and all the evidence that we could obtain from officers and ratings, including those who took part in the subsequent docking trials and diving trials at sea, testify to a submarine in normal condition in which all had confidence. There remained the possibility of faulty workmanship or even sabotage but these, of course, could not be pursued and in view of our subsequent knowledge that the snort mast had broken away, the points become of less importance.

The Board considered

the likelihood of HMS *Affray* having been lost due to some failure in the handling of the submarine on the part of those embarked. Naturally such a cause was bound to be conjectural and our inquiries were directed merely to establish the efficiency or otherwise of those embarked.

The officers of the ship were men of the first calibre as regards their professional attainments. While a high proportion of the ship's company were experienced submarine ratings, nearly half of them had not been to sea in the ship before. This state of affairs, together with the number of passengers on board, though unlikely to be the cause of the accident, might well have been a contributing factor once a dangerous situation developed.

As to the possibility of the submarine hitting a mine 'and the intact state of the hull of the submarine, we considered that the possibility of this being a cause was one that could be eliminated'.

The question of the submarine coming into collision with another ship was also considered 'but for the same reason as above, and in view of the fact that there is no sign of the submarine having been in collision nor of the snort mast having received a blow of the severity that could come into that category, we consider that this cause can also be eliminated'.

However, the Board did 'consider the possibility of a "soft" collision – such as from contact with waterlogged fishing nets floating on the surface or even some distance below the surface'. They also examined letters referring to the loss of nine men on board a trawler called *Twilight Waters* which disintegrated at sea near Dodman Point and the Cornish fishing village of Mevagissey. The trawler was lost before *Affray* had sailed. 'It is, of course, possible that her trawl was floating about, although we have no evidence that she was in the vicinity of the *Affray*,' said the Board. 'An examination of the snort mast does not show any markings which could be definitely attributed to that cause.'

The report acknowledged that 'there were some small black marks but these might just as well have come from the 5in tarred hemp shot-rope from *Reclaim* which is known to have been in contact with the snort mast. It is also worthy of remark that no netting of any kind was found entangled with the wreck.'

The Board's conclusion stated: *'It is thus our opinion that HMS* Affray *was lost due to the snapping of her snort mast and that this was due to a failure of the material of which that mast was made.'*

It continued:

Our reasons are based on the report of the examiners of the snort mast carried out in the Admiralty Central Material Laboratory, Emsworth. The break in the mast occurred just above the point where it is housed in its crutch and where the bending moment is greatest and where the number of welds are present. The failure probably started in a brittle manner at the point at or near the longitudinal weld between the circular tube and the port fairing plate and once started, the brittle condition of the metal of the circular tube caused a crack to run round the whole cross-section instantaneously by way of the transverse welds.

The mast then fell over to port, the remaining portion of the whole section being twisted off so that the upper portion was only held by a small piece of metal as it lay down over the port side of the submarine. The circular tube was found to have been scarf forge welded and its material, though of satisfactory composition, was found to have been of an exceptionally coarse grain structure indicative of gross overheating and had clearly not been heat treated after being welded at a very high temperature. This would account for its extreme brittleness at normal air and sea temperatures.

In a report full of cold facts and data, the following passage is probably the most chilling:

As a result, a 14in hole was suddenly open direct to the sea, flooding the Engine Room. A delay of three seconds in closing the valve could allow enough water to enter to produce a stern-down angle of 16 degrees if not quickly rectified.

If she had been snorting through the night, she would have reached her actual position somewhere between 0500–0700. It would have been quite reasonable and in accordance with submarine practice for the majority of officers and ship's company to be turned in and the submarine to be at watch snorting stations. The Commanding Officer would very likely have turned out at dawn (about 0530) and having satisfied himself that all was well, have turned in again.

The submarine was, therefore, not at the maximum state of alerted efficiency.

In consequence, those inside the submarine started at a disadvantage. That something serious had happened would be evident, but precious seconds would be likely to have been lost in diagnosis . . . Our evidence shows that unless remedial action was taken within 15 – and possibly 10 – seconds, the situation would start to get out of hand . . . There would have been little chance of escape or even of releasing the indicator buoys or firing smoke candles due to poisonous fumes, pain in the ears, exhausting effects of pressure and lack of concentration and coherent thinking. There would also have been a short-circuiting of electrical equipment causing loss of power and lighting throughout the submarine at an early stage. There would have been electrical fires and fumes.

The chances of escape at a depth of over 250ft have to be regarded as virtually negligible. Perhaps the odd exceptional man might reach the surface and survive, only to die from the effects of air embolism (known to divers as 'the bends). From 200 – 250ft the escape route is down to 10 per cent and at over 150ft the survival rate using the 'twill trunk' method is negligible.

All on board would have died within a very short time. If any personnel had managed to shut themselves into the foremost watertight compartment, they in turn would very rapidly have lost their lives.

Chapter 17

THE BOARD CALLS WITNESSES

T he first witness called before the Board of Inquiry was Rear Admiral Sidney Raw, Flag Officer, Submarines, at the time of the loss of *Affray*. Raw had come to the Inquiry armed with a detailed report. He began by telling the Board that in his opinion 'HMS *Affray* was sufficiently worked up and in every way in a fit condition to undertake the training war patrol "Exercise Training Spring" for which she was detailed by the Captain, 5th Submarine Flotilla (Captain Hugh Browne).'

Raw made it clear to the Board that although the exercise had been called a 'training war patrol' it had been put together

largely for the benefit of the young officers of the training class and it cannot be considered a war patrol in the true sense of the term since everything was done in 'slow time' meaning there was no sense of urgency in any of the operation, plenty of margin of time allowed for everything that had to be done, there was no opposition of any sort and the submarine was not intending to carry out any attacks.

He added:

The war patrol is a routine affair designed to accustom training classes to the living and routine conditions to be expected in a submarine in time of war and to give the instructors who accompany them an opportunity of showing them at first hand at sea what they have been taught in the classroom. It has been the custom, therefore, that these routine training patrols are carried out by submarines of the 5th Flotilla, usually a submarine from one of the Reserve Group whose complement is brought up for this purpose. . . . It so happened that HMS *Affray*, who had only just recently been up with the Home Fleet during the Autumn Cruise, had the great majority of her officers and ratings still in her and she was thus in a more advantageous condition.

Asked to clarify the point that in her orders she had been instructed to 'carry out dummy attacks on shipping' Raw replied:

It is normal practice for all submarines to be given permission as a matter of routine to carry out dummy attacks on single merchant ships if the opportunity occurs. Submarines are warned that it is most important that merchant ships should not be alarmed in any way and not be approached too closely.

QUESTION: The Commanding Officer had only been with the ship for one month – do you consider this factor would in any way influence the decision to embark a large training class for a patrol such as that was in fact intended?
REAR ADMIRAL RAW: Lieutenant Blackburn was an experienced Commanding Officer of whom I had a high opinion and who had shown by his previous records that he was steady and extremely reliable. There is nothing abnormal for a Commanding Officer who is fully qualified and experienced to move to a submarine at short notice and take her on a cruise such as a training war patrol. He had expressed his keenness to carry out this particular duty as a good way of working up the majority of his crew. On the day of sailing he said he was entirely satisfied with the state of his submarine and his ship's company. He also stated that he fully understood and was happy about his orders.

Next to be called was Captain Hugh Browne of the 5th Submarine Flotilla who reminded the Board that the Engineer Officers' Training Class had completed twelve weeks out of their fourteen week-long submarine course and that all sub-lieutenants, except one, had served 'three months small ships' time in submarines' and completed nine out of their fourteen weeks' training. Asked how much actual sea experience they had had, he replied: 'An occasional day at sea.'

QUESTION: Can you give us an opinion on their (sub-lieutenants) competency as compared to the able seamen whom they replaced to carry out the necessary duties in *Affray*?
CAPTAIN BROWNE: In my opinion they would be every bit as efficient as able seamen and probably more so at this stage of their training.
QUESTION: How are sub-lieutenants likely to have been employed?
CAPTAIN BROWNE: On various duties throughout the ship, such as 2nd Officer of the Watch, 2nd Petty Officer of the Watch and Able Seaman duties. In every case they would be under the supervision of either an officer or petty officer.
QUESTION: What was *Affray*'s complement?

CAPTAIN BROWNE: Peacetime – 62; wartime – 65/66. She actually had 75 on board.

QUESTION: Were you satisfied that the excess in the complement was reasonable?

CAPTAIN BROWNE: Yes, Sir, entirely satisfied.

QUESTION: Were there any special arrangements made for the messing of the sub-lieutenants?

CAPTAIN BROWNE: They would normally be accommodated in the forward torpedo stowage compartment.

QUESTION: Have either 'T' class or 'A' class submarines been to sea with ten men more than their normal complement?

CAPTAIN BROWNE: Yes sir, on frequent occasions.

QUESTION: Will you confirm that the complete engine room complement had been on board long enough to be familiar with the submarine?

CAPTAIN BROWNE: I consider they had been long enough on board to know sufficient about the ship to take her to sea for an independent cruise.

QUESTION: Were you fully satisfied that the short time that the commanding officer had been in command presented no difficulties to him taking out a high proportion of passengers who had not been previously embarked in his submarine?

CAPTAIN BROWNE: I am entirely satisfied with this. Lieutenant Blackburn was a very sound and most capable commanding officer.

Commander Edward Stanley, Commander (Submarines) at HMS *Dolphin* in April 1951, was called to the stand.

QUESTION: Can you confirm that there was sufficient DSEA apparatus on board for everyone?

COMMANDER STANLEY: Yes sir. I know that there were more sets on board than men.

QUESTION: Do you know why the electrical artificer was left behind?

COMMANDER STANLEY: I was rather surprised at him being selected to stay behind, sir. I can only assume that the first lieutenant or commanding officer was very confident of the state of their electrical equipment. About 18 months ago, a trial was made running submarines without electrical artificers. Two submarines in a relatively bad state were selected and it was considered that the extra work which came to the Flotilla Electrical Workshop made it undesirable to dispense with electrical artificers in submarines. An electrical artificer is essentially borne for repair duties and frequently does not have a job on the watch and probably for this reason it was considered he could be dispensed with.

Chief Petty Officer Francis Gordon Selby was next to be called forward. He was asked to tell the Board where the training classes would have been accommodated on board the *Affray* and he replied that they would have been billeted in the seaman's mess.

QUESTION: What was your duty at the time of the *Affray* incident?

CPO SELBY: Instructor to the executive officers' training class, sir.

QUESTION: Can you give any indication at all of how much practical training in 'A' class submarines the class had had?

CPO SELBY: Not a great deal without supervision, sir. They had had instruction on the majority of systems in a submarine, but would not have been allowed to have operated them without someone supervising them.

QUESTION: The class would have been familiar with the layout and workings of an 'A'; class submarine?

CPO SELBY: Yes sir.

QUESTION: You were taking through this training class, only did not go to sea as you went sick?

CPO SELBY: Yes sir.

QUESTION: Can you express an opinion on the general efficiency or otherwise of this class?

CPO SELBY: Above average, sir. We had anticipated it being one of our best classes since I had been here.

QUESTION: What duties would have been carried out by the training classes once embarked?

CPO SELBY: General duties of the ship's company with very little evolution work for the first 24 hours. The policy was not to give them anything other than routine work for the first 24 hours, Sir.

Engine Room Artificer John Summers who had served on *Affray* between June 1950 and January 1951 was called to the stand:

QUESTION: Would it be true to say that in your experience, the *Affray* was a normal running submarine in which those on board had general confidence?

ERA SUMMERS: Yes.

QUESTION: What were your duties on *Affray*?

ERA SUMMERS: I was in the engine room.

QUESTION: What was the general opinion of HMS *Affray* as a submarine?

ERA SUMMERS: I cannot remember anyone who was particularly worried. Everyone was, as far as I can recall, quite content in the boat.

Able Seaman Stanley Crowe, one of the crew sent ashore before *Affray* sailed on 16 April, was called to the stand.

QUESTION: What was your duty on HMS *Affray?*
A/S CROWE: I was the gunner – although she did not carry a gun.
QUESTION: What was your job at diving stations?
A/S CROWE: At the wheel.
QUESTION: Have you any suggestions or comment to make about the loss of HMS *Affray*, observing that you had been in the ship for some time and was one of the last people to leave her?
A/S CROWE: The only thing I have got to say is why did she go to sea in the conditions?
QUESTION: Which conditions?
A/S CROWE: She had not done any dry diving before she went to sea.
QUESTION: But she did dive on 11 April . . .
A/S CROWE: I came back off leave on 15 April and I believe she dived on 11 April for about a quarter of an hour, just enough to wash her casing. That was the first dive she had done since we did one on the way back from Gibraltar.
QUESTION: Would you say the officers and ship's company were quite happy with her as a submarine?
A/S CROWE: The officers were a grand lot. I had served with the Captain before.
QUESTION: Would you say that the officers and ship's company had confidence in the boat?
A/S CROWE: Definitely.

Captain Browne was recalled and reminded that in orders he had written for Lieutenant Blackburn he had stated that *Affray* was required 'to conduct herself as she would in wartime'. He was asked: 'What would this involve?'

CAPTAIN BROWNE: Her acting so as not to be sighted by other shipping. This would give practice in periscope and snort mast drill. It would also involve her not being sighted by aircraft. She would, therefore, probably be dived most of the daylight hours and at any time when on the surface by day or night would be in instant readiness for diving. Navigation lights would not normally be burned except in cases where it was necessary for safety. Opportunities were taken of carrying out dummy attacks on shipping encountered.
QUESTION: Have you any idea as to when the folboat exercise was likely to be carried out?
CAPTAIN BROWNE: No sir. The whole idea in the orders was to give the commanding officer as free a hand as possible to carry this practice war patrol

for the best advantage in working up his crew and giving instruction to the training class.

QUESTION: Would you agree that it is a reasonable assumption that *Affray* would be likely to carry out the folboat exercise when approaching the coast of Falmouth?

CAPTAIN BROWNE: I think it highly probable that he would have done so at that time. . . . Weather permitting he would land his Marines on his second night out before his call into Falmouth of 19 April.

Leading Seaman John Goddard, a member of *Affray*'s crew from mid-March 1951 until 1600 hours on 16 April when he was ordered to remain behind after the submarine had sailed, was asked by the Board if Lieutenant Blackburn had mentioned anything about his intentions for sailing during the first night at sea. Goddard replied:

No sir, he just told us that the patrol was going to be carried out under wartime conditions and said we would be diving at night and act independently and carry out some 'cloak and dagger' stuff. He mentioned going into Falmouth on Thursday, I think it was.

QUESTION: You had been in the ship a month, you say, did you hear of any trouble or difficulty of any sort?

L/S GODDARD: Yes, Sir. Once we were in the dockyard, I was living down the after end with Leading Electrician's Mate Herbert Wood – he was on the boat when it went down. He came aft one night and said there was a possibility of our refit being extended as part of the number one battery tank was faulty and he said in doing rounds had found some water in them and reported it to Lieutenant Foster.

Goddard said that on the day Lieutenant Blackburn addressed the crew and informed them about *Affray*'s future movements, he had also told them that on returning to Portsmouth 'we might be going back into dock'.

QUESTION: Did he give any explanation why you might be going back into dock?

L/S GODDARD: No, Sir, I can't recall any.

Referring to the water found in battery tank number one, L/S Goddard was asked if this was the only trouble in the submarine he was aware of.

ANSWER: Yes, Sir.

QUESTION: Otherwise, what was your opinion of the submarine in general?

L/S GODDARD: The boat itself seemed quite all right, the crew were new and that Monday [16 April] was the first time they had got together.

QUESTION: Anything else?

L/S GODDARD: The week previous when we went to sea, we had to flood seven and eight tubes in order to get the trim and whilst we were in dock there was no maintenance carried out on the ASDIC.

QUESTION: Did you get the impression from the captain's speech whether the submarine would be on the surface at night or snorting?

L/S GODDARD: Snorting, sir.

QUESTION: When did you get that impression?

L/S GODDARD: As far as I can remember he said we would be snorting most of the night.

QUESTION: Can you say at all whether the watertight doors and hatches were worked in accordance with the weekly routine?

L/S GODDARD: The torpedo hatch was open when we sailed. The after escape hatch was closed from the week previous. I clipped the torpedo hatch shut and put the diving bars on. Also aft there was an extra box for DESA equipment brought on that day.

QUESTION: Do you know when the last DSEA practice trial was carried out?

L/S GODDARD: It was not done during the month I was on board.

Rear Admiral Raw was recalled and was examined for nearly one hour. He reminded the Board that *Affray*'s orders had been 'very flexible and she was allowed to proceed on the surface or snorting at her discretion'. He said:

I do not think it is a fair assumption to presume that she would necessarily have surfaced at daylight after snorting for such a short period as about eight hours. It was normal practice (in recent exercises) for submarines to remain submerged as a matter of routine for much longer periods. By her orders, *Affray* could, in fact, have got as far as Falmouth, have practised her folboat crew and returned to her position for exercises about 0600. Alternatively, she could have gone down to the Channel Islands and Ushant [an island marking the southern entrance to the western English Channel] and again have returned. It was strongly suggested to me that she had, in fact, been practising these folboat operations on the first night, but I discard this as being extremely unlikely.

QUESTION: You do not feel that the presence of a number of men relatively unused to submarine conditions and ten in excess of complement would be a factor in deciding that commanding officer to surface at dawn?

REAR ADMIRAL RAW: Definitely not. It is true he might decide to do so . . . to toughen up trainees he might well decide to keep them down to impress upon them some of the discomfort of submarine life. He would have no physical reason for having to surface at dawn.

QUESTION: Where would you have expected *Affray* to carry out her compressibility trial (a deep diving exercise to test water pressure on a submarine's hull) as stated in paragraph 10 of her orders?

REAR ADMIRAL RAW: The possibility of *Affray* carrying out these trails in the Hurd Deep was discussed before formulating the probability area and discarded. The only time she could have carried out those trails which require a great deal of accurate observation and calculation was on her first night run down the Channel and this was considered an extremely unlikely contingency. Her patrol area South of the Lizard and Scilly Isles gave her ample water to carry out these trials at any time later during the cruise.

Raw was asked to take the Board through the entire hour-by-hour search operation for *Affray* and on reaching the point where hull tappings and SST signals had been picked up by submarines *Sirdar* and *Sea Devil* and indications that *Affray* had been found, Raw stated:

In the early morning of 18 April, *Sirdar* at 0010 and *Sea Devil* at 0014 both reported SST. Sirdar also stated that she had gained ASDIC contact and had heard what appeared to be the letters A and M which means 'am stuck on the bottom'. This was followed at 0034 by *Sea Devil* and *Trespasser* who also reported hearing loud transmissions. So definite were these reports that they led to the firm belief at my headquarters that *Affray* had been found and I informed the Commander-in-Chief, Portsmouth, to this effect and he, in turn, informed the Admiralty.

I would like to emphasise that there was at this time no doubt in the mind of everyone at sea in the searching force or conducting operations from Fort Blockhouse that *Affray* had, in fact, been located. Almost simultaneously *Sea Devil* reported that she was still receiving SST signals and that they were loud and close and HM submarine *Ambush* reported hull tappings in this vicinity.

The Board heard that more hull tappings had been heard at 0605 and that a twelve-charge signal had been fired instructing survivors to make good their escape – but no members of *Affray*'s crew were seen on the surface.

A signal addressed to *Sirdar*, *Sea Devil* and *Trespasser* asking them to categorically confirm they had established communication with *Affray* was described by Raw as 'perhaps one of the most important signals during the search'. It had produced affirmative responses from the first two vessels and confirmed that 'signals too feint to read' from the third. Raw said:

Although hopes were fading at Submarine Headquarters, the general confirmed impression remained that *Affray* was somewhere in the vicinity of the diving position. It is of interest to note that this impression held for many weeks after the initial search . . . and this impression still remained despite the fact that detailed analysis after the return of the searching submarine to harbour had shown that it was unlikely that in fact their reports of SST were correct.

Lieutenant-Commander Reginald Clarke, Captain of HMS *Artemis* – a submarine 'as near as possible the same as *Affray*' – and with five years experience of snorting, told the Board about an occasion while snorting in rough weather:

A certain amount of water was continually coming into the snort induction and then into the engine room bilge. With the boat rolling slightly from side to side, the water in the bilge swished from one side of the boat to the other, making it very difficult to control. This made the trim of the boat rather difficult to control due to the free surface and the boat eventually took a stern-down angle which was increased when the water ran off.

Asked by the Board how much water he thought might have entered *Affray* through the hole created by the broken snort mast, Lieutenant-Commander Clarke said:

Assuming no action was taken to shut the snort induction valve for 10 seconds, approximately 10 tons of water would have entered the submarine . . . this water would flow rapidly aft as a result of the consequent stern-down angle given by the sudden entry of 10 tons of water . . . If the snort exhaust valves were not shut, the engines would flood immediately and considerable water would find its way through into the engine induction system and hence into the engine room.

The question of whether a snort mast being separated from the hull of a submarine could actually be heard in an engine room was met with a mixed response from experienced submariners. Chief Engine Room Artificer Ronald Manning, with more than sixteen years' experience in submarines, told the Board that the sound would not be heard, while Engine Room Artificer Kenneth Finney, with seven years' experience, said, 'Yes, definitely'. Lieutenant Leafric Temple-Richards, commander of *Affray* from April–December 1950 said, 'I should imagine so.'

The truth was that no one had actually been in a submarine in which the snort mast had suddenly, unexpectedly and violently been torn from the hull and lived to tell the tale. Those questioned could only speculate from their own experience and the answer should really have been that they simply didn't know. Asked if anyone might have an idea what might happen in the event of a snort mast suddenly being ripped, jolted or torn away, Lieutenant Temple-Richards replied:

They would know very quickly that water was coming in because you would feel the change in pressure. I think you would feel something in your ears that would tell you something was happening.

QUESTION: Observing that you commanded HMS *Affray* for a year, have you any suggestions or comments that you would like to make?

LIEUTENANT TEMPLE-RICHARDS: She was quite sound. I never had any doubt about her myself. I think we had rather more small defects than other submarines that I have been in, but none of them gave me any worry at all and they were definitely very small defects, which are, I should say, not relevant to this accident.

QUESTION: Can you say whether your confidence in HMS *Affray* was shared by the remainder of the officers and ship's company?

LIEUTENANT TEMPLE-RICHARDS: Yes, I think so, Sir. The engineer officer (Chief Petty Officer David Bennington) was the type of man who is easily depressed and quite often used to say that we were getting too many defects, but he was what I'd call a 'natterer' and I did not attach any particular importance to it, because the defects we had were nearly all engine room defects and in no way affected the safety of the ship. I would like to add that he was a most competent officer and I had every confidence in him.

QUESTION: Can you state that up to the time of leaving the ship in December 1950, you received no complaints or reports of misgivings as regards the ship from any officer or man on board?

LIEUTENANT TEMPLE-RICHARDS: Yes sir. I can confirm that.

QUESTION: Did you have any main engine failure while at sea or did any other serious defects develop?

LIEUTENANT TEMPLE-RICHARDS: Some of the defects that I mentioned appeared while we were at sea and one of them did entail stopping the engine and not using it again until we returned to harbour.

QUESTION: Was it necessary for the engine room staff to work very long hours making good these defects so as to carry out the exercise programme?

LIEUTENANT TEMPLE-RICHARDS: They worked long hours but not particularly long and a great deal of assistance was given us by the Gibraltar dockyard.

QUESTION: It has been stated that on one occasion during the autumn exercise *Affray* had to go to sea with only one engine in working order. Also, on another occasion, one engine broke down while at sea and that the other failed upon arrival in harbour. Do you agree with this statement?

LIEUTENANT TEMPLE-RICHARDS: As regards the first one, Sir, one engine could not be started due to some small defect on the fuel pump and it took some four to five hours to discover what the defect was, but once discovered it was very easily put right and the engine was started. Yes, one engine did break down at sea when a piston cooling pipe fractured and on return to harbour was, as far as I can remember, a separate defect on the other engine . . .

QUESTION: It has been stated that the *Affray* leaked like a sieve and when doing a deep dive, water poured into the engine room faster than it could be kept out, so that the submarine had to surface at once. Would you comment on this?

LIEUTENANT TEMPLE-RICHARDS: The whole of that is quite untrue, Sir. In nearly all of our exercises, we went to at least 300ft every time for some hours and I don't remember any leaks at all. We never had to surface in a hurry because of water coming into the ship.

QUESTION: Can you think of any occasion, which might confirm this story of water leaking in?

LIEUTENANT TEMPLE-RICHARDS: No, Sir. We frequently had quite bad weather and in bad weather when on the surface quite a lot of water came down the conning tower hatch, as it always does in any submarine. There was one occasion when we surfaced in a hurry, but it was nothing to do with water coming into the ship. It was due to one of the telemotor pump starters which fused at plant and it was during an attack and you use a great deal of telemotor pressure and we were not able to keep our depth properly and I was particularly anxious not to be hunted by a destroyer which was about to start hunting me and I fired a grenade and surfaced.

QUESTION: A further statement was made about water and oil pouring every-where and everything falling over. Would you like to comment on this statement?

LIEUTENANT TEMPLE-RICHARDS: I can only say that is an exaggeration of what it is like in a submarine under normal conditions.

Engine Room Artificer John Summers was recalled and asked if, during the previous year's exercise in the Atlantic and Mediterranean, he 'got the impression that HMS *Affray* developed any more defects than is usual in a submarine in similar circumstances'.

ERA SUMMERS: Yes, Sir, we had rather more defects that I have been used to on a boat.

QUESTION: Large or small defects?

ERA SUMMERS: Well, we had one or two large ones, but they were mainly small defects.

QUESTION: Did you have any main engine failures while at sea, or did any other serious defects develop?

ERA SUMMERS: Our trouble with the main engine room was caused by the breaking of bridge-end bolts and we had some trouble with the water system which subsequently we had to remove when we arrived in Gibraltar.

QUESTION: Did any of these make it necessary to return to harbour immediately?

ERA SUMMERS: No, Sir.

QUESTION: It has been stated that on one occasion during the autumn exercises HMS *Affray* had to go to sea with only one engine in working order. Is this so, or did you know what happened?

ERA SUMMERS: I can't remember going to sea with only one engine, Sir.

QUESTION: It has also been said that on one occasion an engine broke down while at sea and that the other failed upon arrival in the harbour – is this correct?

ERA SUMMERS: Well, we had one or two occasions when one engine did fail at sea.

QUESTION: And the other breaking down in arriving at harbour?

ERA SUMMERS: I can't remember that, Sir.

QUESTION: It has also been stated that HMS *Affray* was being used so much during the exercise that there was no time to keep her in good running repair.

ERA SUMMERS: Yes sir. That is true. We had two occasions when we had to stay in harbour and miss exercises in Gibraltar for about five days to a week.

QUESTION: From your last answer, I understand you mean that it was not so much that a ship had to go to sea with repairs uncompleted, but that on a couple of occasions because the repairs were not completed the ship remained in harbour so as to bring herself to seagoing efficiency?

ERA SUMMERS: Yes, Sir.

QUESTION: Also, another statement made said that the ship leaked like a sieve and when doing a deep dive, water poured into the engine room faster than it could be kept out, so that the submarine had to surface at once.

ERA SUMMERS: We had several occasions when this happened . . . but we did not consider ourselves to be in danger. There was a valve left open on the water system which we could not trace soon enough to stop the main engine relief system. The group exhaust was the other big trouble and we remained in harbour to have this done.

QUESTION: What was the precise trouble with the group exhaust channel?

ERA SUMMERS: We had trouble in this system which caused the exhaust jackets to become hot and on one occasion we had to leave the door open on the jacket which let out some more steam, which probably gave the impression that the interior leaked like a sieve.

QUESTION: A further statement was made about water and oil pouring everywhere and everything falling over. Can you explain this?

ERA SUMMERS: I would say that it was an over statement, Sir.

QUESTION: To sum up your replies, you have mentioned various defects, which are large and small, and with all these in view, would you confirm your general opinion about the ship?

ERA SUMMERS: What I have said so far, in my opinion, is quite correct, but all defects that I know of on HMS *Affray* would not cause any serious harm to the ship. We had rather more defects than I have been used to on a boat, but we all worked to get this ship in a seaworthy condition and on both occasions when the ship was not considered fit to go to sea, we remained in harbour.

Asked about the consequences of a battery explosion in *Affray*, Lieutenant Robert Camplin of HMS *Acheron* told the Board that if the main fuses blew 'you would lose all essential services, lighting and electrical power. There would be a fair amount of smoke but you would not get chlorine until you mix salt water with your batteries.'

The Board took this point a stage further when it called Acting Interim Surgeon Commander William Davidson from the Royal Naval Medical School to give evidence. Davidson was asked what the physiological effect would be if the submarine was at a depth of 290ft with some compartments open to the full pressure of water. He replied:

Crew who are untrained in high pressure would suffer from nitrogen narcosis (putting the crew in a drunken-like state). The action of this is similar to the early stages of an anaesthetic. The men would be incapable of carrying out even simple tasks. This condition would arise very rapidly on equalisation of pressure.

QUESTION: The effect of this nitrogen narcosis would be that in a matter of seconds after the equalisation of pressure, any man who had been unable to get into a DSEA and who was in the compartment affected would be incapable of thinking about carrying out any duties?

COMMANDER DAVIDSON: Yes, Sir. When the pressure was equivalent to 180ft, the nitrogen narcosis would begin to affect the crew. Even those with DSEA sets would die unless they escaped within ten minutes, because of oxygen convulsions.

QUESTION: What would be the early effects of nitrogen narcosis starting at 180ft?

COMMANDER DAVIDSON: The first effect would be to remove any worry from the minds of the individual. . . . the effect would get progressively worse as the pressure increased, until the men would be completely incapable of carrying out even the simplest tasks or even giving routine orders. . . . The chances of escape becomes greatly reduced at depths in excess of 150ft.

Commander Davidson added:

On the assumption that the accident happened at night, the majority of the crew would have been asleep. This, coupled with the conditions I have described, would, in my opinion, lead to great confusion and men would be less likely to carry out their duties as they would under normal circumstances. As pressure increases, the voice becomes nasal due to the altered vibration of the vocal chords and the denser air. This causes a squeaky effect and adds to the general unusualness of the situation.

Commander Stanley was recalled and asked by the Board to give his impression of *Affray*'s hydroplanes – the movable 'wings' on the stern, which control the angle of the dive – set at 'hard to rise', meaning the boat was making an effort to surface.

COMMANDER STANLEY: Either she was going down on an even keel or they had been put to rise by someone in a panic not thinking very clearly.

QUESTION: Would you agree that if the submarine were sinking relatively rapidly by the stern, that it was incorrect to have the planes at hard to rise?

COMMANDER STANLEY: Yes, I would agree, Sir.

QUESTION: How would you expect the planes to be?

COMMANDER STANLEY: Amidships, Sir.

The final witness to be summoned had already been called before the Board of Inquiry on three previous occasions and made more appearances than anyone else. Captain Hugh Browne, Captain of the 5th Submarine Flotilla, was asked if he had any final comments to make. He had.

He stated that 'the decision to send *Affray* to sea with the crew as it was, was carefully weighed beforehand' and reminded the Board that the principal officers were all experienced submariners. Captain Browne also said that that the two training officers on board were also experienced and out of the forty-four crew members, thirty-eight were 'thoroughly experienced in this submarine or on HMS *Alaric*, which was identical'. Of the remaining six ratings, only one had been in submarines for many years.

He reminded the Board that *Affray* had been sent to sea to take part in an independent exercise 'similar to those she would have carried out had she been newly commissioned with a crew who had not been to sea together before'.

The Board heard that sub-lieutenants and engineer officers, taken in lieu of certain ratings sent ashore, 'were by no means new to submarines'. He said that engineer officers had been

> right at the end of their training and within a week or two would have been appointed as engineer officers of submarines. Of the sub-lieutenants, all except one had had three months' submarine experience while doing their small ships training; four of them had had this experience in 'A' class submarines. Three sub-lieutenants were nearing the end of their training; they were, therefore, considered to be quite as useful, knowledgeable and intelligent – and probably more so – than the junior ratings they were replacing.

Captain Browne told the Board:

> I wish to emphasise that in the exercise *Affray* was to carry out, there was no sense of urgency or hurry, evolutions could be carried out as slowly as the Commanding Officer wished and I have no doubt that for the first few days everything would have been carried out in a very slow time, in the same way as working up exercises would be carried out by a newly commissioned submarine. . . . Before *Affray* proceeded to sea I knew, and Lieutenant Blackburn knew, that standard of training and work up of his crew. He knew about all the drafting changes that were taking place and when they were taking place.
>
> On the morning before he sailed he expressed himself perfectly satisfied with both the submarine and the crew and stated that he was looking forward to working them up into an efficient team. He looked upon this period of independent exercises as an excellent way of working up the majority of his crew for the time when *Affray* would become fully operational.
>
> QUESTION: Would you not consider it preferable for the submarine to go to sea once with her ship's company on board, if that is possible?
>
> CAPTAIN BROWNE: I would consider it preferable, but not necessary.

❖   ❖   ❖

On 7 August, Admiral Power submitted the Board's finished report in full – more than 900 pages with appendices – to the Secretary of the Admiralty with a covering note stating:

> I am convinced that this theory (the broken snort mast) still presents the most possible solution to the accident and fits most nearly with those facts which have become available. There are certain points which remain unexplained, but on balance there is more supporting evidence and probability about the theory put forward than about other ideas.

The three members of the Board of Inquiry were now allowed to return to their normal jobs within the senior service, but placed on forty-eight-hour call for re-assembly in case last-minute evidence came to light.

Admiral Power concluded: 'I wish to take this opportunity of emphasising the admirable manner in which Rear Admiral Dick and his Board have conducted a long and difficult investigation.'

Chapter 18

'WE DO NOT CONCUR' AND A QUESTION OF SALVAGE OR SCRAP

Not everyone agreed with the Board of Inquiry – or Admiral Power's – conclusion that the broken snort mast was to blame for the loss of *Affray*. Senior Admiralty officials were annoyed that the Board had failed to identify a single person – dead or alive – to take their share of the blame for the accident.

Ten days after receiving his copy, A.O. Osley, Acting Head of the Navy's Law Branch, accused the Board of 'closing its eyes' to other possibilities which might have caused the disaster. He wrote in a memo widely circulated to Admiralty personnel:

It [the report] dismisses, for instance, the possibility of battery explosion more readily than the evidence – or lack of it – justifies. It strongly supports what can be conveniently termed the Flag Officer Submarine's hypothesis . . . The essence of it is that the snort mast snapped while the submarine was snorting near the surface, the water rushed in before anyone could do anything about it and the vessel sank stern down, striking the bottom at an angle of 65 degrees.

This theory has not yet been generally accepted at the Admiralty, because it cannot be readily reconciled with the assessed damage to the submarine and leaves unexplained why the material failure happened when it did. Personally, I have felt for some time that these difficulties could better be resolved by the theory that the breaking of the snort mast was a secondary factor and took place at a much greater depth of water. Owing to some failure of drill (i.e. the opening of a valve) the submarine may have got into trouble, started to sink with the snort mast still up and this eventually collapsed under pressure of water, thereby making the loss irrevocable.

But this is pure speculation by an unqualified layman. Whatever the real cause was, it has been approved for *Reclaim* to grope for further clues and on the evidence so far available, an open verdict must be recorded.

In another response, the Navy's Director of Torpedo, Anti-Submarine and Mine Warfare, G.F. Maunsell stated:

As *Affray* was in dockyard hands from 1 January – 10 April, I consider that a working up period of one day (11 April), which included a dive of only 30 minutes and in which only half the proper crew were on board, is not sufficient for any submarine, even with her normal complement on board.

During a short dive of 30 minutes, very few of the emergency drills could have been carried out and these should have included 'snorting drill' and 'Emergency – stop snorting,' particularly with a new Commanding Officer . . . I also consider that neither the hull or machinery could have been given fair trial during this period and that, therefore, her CO could not have honestly reported that he was entirely satisfied with his submarine and with his ship's company.

The report indicates that the disaster was most probably caused by the breaking of the snort mast. Although I admit that this *may have been the cause,* I consider that there is a considerable volume of evidence against it . . .'

V.G. Shepheard, Director of Naval Construction, also did 'not concur with the conclusions of the Board'. He said that inspection of the wreck 'has revealed nothing amiss except the broken snort mast, which may have broken off after the submarine had come to rest on the bottom – in fact, the position in which the mast was found and examination of the fracture suggests that this was so'.

He noted that 'many possible sources of flooding could never be revealed by internal inspection and it is considered that the evidence against the Board of Inquiry's conclusions has not been given the weight it deserves'.

Shepheard said there was no evidence as to the state of the valves in the snort induction system, 'but the Board's conclusion implies that neither of them was closed. To accept this, the Board have accepted Flag Officer Submarine's hypothesis "how it happened". . . . If the hypothesis does not fit the fact, it follows that grave doubt must be cast on the premise.'

❖   ❖   ❖

While the Board was in session, Parliamentary Secretary to the Admiralty, James Callaghan, met Admiralty officials to discuss whether or not *Affray* could be salvaged. This would be Callaghan's final meeting with the Admiralty regarding the *Affray* as his Labour Party would soon be voted out of office in a general election which would return the Conservatives – and Winston Churchill – to power.

The meeting generally agreed that raising the submarine was the only way to finally ascertain for once and for all what had caused the fatal accident. It would also allow families of those lost on the submarine to receive their loved ones from their present watery grave and give them a proper funeral and final resting place close to their homes.

Unfortunately minutes of this meeting only identify Callaghan and his questions, but not Admiralty officers answering them or offering viewpoints. When asked if it were possible to salvage the submarine, a senior official told Callaghan: 'It could not be said that it was impossible. It would certainly be difficult and there would be no guarantee of success. It could not be done this summer and there would be great dislocation to other important work.'

Others sitting around the table that day were against raising the submarine 'because of the effort involved. If salvage work is not completed in 1952, I calculate that the task cannot be done as each new season means an entirely new start.' Someone at the meeting stated that 'the relatives, too, have been against a salvage attempt on the submarine' while another added that 'this opinion is not unanimous'. (Author's note: several *Affray* relatives have told this author that they were never once consulted about bringing the bodies of their men back to dry land.)

The actual cost of salvaging *Affray* was never brought up and it would be another four months – and a change of government – before the matter was raised again.

Callaghan was replaced by James Thomas, who took the title of First Lord of the Admiralty. Callaghan shadowed the position in opposition. Churchill took a special interest in all naval matters having served two terms as First Lord of the Admiralty in 1911–1915 and 1939–1940. In November 1951, the Prime Minister asked Thomas to update him on plans to salvage the *Affray* – and how much it might cost the Navy. Thomas replied:

I have been advised that the task would be extremely hazardous and that it would only be possible to send down divers for a day or two during each slack water period, this accounting for the estimate of the length of the salvage operation. The probability of failure is stated to be extremely high. The cost of the salvage operation would be a minimum of half a million pounds – and the scrap value of *Affray* no more than £5,000. If the vessel were salvaged and we contemplated further use, there would be very heavy expenditure on refit.

In contrast to the above, you will be interested to know that the cost of a new 'A' class submarine is estimated to be about £880,000. In the circumstances, I have no hesitation in saying that these considerations weigh very heavily against any inclination to attempt salvage.

Mary Henry, Lieutenant Foster's widow, was distressed when she heard the news:

Why the devil didn't they bring the submarine up? The truth about what had happened to her could have been found out. Why couldn't they? Those of us left behind after *Affray* was lost felt – and still feel – as if we've been swept under the carpet. The loss of the *Affray* was an embarrassing episode that the Navy wishes had never happened. As far as the Navy is concerned, families of men lost at sea are a nuisance.

Leading Seaman George Cook's widow, Joy, said she was never approached by the Navy and asked that if she had a choice, would she prefer her husband's remains to be brought to the surface or remain on the seabed.

It was said in Parliament that the relatives had unanimously agreed that they should stay together in the wreck of the submarine, but that wasn't true. Nobody asked and nobody wrote seeking my opinion. I wrote to the Navy and told them that my wish was for George to be brought home. But I had to ask them, they never asked me. And then I never heard another word.

While they were still searching for *Affray*, we had been told that no expense would be spared to raise her once they had located her. After they had found her I naturally expected her to be brought up. Other countries offered to help and provide the correct boats and lifting equipment to raise her, but the Navy didn't take up their offer. I understand that they could have blown air into her, which would have helped bring her up.

Today, I feel that the Navy didn't want her brought up. They wanted her to stay down at the bottom of the sea. Was there something about the submarine that they didn't want us to know?

Chapter 19

NO MARK UPON THEIR COMMON GRAVE

Ever since an underwater television camera had positively identified *Affray*, the Admiralty had been under pressure from the public and the press wanting more details about how the wreck had been located and how the Navy knew so much about it. The television camera and information about those responsible for developing the equipment had never been publicly acknowledged as it had been deemed 'an experiment' by the Admiralty, whose policy was never to publicise its experiments.

Five months after *Affray* had disappeared and three months after she was discovered, the Admiralty bowed to pressure and released a statement admitting that a television camera had been responsible for the discovery. The Admiralty would have preferred the information to remain secret, but Atlee's government was on its way out and Churchill's new government on the way in. Rumours spread throughout the Admiralty's Whitehall offices that if their Lordships insisted on remaining silent about the television camera, the incoming First Lord of the Admiralty, James Thomas, would do the job for them. They issued a statement:

> It can now be stated that His Majesty's submarine *Affray*, which was lost in the English Channel, was first identified by means of underwater television.
>
> After the loss of the submarine, a team of four members of the Royal Naval Scientific Service worked night and day for three weeks to produce the unit which eventually proved to be of such great service.
>
> Portable television equipment, similar to that used for outside broadcasting, was obtained from the Marconi Wireless Telegraph Company, whose prompt cooperation was greatly appreciated. The naval scientists not only had to mount the camera in a specially welded watertight container, but

also had to design and incorporate the various remote controls for operating the set.

The container had to be set in a specially designed frame along with underwater lighting apparatus which had previously been designed to facilitate the work of underwater photography.

The equipment was taken as soon as it was completed to the salvage ship *Reclaim* and lowered over the side for testing. Results proved sufficiently satisfactory to warrant the use of the equipment on the actual search.

The television equipment had been in use for some weeks before success was achieved. After location by ASDIC equipment, a number of wrecks had been investigated by this means and when there was uncertainty, it had proved of great value to the divers, particularly in assisting them to be lowered into the best position for surveying or otherwise working on the wrecks.

Early in June viewers in the captain's cabin saw various parts of the *Affray* coming into view and the climax was when they read the name *Affray* on the screen. Some hours later divers were able to identify the submarine by normal methods.

The Marconi people were delighted that their equipment had been identified in such a public way as it would make the Royal Navy even keener to buy their technology as a permanent fixture on *Reclaim*.

A Marconi spokesman told the *Daily Telegraph*: 'The equipment used was a perfectly normal outdoor television camera and associated controls – such as the BBC have used in their big outside broadcasts. It can be packed into about five suitcases.'

The underwater television camera had more than proved itself to the Royal Navy, who asked Marconi if they could hold on to its equipment while further tests were conducted at sea. At the end of the year, the Navy informed Marconi that it planned to carry an underwater camera permanently on board *Reclaim* and would be asking several companies in Britain and Europe to submit proposals and competitive prices. The news came as a shock to Marconi who had not earned a penny and only a little public prestige from loaning their technology to the Navy for free. They thought they had secured a Navy contract, only to discover that they had opened the door for their competitors to walk through.

The Navy's specifications for permanent underwater camera and support equipment for *Reclaim* was a difficult one for the television camera manufacturers to match. To date, their experience had been limited to working with broadcasting companies, such as the BBC, not official bureaucracies like the Admiralty. In the end the Royal Navy awarded its contract to Marconi's principal rival in Britain, PYE, which produced a camera almost identical to the one developed by Marconi and mounted in a special container with its distinctive branding on the side. Apparently it was all down to price. PYE was the lowest bidder.

❖   ❖   ❖

The House of Commons was crowded, but sympathetically silent on Wednesday 14 November when James Thomas, the new First Lord of the Admiralty, announced that no further operations would be carried out on *Affray*. There was not, he stated 'sufficient evidence to say with certainty why the submarine was lost'. He told the House:

> The wreck of HM submarine *Affray* was located by ASDIC equipment on 14 June after a search lasting two months. She was lying in 288ft of water and was identified by means of underwater television. This equipment was used also to help in directing the divers during their painstaking examination of her hull.
>
> Since the last statement in this House on 1 August, the diving vessel *Reclaim* has worked on all possible occasions and has made every effort to obtain further evidence about the cause of the disaster. I am sorry to have to tell the House that all her work of the last three months has been in vain and that one of my first duties on taking office was to agree that there was no reasonable hope of obtaining any further light on the problem through this means.
>
> The continued use of *Reclaim* on these special duties for so long has already interfered to a serious extent with the training of deep-sea divers. While there was still a chance that useful evidence would be forthcoming, this was accepted. Weather conditions in any case would have made further operations impossible in the winter.
>
> I have studied very carefully the final report of the Board of Inquiry and the results of tests that have now been made on the snort mast of *Affray* and those of two other 'A' class submarines.
>
> I have concluded that there is insufficient evidence to enable me to say with certainty why *Affray* was lost. Many theories have been put forward, among them the possibility that her snort mast snapped while she was snorting and that she filled rapidly through failure to close the valves provided against such an emergency. This would have resulted in her sinking stern first, but there is evidence that *Affray*'s stern was undamaged.
>
> It is possible that a major battery explosion started a shock wave in her hull and that this ruptured her pressure trunking which lies amidships under the casing, but external to the hull. Damage of this type could have resulted in the submarine sinking on an even keel. Such an explosion could have started

1. The schnorchel, or snort mast (left), and periscope of an 'A' class submarine photographed during sea trials in 1949. *(The National Archives)*

2. HMS *Affray*, one of the Royal Navy's 'A' class large patrol vessels, launched on 2 May 1946 and lost with seventy-five officers and ratings on board during Exercise Training Spring on 17 April 1951. The submarine is photographed from the starboard bow before leaving for Australia in October 1946. *(Wright & Logan, Royal Navy Submarine Museum)*

3. *Affray* at Simonstown, South Africa, in December 1946 with HMAS *Australia* in the background. *(Cay's Photo Service Agency, Cape Town)*

4. An off-duty moment at sea: crew from *Affray* smile for Jeffrey Barlow's box Brownie camera on route to Gibraltar during the submarine's Autumn Cruise exercise in September 1950. *(Jeffrey Barlow)*

Below left: 5. Jeffrey Barlow (centre, white pullover) and shipmates stand next to *Affray*'s radar aerial and periscopes as the submarine approaches Gibraltar. *(Jeffrey Barlow)*

Above: 6. Six members of *Affray*'s crew down in the confined space of its engine room. *(Crown copyright)*

7. *Affray*'s control room was positioned directly beneath the conning tower and contained practically everything necessary to dive and navigate the submarine. To newcomers, the space was a confusion and complexity of pipes, valves, electric wiring, switches, dials, wheels, levers, pressure gauges, depth gauges, junction boxes, navigational instruments and other mystery gadgets. *(Mary Henry)*

8. Officers and ratings from *Affray* don their tropical kit on deck for a group photograph in Casablanca in October 1950. *(Jeffrey Barlow)*

9. *Affray* berthed alongside HMS *Tiptoe* during its Autumn Cruise, Gibraltar 1950. Snort masts from both vessels can clearly be seen in their 'lowered' positions running along the deck. *(Jeffrey Barlow)*

Above left: 10. *Affray* at Tangier, Morocco, October 1950. (*Jeffrey Barlow*)

Above right: 11. The most popular pastime on British submarines was a game of 'Uckers,' played by four submariners using a traditional Ludo board and two dice instead of one. (*Alan Gallop*)

Left: 12. Down the hatch: an unidentified crew member of *Affray* prepares to disappear down into the submarine from the bridge. The holes in the floor are designed to drain water away from the bridge after the submarine resurfaces. (*Mary Henry*)

Below: 13. Lieutenant-Commander John Blackburn, taking a sun sight reading on board HMS *Sea Scout* during Exercise March Flight in spring 1950, a few weeks before taking command of *Affray*. (*Royal Navy Submarine Museum*)

14. Following the 'Subsmash One' alert on 17 April 1950, a full-scale sea-air search was launched. A Church of Scotland padre joins naval ratings from HMS *Starling* as they board a lifeboat to join HMS *Boxer*, leader of the *Affray* search party. *(George Ransome Collection)*

15. Search-and-rescue pilots prepare for take-off. The first air-sea search aircraft hoping to find *Affray* took off forty-five minutes after the 'Subsmash' signal was initiated. *(Crown copyright)*

16. Vessels take part in the massive search in the English Channel for *Affray* involving seventeen rescue ships and submarines, April 1950. *(George Ransome Collection)*

17. HMS *Amphion*, sister submarine to the missing *Affray*, searches the English Channel for signs of survivors or wreckage. *(Author's Collection)*

18. 'A' class submarine searching for *Affray* in the English Channel. *(Skyfoto)*

19. Newspapers published detailed photographs of *Affray*. *(George Ransome Collection)*

20. Lieutenant John Blackburn, age 28, was noted by the Admiralty for 'his considerable wartime experience, peacetime training experience and sterling character', which made him 'perfectly suitable' for commanding *Affray*. *(Royal Navy Submarine Museum)*

21. Lieutenant Derek Foster from Petersfield, Hampshire, *Affray*'s popular 'Number One', with his wife Mary at a family wedding. *(Mary Henry)*

22. Able Seaman George Leakey from Hayes, Middlesex, whose youngest daughter Georgina (Gina) wants to know why her father lost his life on 'the death ship *Affray*'. *(Gina Gander)*

23. In April 1951, Able Seaman John Goddard from Southend-on-Sea, Essex, was one of thirteen ratings instructed to recover their kit and return to shore minutes before *Affray* sailed for Exercise Training Spring. John is photographed in later years wearing the uniform of a lieutenant. *(Margaret Goddard)*

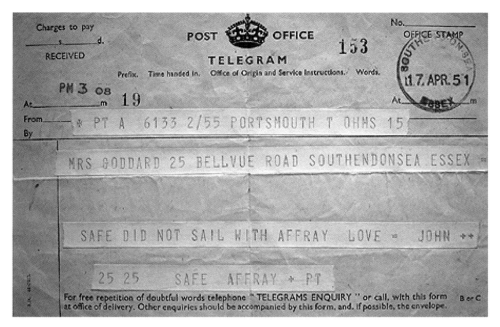

24. Leading Seaman George Cook from Ilfracombe, Devon. *(Joy Cook)*

Above: 25. Telegram sent by Able Seaman John Goddard to his mother with the message: 'Safe. Did not sail with Affray.' *(Reproduced with kind permission of Margaret Goddard)*

Right: 26. Marine Sergeant Jack Andrews from the Royal Marines Amphibious School at Eastney, Hampshire, one of four 'passengers' aboard *Affray* on a 'cloak and dagger' mission. *(Robin Andrews)*

Far right: 27. Telegraphist Harold Gittins (seated) from Wolverhampton, a keen sportsman and popular member of *Affray*'s crew. *(Michael Kenyon)*

28. HMS *Reclaim*, the Navy's 1,800-ton deep-diving and submarine rescue vessel, which played a vital role in discovering the location of *Affray*. (*Author's Collection*)

29. Petty Officer Robert 'Nobby' Hall (seated bottom left), Chief Bosun's Mate on *Reclaim*, had the unbelievable experience of being blown to the surface from a depth of nearly 200ft after a cable linked to his voice-piece had been wrenched from his diving helmet while searching for *Affray*. (*George Ransome Collection*)

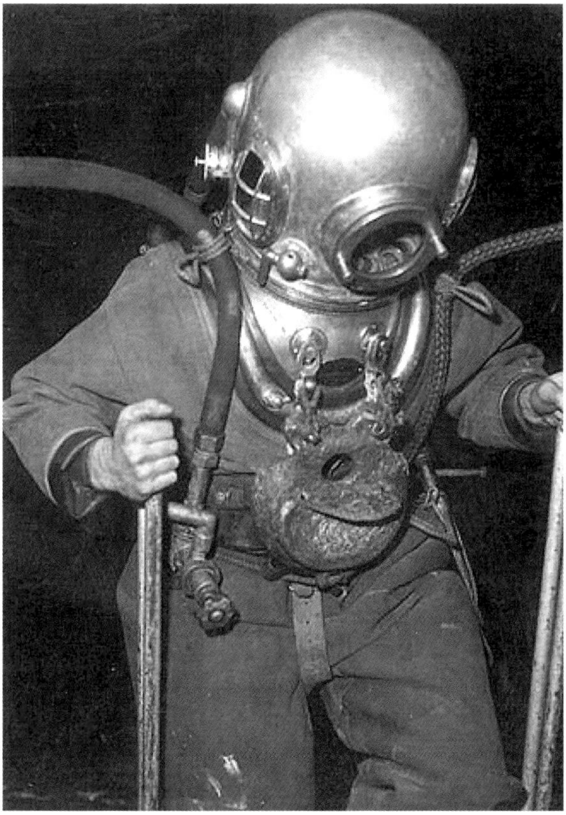

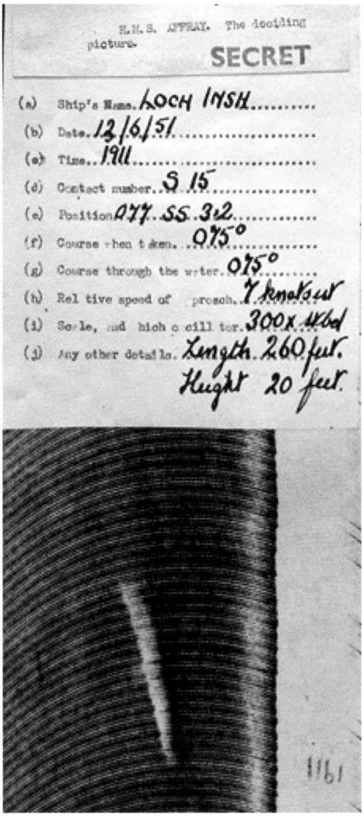
SECRET
(a) Ship's Name. LOCH INSH
(b) Date. 12/6/51
(c) Time. 1911
(d) Contact number. S 15
(e) Position 077. SS. 3.2
(f) Course when taken. 075°
(g) Course through the water. 075°
(h) Relative speed of approach. 7 knots
(i) Length 260 feet.
Height 20 feet.

Above left: 30. Diver from HMS *Reclaim* prepares to go over the side to investigate a wreck which may – or may not – be *Affray*. *(Author's Collection)*

Above right: 31. ASDIC reading which confirmed that at 1911 hours on 12 June 1951 HMS *Loch Insh* had found *Affray* after nearly two months of searching. It showed a long 'cigar-shaped' image sitting 300ft down on the seabed. *(The National Archives)*

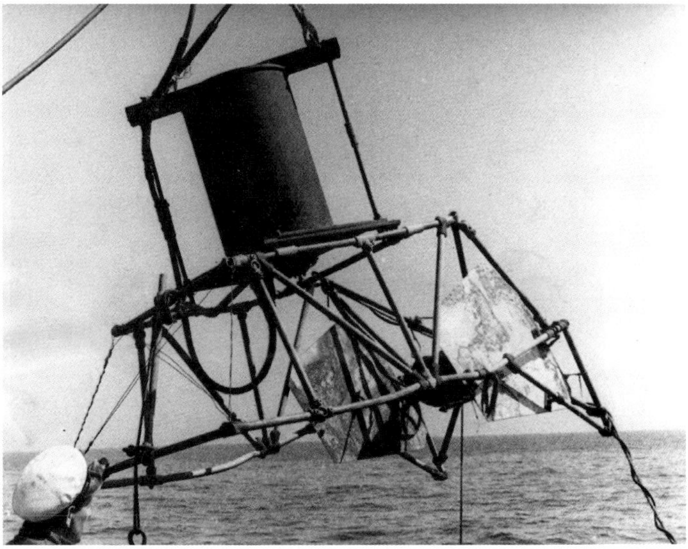

32. 'The Ugly Duckling', an improvised casing containing a television camera which was used to photograph *Affray* on the seabed. The framework underneath provided a base for the device when on the deck of *Reclaim* and held lighting and steadying fins. *(Author's Collection)*

Above top left: 33. Bridge of *Affray* as seen by the underwater television camera. The round white object is the diver's shot weight that guided the special container containing the camera to the submarine's resting place. (*The National Archives*)

Above bottom left: 34. Broken 35ft snort mast seen by the underwater television camera. (*The National Archives*)

Above right: 35. Snort mast is raised onto the deck of *Reclaim* on 1 July 1951. (*Crown Copyright*)

Below: 36. Extensive tests on the snort mast were conducted at the Admiralty's Central Material Laboratory, Emsworth, where it was discovered that the standard of welding at its base 'was far from good'. (*The National Archives*)

37 & 38. Details of the broken snort mast. *(The National Archives)*

39. Collar from the broken snort mast at the Royal Navy Submarine Museum at Gosport, the only piece of *Affray* on view today. *(Alan Gallop)*

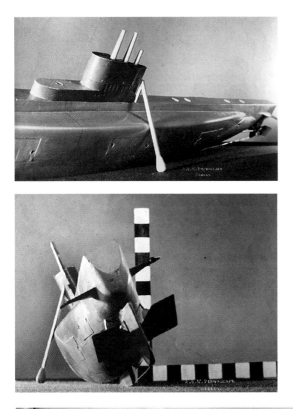

40, 41, 42, 43. Scale model of *Affray* produced for use at the official Board of Inquiry showing the submarine slightly listing on the seabed with the broken snort mast. *(The National Archives)*

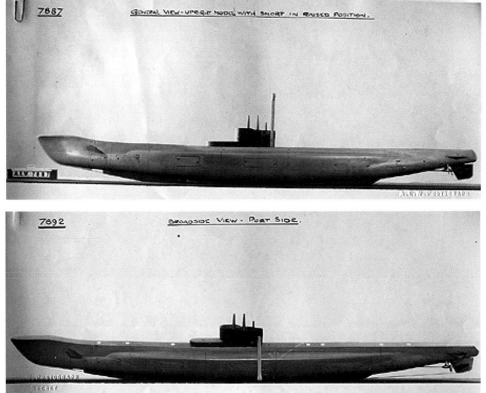

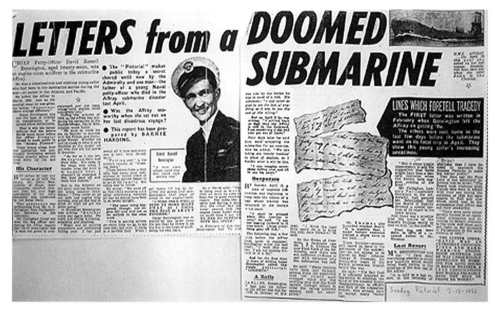

44. 'Letters From a Doomed Submarine': David Bennington's letters to his father telling him about problems with the submarine's engines were reproduced in the *Sunday Pictorial* newspaper in December 1951. (*Author's Collection*)

45: Memorial at the Royal Navy Submarine Museum records the many accidents to submarines between 1904 and 1955. It also serves as a memorial to the 4,334 British submariners who gave their lives in both world wars and to the 739 officers and men lost in peacetime submarine disasters. (*Alan Gallop*)

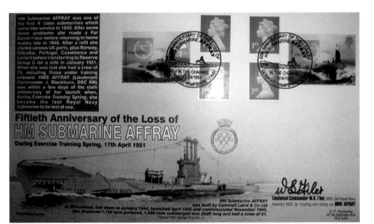

46: Memorial services were held in Portsmouth, Gosport and Chatham in April and May 1951. A service was also held in 2001, marking the fiftieth anniversary of the *Affray* disaster. *(Royal Navy Submarine Museum)*

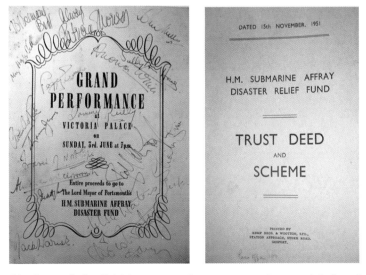

47. Commemorative first-day cover celebrating 100 years of British submarines and the fiftieth anniversary of the loss of *Affray*. *(Gina Gander Collection)*

48. Cover of booklet issued to all dependants of officers and ratings lost on board *Affray* by the *Affray* Disaster Relief Fund Scheme, which raised more than £170,000 in just a few months. *(Royal Navy Submarine Museum)*

49. Stars of the British stage and screen staged a special Grand Performance at London's Victoria Palace Theatre on Sunday 3 June 1951 with all funds going to the HMS *Affray* Disaster Relief Fund. *(Royal Navy Submarine Museum)*

a crack in the snort, which might then have snapped off as she grounded. Whatever the cause of the disaster, it is clear from the survey of her hull that no attempt at escape was made and that the end came swiftly.

The House was informed on 1 August that the metallurgical condition of some parts of *Affray*'s snort and those of her two sister ships was below standard and that some of the welding was not good. Tests just completed on these three snorts indicate that they were well capable of standing up to all stresses other than those associated with an explosive shock. A modified form of snort has successfully passed its tests and is being fitted to 'A' class submarines.

I should like to say that the adoption of an automatic valve has been considered on several occasions. Automatic arrangements for meeting a possible emergency, which might never occur, are apt to induce a false sense of security and it had generally been preferred to rely on a correct drill to meet such situations. We are, nevertheless, considering the technical means of providing a thoroughly reliable automatic device.

The question of salvage has been considered. This would be a very difficult task – perhaps the most difficult ever undertaken. *Affray* lies not only at a great depth but in a very exposed position where weather would be the greatest enemy of the operation. The tides are strong and useful work could only be done in good weather at very limited periods of slack water. There is in these conditions an ever-present risk to men's lives. The material cost is difficult to estimate, but it would be inordinately high since seven or more vessels would be needed.

The operation would be limited to the five fine weather months of 1952 and it might well extend into the summer of 1953, if not found to be totally impracticable earlier. The vessels needed for the operation all have their allotted tasks. Their work is of importance and it has already suffered on account of operations on *Affray*.

I have considered these matters carefully and I have decided that with the high risk of total failure, there is no justification for this substantial diversion of our resources. There will, therefore, be no further operations in connection with *Affray*.

❖   ❖   ❖

Leader comment in *The Times*, Wednesday 14 November 1951:

There will be general approval of the decision of the Admiralty, announced in Parliament yesterday, to leave the wreck of HM Submarine *Affray* in the depths of the Channel, where she has lain since April. Since her position is exposed to every gale, and moreover the tides where she lies in more than 40 fathoms of water are so strong than even in calm weather divers can work for no more than twenty minutes each tide, their attempts to salve her have been attended with no little danger to life and limb. Nevertheless, so important was it to discover the cause of the unexplained disaster – all the more deplorable in that the ship was carrying twenty young naval officers and four Marines under training in addition to her own company – that the attempts have been continued without respite until the onset of winter brings them to a close. The experience so gained has now shown that the prospects of ultimate success are so slender as not to justify resuming the dangerous work next year, especially since it means serious interruption of the Navy's normal programme of training deep-sea divers.

It has not been possible to ascertain the exact cause of the disaster. When the wreck was first located by a triumph of seamanship and the skilful development and use of scientific apparatus, many miles from the position where it was at first thought – erroneously, as it turned out – that signals were being sent out from the sunken ship, it was observed that her 'snort' tube was buckled and broken. It was clear, however, to those acquainted with the equipment of submarines that this could not have been the cause of the loss, since mere damage to the snort would neither cause rapid foundering on an even keel nor preclude release of the marker buoys and use of the escape apparatus. The damage to the snort must have been a result, not a cause, of some sudden catastrophe which disabled all on board, sank the ship and rendered inconsequential all the elaborate devices that provided, as far as human ingenuity can, for the safety of the inmates of a damaged submarine. There would seem to have been no mark of damage by external agency so that the theories that she had been in collision or had struck a mine must be ruled out.

All that can now be said is that the cause of disaster was internal, and that the end was both sudden and complete. The officers and men of the *Affray* will have no mark upon their common grave but, like many brave seamen before them who have gone down in their ships in the course of duty, they will find their monument in the hearts of their countrymen.

❖   ❖   ❖

Against all odds, *Reclaim*'s divers had made every effort to get to the inaccessible snort induction valve on *Affray*'s pressure hull. They were determined to discover if the valve was in the 'open' or 'closed' position. At one stage they began using a mechanical grab – guided by a diver in an observation chamber – to remove a small part of casing housing the valve allowing them to take radio-active X-ray images through the hull – an arduous and highly dangerous process.

A radioactive isotope, no larger than a pea and enclosed in a thick lead container mounted onto a magnetic frame, was pulled into position by a diver armed with a large photographic plate. The diver then removed a lead plug from the radioactive container allowing rays to be released onto the hull. Depending on weather and tidal conditions, divers went down and set the device to take different time exposures lasting between five to twenty-four hours. This was a primitive way of trying to 'see' through the hull, but the technology was new and untried at the time – and results were far from perfect.

On one of the dives, the lead container became detached from its frame and the plug fell off as the diver tried to reposition it, releasing radioactive material onto the wreck site. Fortunately, the diver's sturdy suit protected him from contamination.

The unsuccessful attempt to take X-ray images finally brought underwater investigations on the wrecked submarine to an end in November 1951. On 23 January 1952 the buoys marking the spot where *Affray* lay at the bottom of the sea were lifted and her seventy-five officers and men finally allowed to rest in peace in their grave beneath the waves of the English Channel.

At the time Peter Stephens was waiting to undertake his submarine training at HMS *Dolphin* and working on HMS *Barova*, the boom defence vessel assigned to recover the marker buoys positioned over *Affray*. He remembers:

It was a very eerie feeling, especially at night, knowing what lay below us. On completion, we went into St Peter Port (Guernsey) where we were given the freedom of the town. There were lots of rumours about what had happened, the main one being that the snort mast had snapped because it was so rusty. But this didn't put me off joining submarines.

❖   ❖   ❖

At 1245 hours on Thursday 17 April 1952, the *Affray*'s sister-submarine, HMS *Alliance*, surfaced over the exact spot where twelve months before an identical vessel had come to rest on the seabed nearly 300ft below. A memorial service took place on the deck and more than 100 wreaths from wives, mothers, sweethearts, children and colleagues, delivered to HMS *Dolphin* the day before, were cast over the side by officers and men. The youngest wreath had been sent by 7-month-old Georgina Gander, whose father Able Seaman George Leakey was lost with seventy-four shipmates exactly a year before.

Relatives had pleaded with the Admiralty to allow them to go with HMS *Alliance* to spend a few moments above the site where their loved ones lay and cast their wreaths into the sea. The Admiralty refused, stating that while it was appropriate for a Royal Navy 'A' class submarine to go out to the site, there would be no room for any civilians.

Joy Cook, widow of Leading Seaman George Cook, was bitterly disappointed to receive the news. She had hoped to visit the site with her baby son, Kevin, who was just over 1 year old. 'Why couldn't they have taken another boat out for the families?' she remembers. 'The Navy obviously didn't want us there.'

Thirty-two years later, Joy Cook made her own way out to the site where her husband lies buried at sea with his shipmates. Armed with a detailed chart and the exact navigational coordinates pinpointing where *Affray* lies 16 miles from the shore, Mrs Cook travelled to Guernsey determined to find a boat prepared to take her out to sea. She said:

The local branch of the Submariner's Association advised me to go down to the harbour front and talk to skippers of fishing boats available for charter. As luck would have it, I was put in touch with an ex-Navy man who agreed to take me out in an ex-Navy small boat. He brought his wife along, too, to keep me company.

I took along two-dozen red roses to lay on the water. The flowers were in memory of my husband and his friend David Bennington – who he called Jim – who also lost his life on the *Affray*. They had been to school together and had died together.

I'm so pleased I was able to go to the place above where the submarine lies. But I had to make all the arrangements myself. The Navy should have done this for everybody years before. It wasn't much to ask. It was a small thing, and they couldn't even do that for the families of their own men lost at sea.

Chapter 20

'SHOULD I BE IN HIS SHOES,
I SHOULD ASK FOR A COURT
MARTIAL'

By November 1951 the time had come for the Royal Navy to begin apportioning blame for the loss of *Affray* in the quietest possible way. Strangely no one else – not even politicians or the press – were demanding heads of the culprits to be brought before them on a platter. By the end of the year, *Affray* had disappeared from newspapers and passed into the mists of time in the British public's consciousness. The tragedy was hardly forgotten, but other things had come along to occupy their minds – the Suez situation had worsened, there was growing tension between Jews and Arabs over Palestine, more atom bombs were tested by the Americans in the Pacific and British Foreign Office official and double-spy Guy Burgess had caused a sensation by defecting to Moscow. Seven months after the accident, only widows and children, parents and friends of the dead crew members, Admiralty top brass and submariners in 'A' class submarines, still had the *Affray* on their minds.

James Thomas's Parliamentary statement had managed to destroy the confidence ordinary submariners had in their boats. Up until that time, crews were happy to accept that the breaking of *Affray*'s snort mast had been a 'one-off' and unlikely to happen again. All snorting had stopped while investigations were carried out and masts minutely examined by experts. Steps had been taken to alter interior valve controls and crews were happy that everything possible was being done to ensure safety in their boats. But when it was announced in Parliament that *Affray*'s loss had not been established and that a battery explosion or some other reason might have caused the accident, crews felt they were sitting on top of a volcano waiting to explode. Despite assurances from naval engineers that submarines were safe, the process of restoring crew's confidence in their vessels had to start all over again. Fewer men wanted to serve in submarines, even if it did meaning earning an extra half a crown in their pay packets.

On 7 November, the navy's Head of Military Branch wrote to Admiralty colleagues:

> Investigations into the loss of *Affray* have revealed a most serious lack of care and thought on the part of those responsible for arranging for the officer's training course to go to sea in a submarine. Naval staff divisions concerned have remarked on this aspect . . . and to the layman it is unbelievable that despite the many other important tasks for which operational submarines are needed, a fully worked up one could not be spared for a week or so for the training trip.

The document reminded recipients that the Commander-in-Chief, Portsmouth (Admiral Sir Arthur Power) had earlier praised the manner in which the Board of Inquiry, under Admiral Dick, had conducted their 'long and difficult' investigation. It stated:

> Ordinarily this might well have resulted in some favourable comment from the Board (of the Admiralty). My feelings, however, are that the Admiralty have not been so impressed with the work of the Board of Inquiry as to justify favourable a comment and I suggest that no action need be taken on the Commander-in-Chief's suggestion.

It continued:

> It is within the Admiralty that we encounter an expressed opinion that *Affray* should not have been sailed on the mission in the circumstances and manner that obtained. On balance, I agree that Captain of the 5th Submarine Flotilla [Captain Hugh Browne] should not have sailed *Affray* when and as he did. Equally, I would remark that judging by the firmness of Answer No. 758 by Captain Browne, should I be in his shoes and of his mind and subsequently received his Lordship's displeasure, I should ask for a Court Martial in an honest attempt to clear myself of the blame imputed.

Answer No. 758 had been given to the Board of Inquiry by Captain Browne on 31 July – the final day of questioning to witnesses – when asked if he had any additional comments to add to earlier statements.

He had told the Board that the decision to send *Affray* to sea 'with the crew as it was' had been carefully weighed beforehand and reminded the Board that the principal officers – including the two training officers – were experienced submariners and out of the forty-four crew members on board thirty-eight were thoroughly experienced in a submarine similar to *Affray*.

Browne had stated that before *Affray* had put to sea, both he and Lieutenant Blackburn knew about the standard of training undertaken by the crew and on the morning before sailing Blackburn had expressed himself 'perfectly satisfied with both the submarine and the crew and stated that he was looking forward to working them up into an efficient team'. As Browne left the Board of Inquiry that day, he must have felt a lead weight in the pit of his stomach. He had answered questions put to him as honestly as possible. But now it looked as if the organisation he had honourably served for so long was out to make him a scapegoat, ultimately responsible for killing seventy-five men and the loss of one of His Majesty's submarines.

In December, a top naval lawyer wrote to the Admiralty stating:

there is no doubt that the officer responsible (Captain Browne) for sailing *Affray* in such circumstances is deserving of censure . . . The sailing orders for *Affray* were issued by Captain Browne in a memorandum dated 3 April. The submarine sailed on 16 April in circumstances considered by naval staff to have been unacceptable. Flag Officer Submarines (Rear Admiral Raw) received a copy of these orders and so did the Admiralty.

The orders may have been seen by Flag Officer Submarines personally, but the responsibility for ensuring that the submarine was in a fit state for sea and her crew properly worked up for the operation ordered rests with Captain Browne.

The terms of censure, if it is agreed that censure is required, and the method by which they are conveyed, need careful consideration. It is proposed that the Head of Naval Law should draft a letter in light of Board comments.

It took the Navy two and a half months to draft the letter and send it to Captain Browne. By now Browne had left HMS *Dolphin* to take up a new position at London's Imperial Defence College organising advanced courses for senior officers from all the armed forces. Browne had been waiting for the letter for a long time and here it was at last. His hands might have trembled as he opened the envelope. Would it summon him to a court martial? Would it spell an end to his naval career? Was disgrace waiting around the corner? The letter, marked private and confidential, was signed by J. G. Long from the Naval Law Branch and stated:

Sir, I am commanded by My Lords Commissioners of the Admiralty to state that they have had under examination the circumstances surrounding the loss of *Affray*. Although there is no definite evidence as to the cause of the loss, My Lords consider that you made an error of judgement in sailing *Affray* with a training crew and folboat party embarked on a training patrol before she had been given opportunity for the working up which was clearly desirable after her protracted refit and the many changes in her crew.

Copies of this letter are, in accordance with My Lords' directions, being sent personally to the Commander-in-Chief, Portsmouth, and to Rear Admiral S.M. Raw, the late Flag Officer Submarines.

I am, sir, you obedient servant,

J. G. Long.

And that was it. No mention of a court martial or any official announcement stating that the Admiralty had censured a high-ranking officer. The letter basically meant that Captain Browne would have a black mark on his service file – and nothing else.

Captain Browne was implicated in the death of seventy-five men and the loss a valuable submarine – but only a handful of the Admiralty's top brass knew about it. No politicians were advised or statement made to the press with a view to closing the case of *Affray* for once and for all. The information has never made public – until now.

With that, the Royal Navy quietly closed its files on the mysterious affair of HMS *Affray*.

Chapter 21

A ROLL-CALL OF HONOURS

E ight officers and ratings who had worked tirelessly to find, identify and inspect the wreckage of *Affray* were recommended to receive recognition in the King's 1952 New Year's Honours list. A further twenty-three names were put forward for special commendations by the Admiralty. The submariners received their decorations at Buckingham Palace on 23 February, the first time that Queen Elizabeth II had presented the awards after succeeding King George VI on 6 February. Others receiving awards that day included actresses Flora Robson and Anna Neagle.

Captain of HMS *Reclaim*, Lieutenant-Commander Jack Bathurst from Southsea, was awarded an OBE. His citation stated that on 17 April 1951, the deep diving vessel had been at twenty-four hours notice to sail and much of its crew were on Easter leave.

In spite of this, Lieutenant-Commander Bathurst got his ship to sea in record time when the 'Subsmash' alarm was first raised. The high standard and efficiency maintained in HMS *Reclaim* would have been an important factor in the rescue of survivors, had escape from the submarine been possible.

The citation continued:

In the subsequent search operation, the ship was frequently moored and unmoored over and diving operations carried out over numerous wrecks in the Channel, under difficult conditions. The determination of all concerned and the will to complete the job, especially in the case of the divers themselves, is directly attributable to the high standard maintained by Lieutenant-Commander Bathurst.

When the submarine was finally located on 14 June, diving operations immediately commenced with ingenuity and attention to detail which resulted in the best use being made of special experimental equipment. Lieutenant-Commander Bathurst had himself obtained the services of this equipment due to his close liaison with all departments and experimental establishments concerned with diving.

Others were recognised for 'their outstanding zeal, efficiency and devotion to duty in operations connected with Subsmash and the location and survey of HMS *Affray*'. They included Lieutenant William Filer from Southsea, awarded an MBE, 'he being the first diver to read the name "*Affray*" and thereby positively identifying her. He also carried out the initial survey of the conning tower area. By his outstanding example, zeal, cheerfulness and application to duty as First Lieutenant and Chief Diving Officer of HMS *Reclaim*, this officer has exercised a very great influence on the ship's efficiency and the well-being and morale of the ship's company.'

Senior Commissioned Engineer Arthur Byett was also awarded an MBE 'in recognition of his outstanding achievements in maintaining the machinery of HMS *Reclaim* without the development of any major defects; this in spite of the heavy demands far in excess of normal requirements which had been made on the engine room department.'

Reclaim's Chief Bosun's Mate, Petty Officer Robert 'Nobby' – 'All In a Day's Work' – Hall from Barkingside, Essex, received a British Empire Medal (BEM) 'in recognition of his coolness when trapped feet uppermost at a depth of 210ft. Under these conditions he gave clear and concise directions to his attendants, which subsequently enabled him to be cleared and brought to the surface without injury.'

Able Seaman William Middleton, from Plymouth, received the Order of Merit 'in recognition for his outstandingly efficient initial overall survey of HMS *Affray*. He was down in the observation chamber for a period of seventy-five minutes, during which period he gave a most comprehensive report on the general state of the submarine. Further, as Diving Equipment Storekeeper of *Reclaim*, he had the charge and maintenance of all deep diving equipment for the last 10 months.'

Able Seaman Walter Crane from Ipswich, Suffolk was also awarded the BEM 'in recognition of his constant cheerfulness and unfailing energy in carrying out the various onerous duties imposed upon seamen ratings. At all times when there was heavy manual work to be carried out in mooring the ship under various difficult conditions, Crane has provided a consistent source of inspiration to his fellow junior ratings.'

Engine Room Artificer 2nd Class Peter Bell – already awarded a BEM for his wartime service – received an Order of Merit for 'his outstanding achievement on Tuesday 17 April when HMS *Reclaim* was at 24 hours notice and half the ship's crew on leave. Within two hours of the receipt of the 'Subsmash' signal, the necessary machinery was re-assembled and steam raised, thereby enabling HMS *Reclaim* to proceed to sea.'

Leading Stoker Mechanic Edward Mallion from Maidstone, Kent, received a BEM for 'his happy faculty of always being on the spot when required. In his capacity as Leading Stoker Mechanic operating the stern anchor winches, he proved himself invaluable in interpreting the requests of the officer in charge with speed and efficiency, contributing in a large degree to the successful mooring of *Reclaim* over the various contacts and finally over HMS *Affray*.'

There were no decorations for Rosse Stamp recognising his ground-breaking work using underwater television to find the *Affray*. He returned to the relative obscurity of the Admiralty Research Laboratory at Teddington and continued his work – much of it top secret. Apart from writing a few technical papers for specialist magazines, for which he had to gain permission from the Admiralty before they were published, he never again came into the limelight.

It was a different story for his colleague, Commander Lionel Crabb. Exactly five years after the *Affray* disappeared, Crabb was recruited by MI6 to investigate the Soviet cruiser *Ordzhonikidze*, which had brought Nikita Khrushchev to Britain on a diplomatic mission. It is said that Crabb was instructed to dive under the cruiser and search for evidence of anti-sonar equipment and mine-laying hatches. He dived into Portsmouth Harbour on 19 April 1956 and never returned. Crabb's companion, staying at a local hotel, vanished with all his belongings and even ripped out the page of the hotel registry where they had entered their names.

Ten days later, reports appeared that Crabb was missing and stories claimed he had disappeared while undertaking a covert underwater secret mission. MI6 maintained its traditional silence, while the Admiralty said that Crabb had vanished while testing secret underwater equipment in Stokes Bay. They maintained that he was not engaged in any kind of spying mission. The Russians confirmed that sailors on the *Ordzhonikidze* had seen a frogman near the cruiser on 19 April, but knew nothing of his whereabouts.

Newspapers went into overdrive, claiming that the Russians were holding Crabb in a Soviet prison. Fourteen months after his mysterious disappearance, a body wearing a frogman's suit similar to the type used by Crabb, was found floating off Pilsey Island. The body was without a head and both hands, making it impossible to identify. Neither Crabb's estranged wife, girlfriend or mother could confirm that the body was that of Commander Lionel Crabb. An inquest jury returned an open verdict, but the coroner announced that he was satisfied that the body was that of Crabb, although his mother refused to accept that whoever was buried in a Portsmouth cemetery under a stone carrying his name was her son.

There were reports that Crabb had been seen in Russia, that he was a prisoner in a Siberian gulag, had 'jumped ship' and was now working for the Soviet navy and had been made a 'Hero of the Soviet Union' for his underwater spy work. None of it could be proved, and probably never will be.

Chapter 22

THE *SUNDAY PICTORIAL* EXCLUSIVE

'WE WERE NOT FIT TO GO TO SEA'

There were too many dependants of the seventy-five men lost on *Affray* to allow the accident to remain silent for long. On Sunday 2 December 1951 the *Sunday Pictorial* newspaper – renowned for bringing sensational stories and racy 'exclusives' to the Sunday breakfast table – carried the front-page headline: '*Affray* – Startling Letters From a Dead Son.' The letters were those penned from the *Affray* by Chief Petty Officer Engine Room Artificer 2nd Class David Bennington to his father, claiming that that the submarine 'leaked like a sieve' and was 'just about finished'. Readers were told that the letters

were handed to this newspaper by Mr Oscar Bennington, the father of the author. Mr Bennington, who was extremely disturbed by the letters, has spent much time and money investigating them, both among relatives of those who served in *Affray* and with the naval authorities. He seeks no reward for their publication other than that the fullest publicity should be given to them in the interests of all who go to sea in submarines.

The letters we print today were considered by the Admiralty Board of Inquiry. Later Mr Oscar Bennington was informed that they had been unable to find any clue, which could lead to the supposition that *Affray* was not fully seaworthy. The *Pictorial* prints these letters without comment, believing that the public should have all available evidence.

On pages 6 and 7 of the paper, under the headline 'Letters From a Doomed Submarine', David Bennington's correspondence to his father telling the story of engine failures, mechanical problems and engine room stress were shared with a public hungry for more news about *Affray* after weeks of silence. The double-page spread quoted the young sailor's father as saying that he had done everything possible to avoid any publicity 'which would bring fresh sorrow to the relatives of the men lost on *Affray*. It is only as a last resort in the interests of everyone that I have decided to approach the *Sunday Pictorial* to make the matter public.'

The paper said that two days earlier, the First Lord of the Admiralty had informed him by letter:

> The Board took evidence from friends who were in *Affray* with your son during the exercises in 1950, but were unable to find any clue which could lead to the supposition that *Affray* was not fully seaworthy. There were some minor defects normal to an operational submarine and involving no danger whatever to the crew and those were put right in the dockyard in Portsmouth in the early months of 1951.

The letter added:

> David was an extremely conscientious and hard working Engine Room Artificer and he was undoubtedly depressed by working for long hours in rough weather. A less conscientious man would probably have not been so prone to worry.

The following week brought another sensational *Sunday Pictorial* headline: 'Days of Worry in the *Affray*'. The paper claimed to have received 'new evidence about the condition of the submarine . . . given by a man who served in her in 1948/49'.

After reading the previous week's story about Bennington's letters home regarding the condition of *Affray*, Gerald Smart, an ex-chief petty officer from Birmingham who had been invalided out of the Navy, had contacted the paper to tell his own story. Smart had served in the *Affray* from October 1948 to February 1949 and told the newspaper:

> Not only the main engines but practically all the auxiliary machinery had to be nursed along. During the period I was aboard her, we were not fit to go to sea. Nevertheless, we went and there were many hectic moments.
>
> Our first diving trials in October 1948 were ominous. We plunged towards the bottom at a disconcerting angle instead of planing down. The trouble was in a starboard vent, which got jammed. After that, it went on jamming quite often. And all the crew were sincere when they said they didn't want to sail in *Affray*.

A few days later, the submarine dived again in the Channel and Smart claimed:

a hole suddenly appeared in one of the main pipes circulating water to the engines. It was found to be corroded. Then five hours out of port on our way to the Bay of Biscay we had serious trouble with the steering gear. Back in harbour again a week later, another defect developed but we put to sea just the same.

Again that starboard vent jammed and we went down at an angle that could have been dangerous. On one occasion the skipper called the petty officers together and asked what was wrong with the crew. No one told him.

The newspaper said that Gerald Smart had served in four submarines and 'his naval history sheet shows him as a "competent, intelligent and reliable rating"'.

When asked what were his reactions when he heard that the *Affray* was lost, he replied: 'I was shocked. But I should have been more surprised if it had been any one of the other three subs in which I served.'

Chapter 23

'IT HAPPENED SUDDENLY AND NONE OF US EXPECTED IT,' SAID THE SPECTRE

Scores of books have been written about ghost ships, haunted vessels, strange lights sighted in the middle of empty oceans and other weird tales of the sea – everything from *The Flying Dutchman* to the *Mary Celeste*, tales about strange sightings off the Goodwin Sands and phantom wrecks lured onto rocks along the Cornish coast. Readers who believe in such stories are usually those who want to believe in them.

To this author's knowledge, few phantom sea stories feature submarines, but while researching this book, such material was unearthed written by a highly credible author and journalist. William E. Bennett wrote under the pen name of Warren Armstrong and produced a number of books on maritime subjects, several with the full cooperation of the Admiralty and others with foreword sections contributed by high ranking naval officers.

Bennett's *Sea Phantoms* (1961) is an entertaining read about spooky happenings on the high seas, yet written in a credible and authoritative style. The flyleaf promises: 'Phantom ships scudding unmanned before the wind; wraiths of murdered captains walking the quarter deck; mysterious lights sighted in the midst of an empty ocean; burning wrecks whose fire on certain days lights the sky year after year; haunted vessels, with crew unnerved by ghostly fears . . .'

The last story in the book, *Shadow and Substance*, is about *Affray*, or rather about an unusual occurrence which happened just thirty minutes after the submarine had sent her final signal on 16 April 1951 at 2056 hours stating: 'Diving at 2115 in position 5010N, 0145W for Exercise Training Spring.' Bennett writes that on the night the submarine sailed from Gosport and at approximately thirty minutes after she signalled that she was diving, the wife of a British rear admiral was about to retire for the night at her home in Guernsey, Channel Islands. She told Bennett this fantastic story, which he 'accepted without any qualification':

Quite suddenly, I realised I was not alone in my room and in the half light I recognised my visitor. He had been serving as an Engineer Officer in my husband's ship, a cruiser, at a time when my husband was Engineer-Commander, and we had often entertained him in our Channel Islands home.

He approached me and then stood still and silent; I was astonished to see him dressed in normal submariner's uniform, although I did not recognise this fact until later when I described his clothing to my husband. Then he spoke quite clearly and said: 'Tell your husband we are at the north end of Hurd Deep, nearly 70 miles from the lighthouse at St Catherine's Point. It happened very suddenly and none of us expected it.' After that the speaker vanished.

I immediately spoke to my husband by telephone, for he was then in a shore appointment in England, and to my dismay he told me, first, that he was not aware that this young officer was even in the *Affray*, nor that he had volunteered for the submarine service. It was all very puzzling. We spoke again by telephone to each other a few days later, when my husband told me that the search was being carried out in quite a different part of the Channel from where my visitor had indicated to me – and, as you know, wrongly, as it turned out later. This being so, my husband said, there did not seem to be anything he could do about it.'

Bennett later spoke about the *Affray* tragedy with a group of naval officers and one of them said:

If you had been the husband of that woman, what would you have done? Remember, she was visited by what we can only call the wraith of this young officer *thirty minutes only after the ship dived and before any alarm was raised.* So, what would you have done? Contacted the Admiralty and risk being laughed at? No: in my opinion, though it makes one wonder what *might* have been the result if the telephone call had been brought to the attention of the Admiralty, I imagine that the accident, whatever it was, must have been almost immediately fatal, or else that vision would never have occurred.

A second officer told Bennett:

I've had this same type of vision in my own family, and when checked it was proved to be correct. Death or serious injury leading to loss of life was the cause; but the strange thing was that these visions were not made to the person most closely concerned with the victim but to some near and dear and trusted friend.

Bennett says that 'it was a harrowing experience for this woman, alone in her home and powerless to help'. She told the author:

> I think it would be terribly painful to the boy's family, and to the families of every man aboard the submarine, to read your book. I do not want to tell you the name of the officer concerned and it would be better were you not to mention either my own name or that of my husband, nor the name of his ship, if you can avoid it.

Bennett respected her wish and wrote: 'Incidents such as this . . . are beyond my understanding. Much of what I have written may seem complete nonsense to the average shore dweller. But to the average seafaring man, all things are possible.'

Chapter 24

WHO HAD THE RIGHT TO SEND
MY FATHER TO SEA IN
A DEATH SHIP?

P eople are still angry about the loss of *Affray* nearly sixty years after the tragedy occurred and demanding answers to a number of questions. They want to know why *Affray* was sent to sea when she was reported to be 'leaking like a sieve' and why the submarine was not declared unseaworthy and removed from service. They want to know what mission the four marines were ordered to accomplish had they secretly – and successfully – landed on a beach during Exercise Training Spring. And, most of all, they are curious to know how much money is still locked away and out of sight in the HM Submarine *Affray* Disaster Relief Fund.

Georgina 'Gina' Gander, from Hayes, Middlesex, is the youngest daughter of Able Seaman George 'Ginger' Leakey who in December 1945 joined the Royal Navy at the age of 17 and volunteered to serve on submarines the following summer. When the *Affray* was lost at sea in April 1951, George's wife, Eileen, was four months pregnant with Gina – later christened Georgina in memory of her father.

Gina's interest in the father she never knew has grown over the years. And so has her anger and frustration at being unable to get to the bottom of why he lost his life on what she calls 'the death ship *Affray*'.

Eileen Leakey never spoke about her late husband to daughters Yvonne and Gina when they were children. Yvonne showed little interest in the subject as they were growing up in Scotland and Middlesex, so it was left to Gina to piece together a secret jigsaw picture of her father from her grandparents and uncle over the next five decades – with the disapproval of her mother.

Gina learned that her father had been a freckle-faced, auburn-haired lad – hence the nickname 'Ginger' – with a cheeky grin. He was just over 5ft 3in tall when he joined the Navy as a boy sailor. He loved boxing, both before and after joining the

Navy and had been involved in a number of scraps with his pals while at school. Over the next five years George trained to become a submariner through various postings, including attachment to the submarine depot ship HMS *Montclare* in the Firth of Forth, where he met the girl who would become his wife. He also served on HMS *Alderney*, which travelled under the Arctic in 1949. He returned to HMS *Dolphin* at Gosport in 1950 and on 2 February 1951 George joined the crew of HMS *Affray* while the submarine was still in HM Dockyard, Portsmouth, undergoing her extended refit.

Gina insists that her father was never meant to be a part of Exercise Training Spring on board the *Affray*. A few days before the submarine was due to sail, George was still on official shore leave at home in Glasgow with his pregnant wife and 16-month old daughter. By the time he was due to return to HMS *Dolphin*, the *Affray* would have sailed and he would have rejoined her crew when the submarine returned to base on 23 April. But an urgent telegram summoning him back to Gosport put paid to the remainder of his leave and when he kissed his wife and baby goodbye on that April morning to catch the London train, it would be the last time they would ever see his freckled face and cheeky grin again.

As a member of *Affray*'s stand-by crew, George had to make himself available at short notice in case he was required for any reason. So George returned to Gosport to take over from another sailor who had been suffering from toothache and deemed unfit to take part in the exercise. By the time *Affray* had left her jetty at HMS *Dolphin* on 16 April, the sailor with toothache was still waiting to see the dentist and George had taken his place on board.

Gina picks up the story:

I was very young when I realised that I didn't have a dad at home like everyone else. We lived in Scotland, where I went to school and all the other children had dads who would come to the school – but we didn't. That's when I realised that we were somehow different to the other children.

We used to get yearly visits from the *Affray* Fund trustees and they seemed to have a lot of say in what we did in our house. My mother would tell us that the representative was coming and we had to be on our best behaviour. Mum would clean the house from top to bottom ready for the visit. My earliest recollection of a visit was when I would have been about age 5.

The lady who used to come and visit us was a lovely lady – although I can't recall her name – who reminded me of a schoolteacher, rather prim and proper with her hair tied back. She wore a suit and carried a briefcase. She would sit my sister and I down and ask how we were and what had we been doing. Then we were sent out of the room while she spoke to my mother, who gave her reports on how we were doing at school.

The fund used to pay my mother £25 a month – a lot of money in the 1950s – and that was to cover all our needs. At Christmas and on our birthdays they used to send my sister and I £5 which later rose to £10 as a present from the trustees. Money was paid directly into the Trustee Savings Bank and if my mother needed money for anything else, we had to write and ask for it. But what money we received from the fund had to last us until the next payment.

The trustee representative always asked my mother if she needed more money for anything and they paid all of our school fees and also for our school uniforms.

My mother used to go out to work at two jobs – cleaning in the morning at a local army barracks and later in the day as a cashier in a local tea room. When she bought anything for us, she always bought the best. There used to be a shop in Glasgow called Goldberg's – a 1950s equivalent of Debenhams – and she would think nothing of paying £30 for a new coat for my sister and myself. She always wanted us to be dressed the best. Just because we didn't have a father didn't mean that we had to go without anything.

My sister and I had started dancing classes. My sister wanted to be a ballerina and we used to go to lessons every week. My sister had decided that dancing was going to be her chosen profession, so my mother contacted the trustees and they came to see us and our dancing teacher and it was decided that Yvonne could go for a ballet career. This meant moving from Scotland as Yvonne was going to the Arts Educational School in Tring, Hertfordshire, and we came to live in Hayes, where my dad's family originated.

Prior to this we used to come down to Hayes from Scotland once or twice a year on the 'Flying Scotsman' and spend a few weeks with my grandparents. But of course, although we knew them, we didn't know them particularly well as you would if you saw them every day, like I do with my own grandchildren. When we arrived in Hayes, my mother had this big idea that we would become part of a close-knit family, but this didn't work because my father's family had their own lives and my mother's lifestyle was very different. For example, we never went out, my mother kept everything to herself and wouldn't talk about anything – and never talked about my dad. We never had any photographs of him on show. We only ever heard her cry for him at Christmas and New Year and the anniversary of the accident. Then we would hear her crying at night.

All of the information I have collected about my father and HMS *Affray* came from my grandparents and it got to the stage where my mother didn't like us going to see them. My sister didn't want to go, anyway. She was more interested in her own life at boarding school. But I used to go in secret and this used to end up with me having rows with my mother and as a result I saw less and less of my grandparents. But when I did see them, they would tell stories about my dad when he was a young ginger-haired lad who used to pinch apples from trees in an orchard, get into fights and started boxing, which is something I never knew.

My mother remarried a bachelor when I was age 21. The trust gave my mother the chance to either buy the house in Hayes the trustees had provided or move out. My mother chose to buy the house and as far as I'm aware, the money – £12,300 – went back into the *Affray* Relief Fund.

Years later my grandmother died in Auckland, New Zealand, where she had gone to join her other son – my dad's older brother. I remember she had a certificate framed commemorating my dad's visit to the Antarctic with the Royal Navy and she always said I could have it one day after she had died. She wouldn't let me make a copy or even take it off the wall. She used to decorate around the frame and under no circumstances would she allow it to be taken down. After she died I went to New Zealand to visit my uncle and collected a lot of material about my dad – including the Antarctic certificate.

On that visit my uncle told me a lot about my dad, things my mum had never spoken about. We spent the best part of my ten days in New Zealand just talking about my dad.

At the age of 18, money paid to children by the relief fund stopped. After that, we heard nothing more from either the Admiralty or the trust fund right up until the time I got in touch with them to get more official information about my dad. I wanted this for my own daughter. I felt she had a right to know what happened to her grandfather, so I began a quest to get to the bottom of what had really happened to him, his mates, the submarine and remaining money in the trust fund.

In the last twenty years or so I have written to the Admiralty, Portsmouth Council and the trust fund to find out what is going to happen to money in the fund once they stop paying money out to dependants. Only a few widows of men lost on the *Affray* are still alive today and most – but not all – have remarried.

I believe that any remaining money in the fund should be divided between remaining *Affray* families, including children and grandchildren of officers and ratings who lost their lives. Widows who have not remarried will still be receiving payments, but I believe their children and grandchildren should also be entitled to some of the money. At the end of the day, we children were deprived of our fathers – and so have our own children and grandchildren.

The appointed trustees and administrators of the trust fund cannot be allowed to get away with sitting on other people's money for a day longer. Think of all the things we lost out on by not having a father to provide for us. Money donated to the fund was contributed for us, the wives, sons and daughters of our fathers. It should, therefore, be returned to the *Affray*'s fatherless children or grandchildren for them to do something in the name of our fathers. They might want to set up a memorial somewhere, a little place of their own where they can go to remember their father or the grandfather they never knew.

If there is still a lot of money in the fund – and I believe there is – some of it could go to a worthy cause such as a seaman's widows and orphans charity or the Lifeboat fund. But some should also go to the sons, daughters and grandchildren of those who died on the *Affray*. That's what the money was given for in the first place.

I have always wanted to go to the place above where *Affray* lies and stop for a moment over the top of the submarine. I don't know how much it would cost, but I'm sure many relatives would also welcome an opportunity to do that. The Navy certainly won't do it for us; I asked them at the time of the fiftieth anniversary of the disaster when a service was held at Gosport, organised by George Malcolmson of the Royal Navy Submarine Museum. But perhaps the trust fund could afford to pay for it. Many came to that service in Gosport, proving there are still people around today who can relate to someone lost in the tragedy.

Since 1978 I have written dozens of letters seeking answers to what really happened to the *Affray* back in 1951 and what will happen to money in the trust fund. I have received very few replies and those who did bother to respond were negative. The Navy and the trust fund just want me to go away. But I'll keep on writing. One of these days someone is going to get fed up with my letters and, hopefully, give me a straight answer.

The public trustees passed my letter across to a solicitor for reply. Now, I'm just an ordinary person and couldn't understand their letter. It was very 'legal' and as far as I can make it out, it states that I'm not entitled to know anything more about this fund, because its existence is no longer any of my business. Well, I happen to think that it is my business. As the daughter of someone who lost their dad on *Affray* and one of the people that thousands of good, honest people donated their hard-earned money to helping, I have every right to know where all the money has gone or what's to be done with it.

I went to see my local MP, John McDonnell (Labour, Hayes & Harlington and a recent candidate for Leadership of the Labour Party), and took all my *Affray* files with me. I asked him to investigate why the *Affray* was sent to sea when she was reported to be leaking like a sieve, why nobody had bothered to declare the submarine unseaworthy, what kind of mission the marines were on – it would appear to have been something very mysterious and secret – and how much money remains in the fund after all these years (I've heard it could be as much as £250,000). I want him to get to the bottom of the whole thing.

I also want Mr McDonnell to find out why my dad was called back from leave to risk his life and go out on a death ship. Who had the right to make that decision back in 1951?

Mr McDonnell has agreed to look into all these things on my behalf and I understand this will be done some time in 2007. It will be interesting to see if he can get some answers after all these years.

Chapter 25

TAKING CREDIT AND THE
CONSPIRACY

Three different people claimed responsibility for locating *Affray*'s final resting place in June 1951. One of them was still making his claim in press interviews given forty years after the accident. At the age of 87, former submariner Rear Admiral Roy Foster-Brown told a newspaper that he still felt 'the burning injustice' for never receiving official credit for solving the problem of where the submarine lay beneath the sea. Without him, the disaster would have remained a mystery forever, he said.

Sitting in his garden in Henley-on-Thames, Foster-Brown told a reporter that at the time of the loss of HMS *Affray* he had been commander of the 6th Frigate Flotilla searching for the submarine. He said that the search flotilla had made 250 ASDIC detections, examined 34 wrecks, 74 rocks, 34 tidal rips and steamed 23,800 nautical miles over a 6,000 square-mile area 'and had not the slightest trace or hint of where *Affray* might be'.

Even though there was no hope of finding anyone alive in the submarine, Foster-Brown 'was determined that the fate of those men would not remain unknown'. He said that in desperation, he 'switched to good old submarine logic and, if you like, my own intuition'. He decided to widen the search area and, drawing on his own submarine experience, was convinced that the *Affray* must be further down-Channel, taking an old route used by submarines in wartime to avoid enemy shipping. Foster-Brown ordered his flotilla 60 miles to the south-west of the original search area – roughly halfway between Portsmouth and Cherbourg – to concentrate on a small square of sea between Start Point and Guernsey.

As the flotilla steamed towards their new position, Foster-Brown retreated to his cabin below the bridge on HMS *Loch Insh* 'and thought himself' into what he considered would have been the position Lieutenant Blackburn would have reached the morning after sailing. Working with a compass, a pair of dividers and a chart, he calculated that after diving on the night of 16 April, Blackburn had continued fully submerged for eight hours at a speed of four knots. He then rose to periscope depth at dawn on 17 April to fix his position by sighting the Casquets lighthouse in the Channel Islands.

Foster-Brown then marked an X in the chart and returned to the bridge. On one occasion HMS *Loch Insh* actually passed over *Affray*, but rough weather prevented the sonar from locating her. Foster-Brown was determined and took the ship back to the search area in better weather.

Knowing that the following day – 12 June 1951 – was going to be fine, Foster-Brown told his navigator, James Diggie: 'Tomorrow we shall search the Hurd Deep and we shall find *Affray*.' One hour after criss-crossing the site and sending sonar signals down to the underwater valley, the ASDIC produced a crude image of a cigar-shaped object, roughly the same dimensions as *Affray*, on the sea bottom.

The Admiralty failed to acknowledge Foster-Brown's report about finally finding the *Affray*, which puzzled him for two years until, as the Navy's newly appointed Director of Signals, he asked to see *Affray*'s file. 'I was shocked and disgusted by what I found,' he told the newspaperman.

A colleague, Captain G.F. Maunsell, Director of Torpedo, Anti-Submarine and Mine Warfare (the second person to claim to have 'discovered' *Affray*'s last resting place) had claimed the credit for himself without ever playing any major part in the search for *Affray*. The final insult was that he even said any action by Foster-Brown was on his orders.

Foster-Brown complained to the Admiralty, but their Lordships were not prepared to listen, preferring to forget the *Affray* affair. 'In effect, they were calling me a liar and this has always hurt me deeply,' he said. At the age of 87, the old rear admiral asked nothing more than to be credited with official recognition of (what he claimed to be) his pivotal role in finding the ill-fated *Affray*. When he died in January 1999, an obituary in *The Times* gave him that credit.

The third person credited for finding the *Affray* never claimed the glory for himself – but for someone else. Seven years after the *Affray* tragedy, British author Marshall Pugh – who wrote the story of Commander Lionel 'Buster' Crabb's wartime diving exploits *The Silent Enemy* – penned a series of newspaper articles retelling the story of the search for the missing submarine. One of the articles states that Captain Bill Shelford, who played a major part in the search from the deck of *Reclaim*, was responsible for the find. Pugh wrote:

Very early in the search, one of the frigates must have swept right over the *Affray* and missed the contact. It was just outside the original area of the search and right on the line, which Shelford had worked out as the *Affray*'s true path. The line, known as 'Shelford's Blue Line', was partly based on a hunch which Shelford had, by putting himself in the *Affray* Commander's place, and mainly by extreme hard work and logical deductions which he had made from a pile of signals four and a half inches thick.

Sounds familiar?

Captain Shelford never made any such claims for himself in his own memoirs or later writings and was probably highly embarrassed by Pugh's articles when they appeared. But he never made any attempt to have the claim corrected in future editions of the newspaper.

❖   ❖   ❖

On Tuesday 17 April 2001, fifty years after the disappearance of HMS *Affray*, a memorial service was held at Holy Trinity Church, Gosport, for remaining family and friends of those lost on the submarine. Despite the passage of time, there were dozens of people who still remembered the submarine or who, as children, heard stories about their fathers or grandfathers from grieving mothers or grandparents. The service was followed by a wreath-laying ceremony in front of the submarine HMS *Alliance* at the Royal Navy Submarine Museum. Wreaths were laid in remembrance of husbands, granddads, uncles and old comrades. A note in the order of service for the occasion stated that this part of the ceremony 'dedicated these wreaths to the remembrance of those who lost their lives in the submarine *Affray* as a tribute to their calm fortitude and courage. May there never be found wanting in this realm a like succession of men of spirit, humble and unafraid. Amen.'

Everyone attending the memorial service found it moving, meaningful and a worthy tribute to the men who died in 1951. It was also a good time to reflect on what had happened to husbands and friends lost with the submarine on that fateful day – and remind the world that the accident should never have happened and facts surrounding the tragedy kept out of the public eye for half a century.

On the same day as the memorial service, an article appeared in *The Times* with the headline 'Survivor Says Navy Hushed Up Sub Disaster'. The article, written by the newspaper's defence editor, was based on an interview with John Goddard, one of the ratings ordered to disembark the submarine shortly before she left on her final voyage. The article said that 'concern is growing that the Admiralty covered up the reasons behind the sinking of the submarine'. It quoted Goddard as saying he believed the Admiralty, in a face-saving exercise, deliberately distorted official documents before sending them to the Public Record Office (now known as The National Archives).

'The loss of HMS *Affray* in April 1951 gripped Britain in the same way that the sinking of the *Kursk* in the Baltic absorbed Russia last year [2000],' said the story, which went on to outline how *Affray* had left for her exercise with 'an unusually high proportion of inexperienced young officers', had failed to surface, was the subject of the largest sea-air search ever mounted in Britain, was eventually discovered on the seabed and 'in spite of the wishes of relatives' never recovered.

Goddard, who left the Navy as a lieutenant after twenty-two years' service, told the newspaper that he 'remained convinced that there was an explosion on board the vessel' and that the House of Commons reported that the two strongest theories for the accident were a battery explosion or the snort mast breaking. 'All records then became Cabinet secrets for thirty years and since 1981 have been released only in small amounts,' said Goddard. 'At the end of 1951 the Navy dropped all reference to the battery explosion and has consistently claimed that the tragedy was most likely caused by the snort mast snapping.'

Goddard told the newspaper that he had given evidence to the Board of Inquiry (reproduced in full in an earlier chapter) and mentioned the faulty battery – 'but when I saw the document in the Public Record Office, the wording was all different. It doesn't mention the battery, but just has me being asked whether I was aware of any other defects, to which I replied "no".'

Official documents relating to the loss and search for the submarine, Board of Inquiry findings and evidence given by witnesses, plus numerous copies of orders, signals, letters, memorandum – even scrappily written notes in pencil – plus maps and photographs are contained in more than seventy different files at Kew. All have been available for public inspection since the 1980s and are stamped 'Top Secret' or 'Classified'.

Two different files contain reports produced by the Board of Inquiry and verbal transcripts given by individual 'witnesses' – but they differ. One file contains the 'interim report' demanded from the Board by the Admiralty after the inquiry had only been in session for a short time. It has been produced in fading blue fluid ink having been copied using a primitive duplicating machine after the text had been typed onto a wax stencil, later attached to a revolving drum which produced copies. The interim report is difficult – often impossible – to read in places. Another much fatter file contains the full and finished report and appears to be the original typescript version. It is clear and easy to read.

Goddard almost certainly – yet unintentionally – examined the wrong file, unaware that a second one existed. Had he perused the completed report, he would have seen the full transcript of his appearance before the board – including his reference to the faulty battery. The report clearly states:

QUESTION: You had been in the ship a month, you say, did you hear of any trouble or difficulty of any sort?
LEADING SEAMAN GODDARD: Yes, Sir. Once we were in the dockyard, I was living down the after end with Leading Electrician's Mate Herbert Woods – he was on the boat when it went down. He came aft one night and said there was a possibility of our refit being extended as part of the number one battery tank was faulty and he said in doing rounds had found some oil in them and reported it to Lieutenant Foster.'

❖   ❖   ❖

Over the years the Admiralty has been accused of a 'cover up' over the loss of *Affray* and the flames of conspiracy have been fanned by some well-intentioned people as well as sensation-seeking journalists. And they are not far wrong.

The Admiralty of 1951 must take responsibility for allowing *Affray* to put to sea in a far from perfect condition. This is underlined by the letter sent to Captain Browne, who was quietly, yet never publicly, blamed for the accident by allowing a submarine to go to sea 'in circumstances considered by naval staff to have been unacceptable'.

Senior officers at HMS *Dolphin* were told about the boat's condition by members of the crew who had been working on her for weeks; men who knew the boat like the backs of their hands, men with knowledge of what the submarine was capable of, what it could and could not do in its current condition. The officers discussed the situation, appeared to ignore the warnings and signed a death warrant for seventy-five men by sending her to sea in an unfit state.

In 1951 the Navy wanted the incident swept under the carpet, locked away and forgotten for all time in order to protect the reputation of its Submarine Service. Thanks to the top secret nature of the Board of Inquiry and official documents produced during and after the search for *Affray*, the Admiralty succeeded in hiding the truth and not taking any collective blame for the tragic accident.

Today the Royal Navy is a very different type of organisation from the one that sent *Affray* to sea in 1951. Safety is paramount in everything it does at sea and on land. No one who served as a senior officer at HMS *Dolphin* in 1951 is still alive to reflect on what happened over five decades ago. And that is exactly the direction the Admiralty of the day envisaged the *Affray* story would go. They knew that in time, people would forget.

The broken snort was a red herring, a convenient cover for an Admiralty who knew it would be impossible to identify any other reason for the accident, unless the Navy raised the submarine from the seabed – which they had no intention of doing on grounds of cost. Fortunately, correspondence shooting the snort mast theory down still exists and examples of it have appeared elsewhere in this book. But if the broken snort mast was not to blame for the loss of HMS *Affray*, how and why did the submarine to sink to its doom?

It's time to consult the experts . . .

Chapter 26

WHAT HAPPENED TO THE *AFFRAY?* A PROFESSIONAL PERSPECTIVE

Commander Jeff Tall, OBE, MNI, RN, joined the submarine service in 1966, served in all types of submarines and commanded four of them following a command course in 1974 – two in conventionally powered vessels (HMS *Olympus* and *Finwhale*) and two nuclear powered (*Churchill* and *Repulse*). He also served with the United States Navy (USS *Pearl Harbor*) and was Admiral Woodward's submarine staff officer in HMS *Hermes* during the Falklands Conflict. He retired to take the position of Director of the Royal Navy Submarine Museum at Gosport 1994, where visitors can trace the history of the British Submarine Service from the tiny Holland 1 to the nuclear powered Vanguard class – the Navy's present-day peacekeepers.

Reflecting on his four submarine commands, Commander Tall can point to specific occurrences where 'it all might have started to go wrong, but where good training, good kit, leadership – and luck – played major parts in averting disasters, bearing in mind that the submarine is always – repeat always – operating in a hostile environment.'

When first approached by this author and asked if he would be willing to answer some questions about the *Affray* disaster from his professional viewpoint, Commander Tall declared he was 'personally unenthused [by your book] because there are still many raw nerves around concerning the loss, not least to relatives'. However, after learning that many *Affray* relatives and friends were cooperating with the project, Commander Tall kindly agreed to share his thoughts, which appear in a question-and-answer format.

QUESTION: Numerous Admiralty experts dismissed the broken snort mast theory after reading the report produced by the Board of Inquiry in 1951. What do you, as an experienced submariner, think happened to the *Affray?* I appreciate that we will (probably) never know, so any thoughts you might wish to share will be your own personal hypothesis. If it was 'human error', what might have happened? Do you think there might have been a chain of events leading up to the disaster (bearing in mind that there were so many inexperienced men on board)?

COMMANDER TALL: Unless you have been a submariner in a conventional submarine conducting a snort at night in rough seas, then it is hard to imagine the debilitating effects it can have on individuals. With the snort mast dipping regularly beneath the surface – either because of waves crashing over it or ship control struggling to keep the boat shallow enough to avoid 'dipping' – then there is a constant change in the vacuum sucking on your ears.

On top of this discomfort, it is physically hard work keeping one's balance. It is also likely that the charge will have to be broken because of excessive vacuum on a regular basis. This entails instituting the whole preparation routine every time you try again (draining down the snort system, preparing the engine room, lining up the electrics). This is both frustrating, and once again, very tiring.

In these circumstances, it is essential for everyone to recognise the growing risks to efficiency and alertness – something that only experience and regular training can instil.

In such circumstances, a boat becomes vulnerable to the dreaded 'three in a row' of failures/mistakes. Could the submarine be getting heavier and heavier because of the accumulated water coming down the snort mast (noting that there was no automatic emergency flap valve)? And could this accumulation have finally exceeded the boat's reserve of buoyancy? Could there have been an uncontrolled flood down the exhaust mast? Could there have been another flood elsewhere (cooling water hull valve)? Could there have been an electrical failure that would have knocked off supplies to the hydraulic pumps? Could there have been a telemotor failure that would have denied control over the hydroplanes? Perm any three from a dozen possibilities and you are in real trouble!

Flooding (possibly cumulative, possibly uncontrollable, combined with a steep angle on the boat which prevented shutting the snort mast back-up valve) seems to be the probable cause.

QUESTION: Several people put forward the 'battery explosion' theory quite forcefully after the report was circulated for comment. Water and oil had been found in a battery sump while *Affray* was in HM Dockyard a few days before her sea trials. Do you personally rule the battery explosion out as a possible cause?

COMMANDER TALL: A number of 'A' class submarines suffered battery explosions, with occasional loss of life. These explosions invariably occurred when the battery was gassing (being overcharged to maintain its efficiency), and came about because someone foolishly lit a cigarette or the battery ventilation system had not been properly lined up allowing a build-up of hydrogen.

I can think of no reason why *Affray* should be conducting a gassing charge so soon after leaving harbour. Although a sign of poor maintenance, the water/oil issue was sorted out before she sailed. I therefore rule out the battery explosion philosophy.

QUESTION: In your opinion, was *Affray* carrying too many men on board when she set out on her last exercise – or was it normal for an 'A' class submarine at that time to carry seventy-five men on board?

COMMANDER TALL: Seventy-five is not an excessive number to have on board. There has to be some doubt about the level of expertise onboard, however, noting the number of trainees being carried. That is the Commanding Officer's call.

QUESTION: Many commented at the time – and since – that it was strange to have found *Affray* so far away from her last known diving position and where she was expected to surface the following day. What are your own thoughts about why she was so far away from where everyone expected her to be – including most of the search and rescue team? Could there have been some kind of compass failure?

COMMANDER TALL: Why strange if she was within (or very close to) her allocated subnote moving haven/exercise area?

Had the Commanding Officer deliberately moved away from busy shipping lanes in order to conduct his snorting routine, thereby reducing the risk of collision with a merchant ship? Alternatively there may indeed have been a navigation cock-up . . .

QUESTION: What about the so-called 'hull tappings' and SST signals that several sources within the search and rescue party claimed to have heard? Do you have any thoughts on what may – or may not – have been heard?

COMMANDER TALL: Morbid curiosity? Being a member of the club, and knowing full well the risks, I prefer to think that death came quickly to all on board.

QUESTION: Lieutenant Blackburn was given a great deal of flexibility in how he interpreted his orders for Exercise Training Spring. Is it likely that *Affray* might have been undertaking a rather different kind of exercise/operation than laid out in the orders? I appreciate that, if this was the case, a certain security aspect would have surrounded the exercise. Is this likely?

COMMANDER TALL: The conspiracy theory? Quite simply – *no!*

❖   ❖   ❖

Engineer Lieutenant Mike Draper, who retired from the service in 1990, has different ideas about what might have happened to the submarine. In April 1951, Mike was a 21-year-old Leading Electrician's Mate serving on the 'A' class submarine HMS *Aurochs*, from where his friend John Denny, an electrician, had recently been drafted to the *Affray*. Mike put in a request to join his pal and would have transferred in May if *Affray* had not gone missing. He remembers:

> We in the *Aurochs* were sent to assist in the search and sailed the day after the Subsmash had been promulgated. My guess is that during the early hours of the day *Affray* was lost. We were in the area for at least a week, possibly ten days, with no results. From the many modifications that took place on all 'A' Class boats following this tragedy, I offer the following possible cause of the mystery.
>
> *Affray* was due for a battery equalising charge which involved about a six-hour overcharge. During the weekend she would have been charging batteries and a long overcharge causes a lot of hydrogen to be liberated.
>
> My guess is that during the early hours of Tuesday 17 April, she dipped below periscope depth and the snort mast float valve closed. The action of the engine room would have been to shut the 'hand-operated' snort mast induction valve and at the same time disconnect the engine/motor clutch.
>
> The action by the person shutting the hull valve was very fast, using a large wheel. Like all actions on submarines, we did things as fast as was humanly possible. It is easy to surmise that the valve was nearly closed before the diesels actually shut down. This often caused the engine relief valves – one on each cylinder – to lift and great flashes of flames to shoot out. With all the hydrogen throughout the boat, an instant flash/explosion would have occurred – sufficient to kill, stun or confuse the crew and also possibly fracturing the weakest point of the snort mast (bearing in mind the float valve was closed and the mast was not meant to be capable of full diving pressure). The hull valve only being 'almost shut' would continue to allow a fair flood of water.
>
> With the crew incapable of taking action, the main motors, possibly at half ahead group up – the name given to the speed setting for the main electric motors – the boat would have continued on course slowly getting deeper until it grounded in the Hurd Deep.
>
> Following the disaster, all boats were modified and routines were changed. All overcharges were prohibited when snorting. The hand-operated induction

hull valves became hydraulically operated, battery compartment fans were always to be run at full speed, hydrogen detectors were mounted throughout the boat and snort masts were reinforced.

I do not feel that human error was the cause. If anything, it was a procedural error, allowing equalising charges to be carried out while snorting. I agree with Commander Tall that circumstances can accumulate very quickly. However, in my own experience, we never allowed trainees to act without supervision.

We will obviously never know the full facts, even if the boat was to be recovered, which of course should not happen. My summary is based on events which we undertook after the event.

❖   ❖   ❖

In a 1999 interview with the BBC, Admiral Tony Whetstone – like Jeff Tall, a former submarine commander and a past Director of the Royal Navy Submarine Museum – was asked what he thought might have happened to the *Affray*. He said:

> Somebody could have been slow to react to an emergency or could have come to the wrong conclusion for the cause of the emergency, which is a very likely thing. At night, in semi-darkness, the engine room is noisy, in the control room one officer is intent on the periscope and it is quite possible that reactions would have been just that bit slower.
>
> Probably by the time most people were awake, the situation would have passed the point of no return.

❖   ❖   ❖

In the magazine *Ships Monthly* (April 2001) Roger Fry observed that the Admiralty's priority

> was to convince its own sailors that British submarines were safe and also to convey to world leaders, and the general public, that Royal Naval submarines were highly effective weapons systems, tasked by efficient leaders and crewed by highly trained experts. The Navy played down their knowledge of *Affray*'s known defects prior to sailing. Questions of negligence in sending the boat to sea were ignored, as were certain aspects of the first search and even

recommendations of court martial. The Navy believed it best if the incident was forgotten.

What is clear is that the *Affray* was not run down by a passing ship, nor involved in some Cold War conspiracy, was not overloaded and was not off course. The fractured snort must be considered a red herring, the break occurring as she hit the bottom with some force.

It seems that Lieutenant Blackburn, an experienced submarine officer, was diligently carrying out his orders as safely as the hazardous operation would allow. With *Affray* tooling along at periscope depth, most likely snorting, some situation within the boat started a train of events which once rolling, no one was able to stop.

Chapter 27

THE STRANGE CASE OF STEWARD RAY VINCENT

O ut of the seventy-five crew on board *Affray*, Steward Ray Vincent was the least experienced with just one week's submarine training under his belt. The only son of elderly parents from Ampthill, Bedfordshire, Vincent had joined the Navy after leaving school at the age of 15. Vincent was one of two wardroom stewards lost on *Affray* – the other was Leading Steward James Barlow. They had been detailed to work alongside the submarine's cook, Bob Smith.

It was while serving in Londonderry on the Loch Class frigate HMS *Woodbridge Haven* in December 1950 that Vincent had appeared before a Board of Inquiry charged with 'causing malicious damage' to the ship while in harbour. Vincent had gone ashore alone on 23 December and returned to the ship after closing time where he began sabotaging the quarterdeck. It is not recorded if Vincent had downed one pre-Christmas drink too many on top of his rum ration and begun damaging the ship in a drunken state or if his behaviour was due to other reasons. Either way, he was spotted by the duty watch who managed to overpower him and march him down to the ship's guardroom, where he remained under supervision until the *Woodbridge Haven* returned to Portland early in 1951.

A Board of Inquiry recommended that Vincent be transferred to HM Barracks at Chatham, where his arrival was registered on 15 February. Within days of arriving, Vincent had volunteered for service in submarines and his records were routinely checked at HMS *Dolphin*. No mention of damaging a Royal Naval ship appears to have been made.

Vincent joined his submarine training class on 9 April and had undertaken only one week's instruction when he was detailed to serve on *Affray* during Exercise Training Spring. This would be his first experience of going inside a submarine, let alone going to sea in one as part of a demanding wartime training exercise. Because of the large number of officers on board, an additional steward was needed to work alongside Leading Steward Barlow. It was felt that serving on *Affray* would be a good idea and it was designed to become an integral part of Vincent's submarine training. The only other submarine instruction undertaken by Vincent at this time was DSEA submarine escape training, which had taken place in a large tank at HMS *Dolphin* during the week of 9 April.

A note from Rear Admiral Raw to the Commander-in-Chief Portsmouth dated 28 April 1951, states that 'quite correctly' Vincent's service documents

did not indicate in any way that he was unsuitable for service in submarines. In checking Vincent's papers, no one in HMS *Dolphin* or Flag Officer Submarines' Drafting Office could have known there was a special reason why Vincent should not be employed in submarines, since Vincent had not previously served in submarines and no previous drafting records concerning him were held.

A note in Vincent's file from Casper Swinley, Captain-in-Charge, Portland, states: 'When the time comes for investigating the causes of the sinking of *Affray*, it might be of importance to refer to the minutes of the Board of Inquiry held to investigate sabotage to HMS *Woodbridge Haven* by Steward R. Vincent.'

Is it possible that Steward Ray Vincent had in some way been responsible for causing damage to *Affray*, contributing to the death of the entire crew – including himself? And what was the 'special reason why Vincent should not be employed in submarines' that Rear Admiral Raw referred to in his note to the Commander-in-Chief, Portsmouth?

Other notes in Vincent's file from unidentified naval personnel state that this theory was improbable. But personnel had been asked to consider the possibility. A response from the Director of Naval Intelligence states: 'Of the many possible explanations of the disaster which has come to my notice, sabotage by this rating is considered to be the least likely.'

Asked if Vincent might have attempted to sabotage the submarine and the theory exploited as a possible reason for the disaster, another officer states: 'It is probably too good to be true and the cause of the sinking may well have a less dramatic explanation. It is not probable he would have sabotaged *Affray* at the cost of his own life?' But who knows what kind of mental state Steward Ray Vincent was in when *Affray* put to sea on 16 April or how the young steward, with just one week's training under his belt, was coping during his first experience in a submarine submerged and full of strangers?

Chapter 28

A TECHNICAL DIVER REMEMBERS HIS VISIT TO THE WRECK OF *AFFRAY* IN 1998

In the summer of 1990, nearly forty years after the *Affray* disaster, a Royal Navy surveying group preparing new navigational charts of the English Channel on board the M/S *British Enterprise IV* 'discovered' a large shape sitting at the bottom of the sea 46 miles off the coast of Portland. Older charts carried on board showed that they were directly over *Affray*. Younger sailors on board had to be told the story of the *Affray* by older officers, most of whom had not been born themselves when the submarine was lost at sea.

A print-out of the sonograph showed that *Affray* was still lying intact and upright on the seabed. She had not toppled over and slid further into Hurd's Deep as many had predicted four decades earlier.

In November 2001, the Royal Navy was granted official permission to protect sixteen sunken British ships and submarines from disturbance by trophy-hunting divers. Dr Lewis Moonie, Under Secretary of State for Defence, announced that the ban on diving had been instigated under the auspices of the Protection of Military Remains Act 1986. Anyone disturbing or removing items from designated military wrecks could be prosecuted, with convicted offenders possibly losing their diving equipment and boats and being fined up to £5,000.

The wrecks are all located in controlled sites and include *Affray*. Five other sites, in international waters, have also been designated 'Protected Places,' where diving is allowed on a 'look but don't touch' basis. These include the battle cruisers HMS *Hood*, HMS *Repulse* and the battleship HMS *Prince of Wales*.

The announcement followed an extensive public consultation process and those contributing included ship associations, veterans' groups and diving organisations. Dr Moonie said: 'I hope that those who have disturbed or plundered the last resting place of those whose lives were lost in the service of their country will now realise that this vile and abhorrent practice will not be tolerated by this Government.'

Permission to dive on *Affray* is now almost impossible to obtain, but in August 1998 – three years before the ban was introduced – a group of eleven leading technical divers became the first group to set eyes on *Affray* since *Reclaim*'s divers left the site for the last time in November 1951. The divers were far from being irresponsible 'wreck robbers' hunting for historic trophies to snatch from the deep and sell for profit; quite the opposite, in fact. Collectively known as 'The Starfish Enterprise', they were carrying out a series of build-up deep dives in preparation for a later expedition to the wreck of HMS *Britannic*, sister ship of the RMS *Titanic*, which had been lying in 120m (394ft) of water in the Aegean since an explosion ripped her open in 1916. The Starfish Enterprise is a pioneer of UK deep wreck diving, having conducted the first amateur dives on the RMS *Lusitania* in depths of 87–93m (285–305ft) in 1993/4 along with some leading American deep diving experts. One of the divers, Geraint Ffoulkes-Jones, from Northampton, takes up the story:

A fellow diver and marine archaeologist, Innes McCartney, suggested the *Affray* site as a possible target for The Starfish Enterprise on one of the weekends we had booked out of Weymouth. The trip was organised by Christina Campbell, who set a record for the deepest amateur wreck dive by a woman when she later attained a maximum depth of 118m (390ft) diving onto the *Britannic*.

We travelled out to the *Affray* site on the charter boat *Skin Deep*, skippered by the late Andy Smith. HMS *Affray* sits in about 86m (282ft) of water and provided a good stepping-stone towards the depths we would eventually reach on the *Britannic*. *Affray* was quite a deep wreck to be dived at the time.

Preparations for the dive had been going on a long time. It takes years of training and experience to get to a level where we could safely dive down to an 86m wreck. The training for this probably started in about 1991, when mixed gas diving first made its way into the UK.

Our skipper, Andy Smith, was instrumental in all our preparations. Without experts like him we would never have got there. Andy was a true pioneer. Probably his biggest legacy to UK diving is his development of the cage lift on the back of his boat that lowered into the water so we could step in and get lifted back up to boat level. Prior to that we had to use ladders and Andy kept on complaining that all the extra gear we would bring was bending them too much.

At the time we were using 'open circuit' diving equipment and not the 'closed circuit' types used today where gas is recycled in a loop. This involved a large twin-set (2 x 15 litre) of back mounted HeliAir (Helium + Air mix). This reduced the narcotic effects of Nitrogen in the breathing mix to a manageable level. In order to keep our decompression obligation down to a manageable level – less than two hours – we used a side-mounted 10 litre cylinder of 36 per cent Nitrox from depths of about 33m to 12m (108ft to 39ft) and then another side mounted cylinder of 80 per cent Nitrox from 9m (30ft) to the surface.

We also used what we call the 'Starfish Decompression Station Lazy Line' module to keep everyone together when decompressing. It works like this: the first pair go in and confirm that the shotline the skipper has put in is on the wreck. If it is, they tie the grapnel in place with a short piece of sacrificial line and they release some form of floating marker telling the surface that all is well and worth sending down other diving pairs.

The second pair takes the 'lazy line', which they attach to the main shot line at about 45m (148ft) depth via a prussock loop and quick release shackle. All divers leave a marker at this break away point. On ascent and when all markers have been removed, the lazy line is released and the divers then all float off down tide decompressing as one group. This makes it easier for the boat to follow us and we can help each other out if a problem occurs. It is not uncommon for us to surface up to 8 miles down tide of where we got in during spring tides. We time the entry so that we are on the wreck in slack water so the tide builds throughout the decompression period.

We can descend at between 20–30m (66–98ft) per minute, depending on how much tide is running – so that's 3–4 minutes to get down. On the way up, the fastest we go is about 10m (33ft) per minute and then we get progressively slower as we get closer to the surface. For a 25-minute bottom time (that's the time spent from leaving the surface to leaving the bottom) dive on *Affray*, we do our first decompression stops at about 55m (180ft). These stops then occur every 3m towards the surface. The initial stops would only be a minute and they get exponentially longer towards the surface with the final stop at 3m (10ft) being about 30–40 minutes. Total decompression could be about two hours, giving an in-water time of two-and-a-half hours. The decompression times get longer with increased depth, and increased time. With increased depth, the stops start deeper.

Ideally, we don't spend any time down there looking for a wreck. There is no way we can free descend 85m (279ft) through murky water and expect to land anywhere near where we intended. It's very dark down there and without lights is almost pitch black as the sun doesn't penetrate through the layers of plankton, suspended particles, silt, etc.

All research is done beforehand to come up with some possible targets to look at. The boat skipper then locates these on the surface using GPS (or DECCA back in '98) and an echo sounder. He then puts a shotline down onto the wreck. The 'shot' is a length of rope with a grapnel on the end. Grapnels are typically homemade and have flexible prongs made from steel re-inforcing bar so that after diving is finished it will easily pull out of the wreck as the prongs straighten. Ideally, the first pair goes down the shot and swims straight into the wreck. This was the case with the *Affray*.

Submarines are notoriously difficult to shot as the rounded hull doesn't give much for the grapnels to grab on to. Most skippers aim for the conning tower as the highest point. If the shot is off the wreck, then we will do a small search looking for it, but unless it's within 30m (98ft) we probably won't find it.

We never really expect anything when going to look at a new wreck. When we found the *Affray*, she was sitting upright, pretty much intact and tilting slightly to starboard. On both of our dives, the shotline we descended was at the conning tower so its distinctive shape with the periscopes sticking out was the first thing that came into view. In-water visibility was quite good, but it was very dark, so what we could see depended on how bright our lights were. Innes, being the submarine expert he is, could identify that the snort mast had been broken off.

She was pretty much intact, apart from the damage to the snort. There were no obvious breaches in the hull and I don't remember anyone saying that they saw any open, or partially open, hatches. I have to say she's the most impressive looking submarine that I've ever dived on, but then she is the newest and hence probably the largest. I also remember a ladder on the outside of the conning tower.

Like HMS *Affray*, a significant number of shipwrecks we visit will have involved some loss of life. A few, such as the *Lusitania* and wrecks from the Battle of Jutland site have involved massive loss of life, in the thousands, so each situation generates different types of feelings.

For me, submarines always generate a different type of feeling as you know that submariners are still inside her. The submarine's long thin shape takes on the air of a large coffin or tomb and divers are reminded of this more than in normal wrecks. I do think about what it must have been like inside when it sank, and hope for the sake of the guys inside that the outcome was fairly quick. With HMS *Affray* and its broken snort, I imagine it would have filled up fairly quickly.

On my second dive on *Affray*, I remember that I wasn't diving with a partner in the sense that we stayed together all the way through. I recall returning to the conning tower near the end of the dive to take a closer look and noticed that there were other divers in the vicinity. After a few minutes I got this very eerie feeling of being very alone and realised that all the other dive lights had gone. I took this as my queue to leave too and slowly started to ascend the shotline. As I looked down she looked very peaceful. And then the conning tower and then the periscope slowly faded out of my torchlight. After another 10 or so metres (33ft) the ambient light started to kick in, and as I usually do, I turned off my light, which generates a very calm atmosphere. The ascent time gave me plenty of time to contemplate where I'd been and what I'd seen.

Innes took some video footage and showed it to someone in either the Navy or the Admiralty and told me that people were in tears when they saw it.

Chapter 29

QUESTIONS DEMANDING ANSWERS

R eaders will probably have mentally asked a multitude of questions regarding the loss of *Affray* as they made their voyage through this book. There are, indeed, many things that remain unknown about the submarine before she left Gosport, while at sea on her training exercise, during the sea-air search, after her discovery, while divers and a TV camera investigated her, during the Board of Inquiry and over the five decades that followed. The actions of senior Admiralty officials and politicians of the day are also called into question and why the public in 1951 was supplied with misleading, inaccurate and untruthful information about the condition, search and discovery of the submarine.

These are questions that demand answers, but we are unlikely ever to receive any due to the passage of time which had passed since *Affray* disappeared under the waves for the final time in April 1951. There are no survivors to tell the tale and few people are still alive today who can throw further light on the subject based on first-hand experience working with the submarine.

Why do so many statements made by Admiralty officials and politicians at the time differ? Why was *Affray* allowed to put to sea in what appeared to be a condition bad enough for a senior naval officer to be censured through a letter – but nothing else. Why were senior Admiralty officials allowed to influence the outcome of the Board of Inquiry before it had drawn its own conclusions? Why was the reason for finding oil in the submarine's battery sump not minutely investigated? Why was such an inexperienced crew allowed to go to sea? Why could the departure date of Exercise Training Spring not have been postponed until the submarine could leave the dockyard in tip-top condition with no need to return?

These and other questions are addressed below. In some cases a reasoned explanation is provided – but there are no hard and fast answers about what happened to *Affray* and never likely to be.

There is discrepancy between Chief Petty Officer David Bennington's first-hand accounts about the *Affray*'s condition during the 1950 Autumn Cruise and verbal evidence given to the Board of Inquiry by other members of the crew. Bennington's letters to his father were dismissed by the Board who stated:

> We are of the opinion that these letters do not represent the condition of the ship and that the trouble to which this rating refers were not the cause of her loss. Indeed, the specific troubles of the engines constantly stopping and similar matters were not ones which would directly affect the safety of the ship and in any event the engine defects in question were made good during the period HMS *Affray* was in the dockyard (January–April 1951).

Although engine problems might have been fixed, issues surrounding her 'leaking like a sieve' and oil appearing in number one battery appear not to have been addressed in the dockyard.

If 'the defects in question' were addressed, why were so many references made to *Affray* needing to return – by Lieutenant Blackburn and others – after the exercise? If *Affray* was passed fit for sea, why did she need to return for more work?

Bennington was described as a 'hard-working, most conscientious and progressively worried man', yet dismissed as a 'natterer' by *Affray*'s previous commander, Lieutenant Temple-Richards. Why did the Board not take Bennington's letters more seriously? They were the only surviving record about *Affray*'s mechanical condition before to going to sea, yet the Board chose not to pay attention to Bennington's comments. Was this because his observations differed to the line the Board was encouraged to adopt and anything directing the line of enquiry down a different route should be dismissed as unsuitable?

Why did it take more than three months to repair *Affray*'s engines and undertake other routine work when she entered the dockyard in January 1951? *Affray*'s logbooks show for that for much of this period, little repair activity was taking place on the submarine. (Author's note: *Affray*'s logbooks for January–March 1951 are available for inspection at The National Archives. The logbook for April was lost with the submarine.)

Why, after more than three months in the dockyard, were *Affray*'s sea trials on 11 April 1951 so short? In the four short hours she was at sea, *Affray* only dived to periscope depth for fifteen minutes – described by one witness as 'just enough to wash her casing. That was the first dive she had done since we did one on the way back from Gibraltar.' Why did Lieutenant Blackburn not dive to a greater depth and for a longer period? Although he had just over half his crew on board, why did Blackburn not use his time at sea to 'work up' those who were on the submarine and put the *Affray* through its paces? If, as has been claimed, *Affray* 'leaked like a sieve', a longer dive to greater depth would have immediately identified this problem, but she was not given a chance to demonstrate her defects in a pressurised situation at any great depth.

What was the true reason for the four young Royal Marine Commandos being on board *Affray* for their 'cloak and dagger' mission? What were they training for? Was it for some kind of covert foreign operation – at Suez, perhaps? It is known that the government was making plans for British troops to invade Suez as early as 1951. Were the marines in *Affray* intending to land on a beach near Falmouth, in training for a similar mission that would have eventually taken them to a beach near Suez to gather intelligence? In 1951 many naval ships were testing new and untried 'top-secret' equipment. Were the commandos hoping to trial new surveillance kit after hitting the beach at Falmouth? And why was Sergeant Jack Andrews so coy about talking about his mission with his brother, a fellow marine, on the evening before *Affray* sailed? Had he been sworn to secrecy?

What had Sergeant Jack Andrews seen or heard down in *Affray* on Sunday 15 April to make him remark to his brother that the submarine was leaking and he was far from happy about travelling in her? Had he met David Bennington in the mess and heard the young submariner sounding-off about the state of the submarine? Or had he physically seen evidence of leaks on board before leaving *Affray* to visit his brother's home for dinner later that evening?

Why did it take Rear Admiral Raw a whole hour after acknowledging that *Affray* was late in reporting to issue the Subsmash signal? Why did he not mount a smaller-scale Subsmash search, using aircraft, ships and submarines already at sea as soon as he learned that the *Affray* was overdue? This could have been stepped up into a full Subsmash an hour later. No doubt he was hopeful that *Affray* would eventually transmit a signal and a plausible reason for reporting in late. Perhaps he thought she might have been experiencing trouble with her radio. It is unlikely that Lieutenant Blackburn had misunderstood his orders, as was suggested early in the search. The orders were clearly written, even though Blackburn was given the flexibility to undertake Exercise Training Spring as he thought best, providing he followed the basic rules set out in his orders.

Why did the Admiralty issue such positive statements to the news media stating that *Affray* had been found following hull tappings and other signals heard on 18 April? An official statement to the news media categorically stated: 'Communication has been established by signal with *Affray*.' A message to Navy ships and Air Force planes said: 'The submarine has been located. Cancel all searches.' How could the Navy have been so sure that they had found *Affray* – and been so wrong? Or were the hull tappings and other signals genuinely from someone inside the crippled submarine, possibly handicapped by some disaster that had overtaken her and not fully trained in the language of Morse code? Were the signals transmitted from a submarine out of control, struggling beneath the surface and drifting in no particular direction?

Why was an order for total underwater silence – including engine shut-down and radio silence – not issued for the duration of the period when hull tappings and signals were heard? With so much noise coming from vessels searching for *Affray*, ASDIC and radio, it must have been difficult – if not impossible – to have properly heard what was assumed to be signals from *Affray*. If total underwater silence had been called for, there would have been better chance of hearing the messages more clearly – but the Navy did not ask for, or consider, total shut-down for even a short period.

Why did the Admiralty not make it clear to the public – and its submariners – that it was impossible to escape from 'A' class submarines in depths over 300ft, even wearing emergency escape apparatus? It was known to the Navy that 'A' class boats were operationally safe in undamaged conditions, but took a large list if heavily flooded while sitting on the bottom.

Why were so many 'inventions and visionary suggestions' sent in by the public claiming to know where *Affray* could be found dismissed? Many suggestions were, of course, submitted by opportunists out to make a fast buck and others came in from crack-pots. But Captain Bill Shelford had stated that the more serious suggestions were entered onto a map 'and I found them meeting in one small area outside the scope of the main search'. Captain Foster Brown sent a ship to investigate and reported such loud echoes on the ASDIC 'that they nearly knocked him off the bridge'. What was going on beneath the water in that small area? And why was it not investigated further, even if it was seventy-five miles from where *Affray* was eventually found?

Why did the ships *Ulysses* and *Contest* fail to make contact with *Affray* when they passed overhead on 17 April – within twelve hours of the accident? And why, on 18 April, did ships from the 4th Destroyer Flotilla, plus *Ulysses* and *Contest*, while carrying out ASDIC searches, fail to detect the presence of a large object – 281ft 9 in long, 22ft 3 in wide and 16ft 9in high – directly beneath them? Admittedly, the weather was rough which made it difficult to pinpoint anything on the seabed accurately. This does not alter the fact that a group of ships fitted with the best equipment of the day twice failed to detect the missing submarine directly beneath them. There is a possibility that men might still have been alive in *Affray* on 17 and 18 April, even if it were not possible for them to escape because of the depth of water. But an air line could have been sent down to her – plus a food line if needed – buying the Navy more time to mount a full-scale rescue. Or did the Navy of 1951 secretly prefer that *Affray* should not been found, knowing the huge difficulties and colossal expense that would be incurred attempting to raise a crippled submarine containing men still alive?

The First Sea Lord, Sir Bruce Fraser and Commander-in-Chief Portsmouth, Admiral Sir Arthur Power, met before the Board of Inquiry went into session to pre-determine its outcome and blame the accident on the broken snort mast. They obviously feared that the Board's eventual findings might discredit the Royal Navy and its Submarine Service and must have had little faith in its ability to arrive at a satisfactory conclusion. So they did the job for them. The three Board members would have found it difficult to mount an objective Inquiry armed with knowledge that senior officers had already decided its outcome – but they went along with it and put forward a 'hypothesis' that the snort mast was to blame, even though other Admiralty experts later dismissed it. The broken snort mast has since been accepted as the most likely cause of the accident, even though First Lord of the Admiralty, James Thomas, told Parliament on 14 November, 'there was not sufficient evidence to say with certainty why the submarine was lost'.

While referring to the discovery of 'a small quantity of oil mixed with water in the sump of number one battery tank', found while the submarine was in the dockyard, the Board stated that 'the defect is neither important or relevant to the Inquiry, apart from it having initially led to an assumption that the submarine may have been returning to the dockyard following Exercise Training Spring which would probably not, in fact, have been necessary.' Several witnesses told the Inquiry that Lieutenant Blackburn had expressly informed the crew that *Affray* would return to the dockyard after the exercise, making it obvious that work still needed to be completed on refurbishing the submarine – work that could not be undertaken before she put to sea for her trials and the fateful exercise. Whether the work mentioned was on number one battery tank remains open to question.

The Board stated that 'while a high proportion of the ship's company were experienced submarine ratings, nearly half of them had not been to sea in the ship before. This state of affairs, together with the number of passengers on board, though unlikely to be the cause of the accident, might well have been a contributing factor once a dangerous situation developed.' In 1951, the Navy did not undertake what is known today as 'a risk assessment', which attempts to anticipate any and every type of problem that could affect a submarine and its crew at sea. Yet in 1951, the Royal Navy had recently been through nearly six years of war and encountered numerous emergencies above and below the waves. So why had they not anticipated problems arising using an inexperienced crew that had not been 'worked up'? The majority of the crew were inexperienced in so much as few had completed their submarine training course. Although described as 'experienced', *Affray*'s crew were not experienced enough to pull together as a team when events turned nasty on their submarine. Or perhaps events happened so quickly, they were never given time to pull together . . .

Why was Steward Ray Vincent allowed to go to sea in *Affray* after just one week of submarine training? And why was this same young man, removed from serving on a surface ship for causing wilful damage, allowed to transfer to the submarine service without any record of his misdemeanours included on his service file?

Why were so many crew members replaced at the eleventh hour? It is known that too many men reported for duty, but why did Lieutenant Blackburn wait until the entire crew had been marched down to the submarine to hear him talk about the exercise before he dismissed some of them? Why were men taken off the submarine not informed earlier and redrafted to other duties?

Why was it so difficult for dependants of *Affray*'s crew to obtain reliable information about the submarine's last voyage for thirty years? By the time they could access official files in The National Archives (released in 1981), the *Affray* affair was long forgotten and senior naval officers and Admiralty decision-makers responsible for sending her to sea, coordinating the search, exploring the wreck and mounting the Board of Inquiry were long retired or dead. During those thirty years it was impossible to lay hands on any official documents about the *Affray*. When released, few people bothered to seek them out and attempt to try and make sense of what happened in April 1951. Today, no individuals working for the Admiralty, serving in the Royal Navy or working for the Ministry of Defence were around in 1951. The world has moved on and so has the Submarine Service. If it was the Admiralty's intention to sweep the *Affray* affair under the carpet and out of the way in 1951, it succeeded. It is only now, more than fifty-six years after the disaster, that the questions are again being asked – those questions being, what happened to the *Affray*, why was it allowed to happen and who was ultimately responsible for the disaster (as opposed to who carried the can)?

Today's technology is vastly superior from that available to the Royal Navy in 1951 and *Affray* still sits at the bottom of the sea in the same position in which she came to rest all those years ago. Despite efforts by divers using primitive X-ray equipment to ascertain whether the valve at the foot of the snort mast was in the 'open' or 'closed' position, they were never able to penetrate the hull to find the answer. But today's technology could easily solve this riddle for once and for all.

Using the same technology available to airport security staff to scan the contents of passengers' luggage for explosives and dangerous weapons, today's deep-sea divers could travel down to the wreck and conduct tests with greater ease than those available to *Reclaim*'s divers in 1951. Despite the passage of time, it is still possible to X-ray the valve and determine its position without disturbing the wreck. But the November 2001 ruling allowing the Royal Navy to ban diving on sixteen sunken British ships and submarines and protect them from disturbance by trophy-hunting divers will have to be overcome.

Permission to dive on *Affray* will be difficult to obtain unless the Royal Navy itself decides that after nearly sixty years it wants to go for final closure and finish the job that it began in 1951.

In March 2007 it was widely reported that up to one billion dollars worth of gold and silver sitting on the sunken seventeenth-century English warship HMS *Sussex* might soon be recovered. The ship took 560 sailors to their death when it sank off Gibraltar in 1694. The ship is sitting in 2,500ft of water and, unlike *Affray*, has not been designated a protected site – probably because half of any treasure discovered on HMS *Sussex* will be returned to the British government. The remainder will go to the salvage company planning to mount the undersea treasure hunt.

Mounting an official dive on *Affray* will not produce any gold or silver for Her Majesty's Exchequer. But it will provide answers to many questions, which, perhaps, is why no official attempt has been made to find the real truth about how *Affray* was lost. Do the British authorities at the very highest level not want us to know what caused the last British submarine to be lost at sea to slip beneath the waves more than half a century ago? And why it was allowed to happen?

Appendix: List of Crew

The following crew sailed in *Affray* on Exercise Training Spring on the evening of Monday 16 April 1951.

Officers:

1. Lieutenant John Blackburn, DSC, RN
2. Lieutenant Derrick Foster, RN
3. Lieutenant William Kirkwood, RN
4. Lieutenant Russell Lansberry, RN
5. Lieutenant Osborn Allen, RN
6. Lieutenant Michael Cole-Adams, RN
7. Lieutenant John Treleaven, RN
8. Lieutenant Jeffrey Greenwood, RN
9. Lieutenant James Alston, RN
10. Lieutenant Frederick Shaw, RN
11. Lieutenant Albert Welch, RN
12. Senior Commissioned Engineer William Bilton, RN
13. Sub-Lieutenant William Longstaff, RN
14. Sub-Lieutenant William Linton, RN
15. Sub-Lieutenant Roderick Mackenzie-Edwards, RN
16. Sub-Lieutenant Robin Tugman, RN
17. Sub-Lieutenant Robin Preston, RN
18. Sub-Lieutenant Richard North, RN
19. Sub-Lieutenant Richard Howard-Johnston, RN
20. Sub-Lieutenant John Strachan, RN
21. Sub-Lieutenant Hugh Nickalls, RN

22. Sub-Lieutenant Colin Mackenzie, RN
23. Sub-Lieutenant Anthony Rewcastle, RN
24. Sub-Lieutenant Anthony Frew, RN
25. Sub-Lieutenant Alan Garwood, RN

Ratings:
26. Andrews, Trevor, Marine Sergeant
27. Ashley, George, Leading Stoker Mechanic
28. Barlow, James, Leading Steward
29. Bartup, Dennis, Electrician's Mate 1st Class
30. Beddoes, David, Steward
31. Bennington, David, ERA2
32. Bridges, Oliver, Stoker Mechanic
33. Burberry, Alfred, Chief Petty Officer
34. Cardno, Robert, Stoker Mechanic
35. Cook, George, Leading Seaman
36. Cooper, John, Petty Officer
37. Curry, Roy, Stoker Mechanic
38. Denny, Frederick, A/Electrician
39. Drury, Frederick, Stoker Mechanic
40. Gittins, Harold, Telegraphist
41. Gostling, Bernard, Stoker Mechanic
42. Green, Walter, Leading Stoker Mechanic
43. Harkness, William, Petty Officer
44. Harris, Leonard, Stoker Mechanic
45. Hiles, Roy, Stoker Mechanic
46. Hodges, John, Stoker Mechanic
47. Hooper, Alfred, Marine
48. Horwell, Eric, Electrician's Mate 1st Class
49. Irven, Alan, Telegraphist
50. Jarvis, Dennis, Marine
51. Larter, Gordon, Stoker Mechanic
52. Leakey, George, Able Seaman
53. Lees, Norman, ERA3
54. Lewis, William, Stoker Mechanic
55. McKenzie, John, CERA
56. Miller, James, Stoker Mechanic
57. Pane, Peter, Able Seaman

58.   Parker, George, ERA2
59.   Pearson, Dennis, A/Petty Officer
60.   Ramplin, Alan, Stoker Mechanic
61.   Rutter, Jack, Radio Electrician
62.   Shergold, Edward, Marine Corporal
63.   Smith, Francis, Cook
64.   Smith, John, Stoker Mechanic
65.   Smith, Ronald, Leading Seaman
66.   Stewart, Anthony, A/Able Seaman
67.   Taylor, Maurice, ERA3
68.   Temple, Norman, Stoker Mechanic
69.   Thirkettle, John, Petty Officer
70.   Trimby, Victor, Acting Leading Stoker Mechanic
71.   Vincent, Roy, Steward
72.   Whitbread, Reginald, CPO Stoker Mechanic
73.   Wood, Herbert, Leading Electrician's Mate
74.   Woods, Frederick, Telegraphist
75.   Worsfold, Benjamin, A/Leading Telegraphist

BIBLIOGRAPHY

Archives

The National Archives (Public Record Office, Kew)

ADM 1/22730; ADM 1/22407; ADM 1/22629; ADM 1/22735, 'Board of Inquiry Interim Report'

ADM 1/22194–22241, 'Visionary Inventions and Suggestions'

ADM 1/31032; ADM 116/5785/116/5821; ADM 116/5867; ADM 116/5899, 'Board of Inquiry Full Report'

ADM 227/665; ADM 254/164, 'Examination of Broken Snort Mast'

ADM 173/20376–22505, 'HMS *Affray* Log Books'

Books

Agar, Cdr Rodney and Johnstone, Capt Murray, *Hold Fast the Heritage* (Woodfield, 1994)

Akermann, Paul, *Encyclopaedia of British Submarines (1901–1955)* (Maritime Books, 1989; Periscope Publishing, 2002)

Anon., *His Majesty's Submarines* (HMSO, 1945)

Anon., 'HMS *Alliance*/Royal Navy Submarine Museum', *Guide to the Royal Navy Submarine Museum* (Gosport, RNSM, 2006)

Armstrong, Warren, *Sea Phantoms* (Odhams Press, 1963)

Shelford, Capt W.O., *Subsunk: The Story of Submarine Escape* (George Harrap & Co, 1960)

Young, Edward, *One of Our Submarines* (Penguin Books, 1952)

Articles

Fry, Roger, 'Disaster Beneath the Waves', *Ships Monthly* (April 2001)

Peel, J.H.B., 'Fifty Years of Submarines', *Everybody's Weekly*, 10 November 1951

Shelford, Capt W.O., 'Underwater Television', *Scientific American* (June 1953)

Stamp, W.R., 'The Search for HMS *Affray* with Underwater Television', *Discovery Magazine* (September 1952)

Newspapers and Journals

Barnsley Chronicle, 28 April 1951

Daily Express, 18–25 April; 2 June 1951

Daily Mail, 18–25 April 1951; 5–8 May1958; 7 May 1991

Daily Mirror, 18–25 April 1951

Daily Telegraph, 18–25 April 1951; 13 September 1951

Engineer, 23 November 1951

Evening News (Portsmouth), 17–20, 23, 28, 30 April 1951; 1–2, 29 May 1951; 2, 14–16 June 1951; 11 January 2000

Hansard, H.C. Deb., 18 April 1951; 9, 30 May 1951; 13, 14, 18, 20, 27 June 1951; 18 July 1951; 1 August 1951; 14, 28 November 1951

News Chronicle, 3 July 1951

Sunday Pictorial, 2, 9 December 1951

The Times, 18–25 April 1951; 13 September 1951; 15 November 1951; 4 February 1999; 17 April 2001

Film

Morning Departure (1950). DVD copies of the film available from DD Home Entertainment, 11 Churchill Court, 58 Station Road, North Harrow, Middlesex HA2 7SA; www.ddhe.co.uk

INDEX